BACKROADS OF PARADISE

UNIVERSITY PRESS OF FLORIDA

Florida A&M University, Tallahassee
Florida Atlantic University, Boca Raton
Florida Gulf Coast University, Ft. Myers
Florida International University, Miami
Florida State University, Tallahassee
New College of Florida, Sarasota
University of Central Florida, Orlando
University of Florida, Gainesville
University of North Florida, Jacksonville
University of South Florida, Tampa
University of West Florida, Pensacola

University Press of Florida
Gainesville · Tallahassee · Tampa · Boca Raton
Pensacola · Orlando · Miami · Jacksonville · Ft. Myers · Sarasota

BACKROADS OF PARADISE

A Journey to Rediscover Old Florida

Cathy Salustri

This book may be available in an electronic edition.

21 20 19 18 17 16   6 5 4 3 2 1

Library of Congress Control Number: 2016946693
ISBN 978-0-8130-6296-9

The University Press of Florida is the scholarly publishing agency for the State
University System of Florida, comprising Florida A&M University, Florida
Atlantic University, Florida Gulf Coast University, Florida International
University, Florida State University, New College of Florida, University of Central
Florida, University of Florida, University of North Florida, University of South
Florida, and University of West Florida.

University Press of Florida
15 Northwest 15th Street
Gainesville, FL 32611-2079
http://www.upf.com

For Barry, who is the second-best thing that ever happened to me, and for my parents, Richard and Ann Salustri, who are the first

U.S. HWY. APOPKA, FLA.   37240

Not all those who wander are lost.

—J.R.R. Tolkien

Contents

Prologue

July 1, 1980

My grandfather's face twisted as we turned off the oak- and pine-fringed interstate and entered the final leg of our southwest journey down US 301. As we passed bleached wood cracker houses, and dingy brown cedar sheds, his tanned forehead furrowed, drawing his coarse eyebrows tighter and tighter together until the bushy lines above his dark eyes disappeared under a thin ridge of curly dark hair.

Perched on stilts, houses sat, no shutters or coverings save grime and webs. Underneath and alongside them, a ragtag fleet of pickup trucks with rusted wheel wells, oxidized roofs, and Bondo fenders shared weed patches with Jon boats, the only difference the boats' marginally better maintenance and the occasional trailer elevating them off dirt patches. Washing machines, sun-bleached farm equipment, and a mise-en-scène of auto parts greeted us anew at each home.

My grandfather sucked in sticky-hot Florida air, his silence crowding our weighed-down 1976 maroon Buick Regal. *"This,"* I can only imagine him thinking, *"is worse than what I left in Italy. This is what I have worked my whole life to give my son? That they should move to a slum in the South?"*

"This" referred to Florida, specifically, the interior parts of the state detailed along US 301, the parts of the Sunshine State not photographed by any Florida tourism board. "They" referred to my father, my mother, and me: a seven-year-old whose greatest adventure in life, prior to the three-day journey to Florida from New York, was a dead heat between a goat eating my coat at the Bronx Zoo and taking a train to see *Peter Pan* on Broadway. In a chain of events too complex for my young brain to comprehend, my parents decided to leave Westchester County, New York, and move to Clearwater, Florida. While my parents knew the drive's end result, a small two-bedroom just miles from then-pristine Clearwater Beach, my grandfather, who had come along to help, did not.

Eventually we turned onto I-275, where the landscape grew noticeably tidier and steadily more sanitized. Our orange-striped moving truck dutifully followed the car as we made our way to Clearwater. The water of Tampa Bay bounced the sparkling sun into our car, and the salt formed diamond crystals on my grubby, sweaty hands.

"Look at that, Cath," my dad said, his voice reverent. "Look at how clear it is, not like Staten Island at all." My father still made the sign of the cross on himself when we passed Catholic churches, but not until this moment had I heard such hushed worship in his voice.

I nodded and peered out the window, feeling something new and familiar inside my chest as I gazed at the sandy landscape offering itself to me. I recognized this, much later, as the sense of coming to where I needed to be.

I fell in love with the water that day, but as I grew older I felt the inexorable pull of the other parts of Florida, too. I have fallen hopelessly in love with the weathered corners of Florida, the bits that don't fit with the Convention and Visitors Bureaus' image. The chambers of commerce and tourism boards want quite keenly to present a fresh and clean land of white beaches and sparkling waters. In turn we have convinced ourselves that we need to make sure our guests never see the other side of Florida: the Florida that is the skeleton, the backbone of all the others.

....

I, like my parents and countless settlers before them, have not tried to claim Florida. Instead I have let the state claim me. Almost forty years later I travel Florida still, looking for parts I may have missed, seeking them out before they fade away under the heavy blight of franchises, strip malls, and rented Jet Skis.

Today I explore Florida on roads that parallel the interstates, rattling along with the same excitement that thrummed through me that afternoon in our maroon Buick. My beaches have changed, and the strip malls may one day win, but as I troll the backroads, I remain forever in search of that secret backwoods state with its sun-bleached roadside shacks. I feel the quickening inside as a sense of the familiar envelops me. It is that same sense of simultaneous longing and recognition I first felt when the salt water of the Gulf opened itself before me.

It is the feeling of coming home.

KEY TO
FLORIDA
HIGHWAY TOURS

This map of Florida appears on the inside front cover of the Work Progress Administration's *Florida: A Guide to the Southernmost State* (1939).

Introduction

Look around any Florida bookstore: You'll find guidebooks to traveling Florida with kids, dogs, or your iguana. You'll find regional guides and even a guide or two about what you'll "see" along the interstate. What you *won't* find is any sort of comprehensive travel guide to the Sunshine State. There's Florida for lovers, for families, for gay people, for bikers, for hikers, but no simple "This is Florida for *everyone*" guide.

Once upon a time, you could not only find such a book, but our government considered its existence so crucial to our economy it sponsored the creation of such a travel guide. In 1935, the Works Progress Administration created the Federal Writers' Project (FWP), which, in addition to documenting folk life and oral histories, left an exhaustive legacy of tour books to every corner of the United States: the American Guide series. The project hired out-of-work writers, librarians, teachers, and historians to research and write driving tours for each state (as well as Alaska, Puerto Rico, and a host of "specialty" guides, such as a guide down US 1). The guide series had a threefold purpose: One, the government wanted to put people to work, even writers; two, the guides would, in theory, stimulate the economy by getting people to travel, at least locally; and three, they captured a slice of life in every corner of America.

The Florida project sent writers—mostly anonymous writers, but also Zora Neale Hurston and a still-wet-behind-the-ears Stetson

Kennedy—into the depths of Florida to reveal its splendor to the world. What they found wasn't always splendid; they encountered mosquitoes, slave-like working conditions, racism, and poverty. But these writers also detailed Florida's beauty. They wrote about thick green forests, white sand beaches, and waters teeming with seafood. In 1939, the FWP and the State of Florida jointly published the work of those writers as *Florida: A Guide to the Southernmost State*. The *Guide* included twenty-two driving tours of Florida's main roads.

The brilliance of these WPA tours became apparent after Eisenhower built the interstates that encouraged drivers to bypass small town after small town in favor of making good time. Today, those main roads now serve as our backroads, and the absence of the *American Guide* series is keenly felt, especially in Florida, where most guidebooks barely scratch the state's surface. These roads lie forgotten by all but the local residents, a few commuters, and dedicated road-trippers actively seeking them.

....

I have a master's degree in Florida—literally. I earned an MLA in Florida Studies from the University of South Florida St. Petersburg. During my first semester there, one of my professors assigned roughly 587 pages of reading a week, and one of our first assignments included a poorly photocopied selection from *A Guide to the Southernmost State*.

Fast-forward a few years. As I neared graduation I wondered how much had changed, how Florida looked now when viewed through the lens of the WPA tours, what I'd find if I followed those backroads.

Roads are living things. To assume you can find a road where someone else put it down almost eighty years ago? Utter folly, especially in Florida—a land whose eternal youth stems from ceaseless reinvention. Florida's roads did not stay where the *Guide* writers left them. Over the years those roads kept growing, twisting and turning and pulsing with Florida's fervor in much the same way her people and land do.

While plotting out the routes, I found no indication that anyone had kept track of which roads used to go where. Simply going by mileage on

Google Maps wouldn't work, either, I discovered, because, especially in more popular and therefore more populous areas like Tampa, development and road widenings have resulted in so much change that I might find the road as far as a half mile away from where the *Guide* writers left it.

The *Guide* used mileage points, but that only helped if you started at the beginning and followed the route exactly, as it didn't list distance between two cities but the distance from the starting point. The saving grace? The writers listed the cities along the path of every road. I used those cities—most still there—and marked the routes in a geographic connect-the-dots through Florida. Many of these roads lay far from the interstate; in some instances, they had new numbers and names altogether. I broke out my shiny, red Florida *Gazetteer* to re-create the Depression-era routes by studying towns, using a rainbow of high-lighters to trace city to city along possible routes, e-mailing transportation historians for guidance, and poring over maps and researching old route numbers until my back ached from leaning over my worn, wooden, dining-room table.

With the surprisingly difficult task of retracing routes completed, my boyfriend, Barry, and I climbed into a twenty-one-foot camper van and spent a month following those tours, guided by a dog-eared, broken-spined, 1950s-era version of the *Guide*, a now-tattered and ripped *Florida Gazetteer*, and (on Barry's part) endless patience. We logged almost 5,000 miles; that camper became home in my quest for the Florida I hoped to see through the mostly anonymous eyes of the Federal Writers' Project. In this book I've combined that 5,000-mile odyssey with our subsequent travels along A1A and US 98, from time to time recalling bits of other road trips I've taken, either with friends or alone. On every trip, though, I've searched for scraps of the Federal Writers' Florida, abandoned along her backroads. Out of those miles grew these tours: the ultimate Florida road trip. These tours share much with the *Guide*, in that we traveled the same roads and saw some of the same things, but they differ, too. This book will not tell you how many miles from Romeo to Juliette, or whether or not you'll find good accommodations in St. Augustine, because you can find that sort of thing more easily—and more accurately—on the Internet. What this book *will* do is show you not one "real" Florida but many Floridas. It follows those long-abandoned tours and writers, bringing to life their Florida as well as mine, and showing you the promise of alternate Floridas, infinitely variable and unbroken, of the twenty-first century.

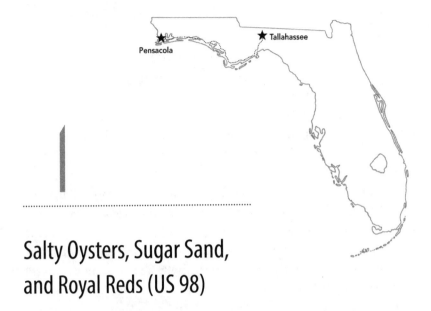

Pensacola

Tallahassee

Salty Oysters, Sugar Sand, and Royal Reds (US 98)

Here are one-street towns, quiet in the sunlight,
their weathered century-old houses still in use.

A Guide to the Southernmost State, 1939

It is far too tempting to see Florida only in snippets of vacation. Every time I read another condescending account from an online columnist ridiculing our notable oddities, my soul cracks a little bit. *That's not Florida*, I want to scream. *That's not who we are at all!* Those writers don't know Florida, don't hold in their hearts the Florida of our dreams, the one we seek but rarely find.

Rambling along the lazy watercolor stretches of US 98, with the windows down and the tangled smell of pine forest and salt air, that dream dances within my grasp. That promised slice of vintage Florida lives here, as if an artist stepped in and created the tropical Technicolor beach town that exists in the unwashed corals and teals of your imagination. From the pine-lined forests of backwoods Florida to the sun-soaked beaches as the road stretches toward the coast, US 98 reveals every magnificent subculture in the Sunshine State.

Even still, the coastal stretch of road between Wakulla and Pensacola Beach takes commitment, because although the cities lie just 212 miles apart and Google Maps will lead you to believe you can make this drive in less than five hours, before you take the drive, you, like Google Maps, may fail to understand the lure of a fresh Florida oyster or the seductive pull of a cold beer to wash down a Styrofoam bowl of Indian Pass Raw Bar gumbo.

We start on the Georgia/Florida state line just north of Tallahassee, on US 319, here called Thomasville Road. North Florida, especially the panhandle, remains vastly untouched from the *Guide*'s portrayal of it, that of a land unlike south Florida, with "rich red clay" soil, gently sloping hills and a marked antebellum feel wholly absent from the state's coastline and southern interior. Floridians often quip, "You have to go north to get South" in Florida, because so much of the state's southern population consists not of generations of southerners but transplants, and much of Florida feels more like a theme park or resort than the South. This is not the case in inland north Florida: Tallahassee feels more like the Deep South than Key West.

In 1939, *Guide* writers noted the Robert E. Lee monument outside of Tallahassee in Bradfordville. The Daughters of the Confederacy built the monument[1] and dedicated it in the 1920s.[2] The inscription reads, "Erected and dedicated by the United Daughters of the Confederacy and friends in loving memory of Robert E. Lee and to mark the route of the Dixie Highway."

Ask a longtime Floridian about the Civil War and you'll receive a grab bag of answers. Some will call it the "War of Northern Aggression" and talk at length about the economy and states' rights. Others will talk about racism and our ongoing debt to society, and still others will blanch physically at your question and perhaps even go so far as to pretend nothing like that ever happened in the Sunshine State.

In *The Burden of Southern History*, C. Vann Woodward argues that the South should not deny its past just because it's shameful. I agree; we need to talk about race. It still lives with us, and not talking about it doesn't help. The monument to Lee still stands. The state moved it up roadside when widening the road, but not as an act of racial sensitivity: it was likely more convenient. I'm not in favor of removing the monument, but perhaps the inscription could reflect more nuanced perspectives, especially as it welcomes northerners to our fine state as they approach the capital.

Tallahassee became the state capital because it sat between Pensacola on the west and St. Augustine on the east back when most Floridians lived less than 50 miles from the Florida/Georgia border. As the route bisects the city, wooded roads and sloping hills turn into massive shade tree–lined streets. Its colonial architecture contrasts with the retail sectors, and beyond the city limits, historic buildings and parks abound, including Natural Bridge Battlefield just outside the city in Woodville.

In 1865, Confederate troops stopped Union soldiers here, helping Tallahassee earn the distinction of being the only capital east of the Mississippi that the Union could not overtake. That's not the state park's only significance, however. At first glance, Natural Bridge appears simply a delightful verdant park, perfect for picnics and strolling. Knobby-kneed cypress trees shade two ponds less than 100 yards apart and cluttered with duckweed. Feathery Spanish moss dangles overhead, shadowing the black water with tiny, arching wisps.

The ponds, however, aren't two disparate ponds at all, but one river: the St. Marks. It flows from the north, vanishes into an underground sink, and reappears slightly south, where it continues until it spreads itself into Apalachee Bay, named for the Apalachee Indians, a tribe with a reputation among other indigenous nations as a fierce and wealthy people. Archaeologists place the Apalachee in Florida around 1000 BCE; they lived between the Aucilla and Ochlockonee Rivers from what is now the Georgia line south to the Gulf of Mexico. Some fifty thousand to sixty thousand Apalachees lived in the area until the Spanish explorer Pánfilo de Narváez showed up in Tallahassee, courtesy of some crafty Indians from the Tampa Bay area who suggested he could find gold in the areas of north Florida more easily than in the peninsula. That was 1528. Within 150 years the Apalachee culture disappeared through one of two means: Catholic conversion and/or murder by British soldiers allied with Creek Indians. Today, fewer than three hundred Apalachee Indians exist. They no longer live in Florida, having moved first to Mobile, then on to Rapides Parish in Louisiana in the mid-eighteenth century.

As US 319 meanders farther away from Tallahassee, the urban traffic, franchises, and planned communities diminish. The western edge of the road borders Apalachicola National Forest, noted for longleaf pines and colorful assortments of wildflowers as well as a plethora of water—almost three thousand acres of freshwater in all. The deep blue of the watery sinks, lofty green and ocher fringes of longleaf pines, and tufts of money-colored wiregrass carpeting the forest floor offer what I can only imagine the whole of the inland Florida panhandle looked like three thousand years ago. Inside the forests of north Florida it's easy to forget the cluttered roads of main cities, the beaches dotted with visiting sunseekers, and the airports importing the next round of travelers hoping to see a scrap of paradise from their climate-controlled, sanitized, Gulf-view motel room.

At every turn the forest offers new vistas. Everything inside the forest feels and smells like it has just rained: a sprouting malachite newness. Saplings and saw palmetto break through the moist ground and stretch for the sky; in swampy parts, chunky cottonmouths bump through the bog while wading birds extend black dainty legs gracefully through muddy waters.

US 319 edges along the eastern edge of the Apalachicola, but just east of the road along the stretch travelers will find Wakulla State Forest and Edward Ball State Park.

The Wakulla Forest once belonged to the St. Joe Company. Edward Ball, the company's founder and member of the Du Pont family, bought broad expanses of the panhandle in the 1920s.

Locals can enumerate the many sins of St. Joe, starting with its having bought land from locals for pennies on the dollar. It opened a paper mill that, while helping employ workers as the Depression gave way to war, emitted significant air contamination from sulfur. The mill used 35 million gallons of water every day, lowering the water table substantially, which led to sinkholes, changes in the land's topography, and significant water contamination as rainfall reached the aquifer too quickly. As St. Joe clear-cut old-growth longleaf pine forests, it replanted the land with the faster-growing and—this is important—biologically different slash pine, reducing the longleaf pine to 2 percent of its population and earning the area a national designation: Critically Endangered Ecosystem.

As "punishment" for the company's environmental sins, the State of Florida paid the St. Joe Company $182 million for ninety thousand acres of prime land, turned it into a state park, and named it in honor of the man from whom they rescued it. When the St. Joe Company turned from growing trees to growing subdivisions, the state rerouted part of US 98 to better suit the needs of the company.

That's what's nice about Florida: there's something for everyone to exploit. We're equal opportunity that way. Today, locals take aim at a larger enemy than the massive St. Joe Company: Nestlé. Bottled water is a $4 billion industry in America, and drinking water is a big deal in Florida for many reasons. The bulk of the state depends, at least in part, on the Floridan Aquifer for drinking water. The Floridan Aquifer is an underground river encased in spongy limestone. For years, Floridians have heard that the water table is low and that we need to conserve water, and the state's five water management districts—initially created to deal with flood-control issues as people, farms, and ranches moved into the state with no regard for its intrinsic swampy qualities and the unbending nature of flowing water—have long limited things like how often a resident can water his vegetable garden or how much water a city can withdraw from the aquifer to deliver to its residents.

Despite the much-hyped shortages, when Nestlé asked the Suwannee River Water Management District for a permit to pump water for bottling in 2010, the same people who had convinced sweet old ladies we'd all die of thirst if they showered daily seemed ready to approve the permit. Nestlé promised to pump no more than 1.6 million gallons of water per day from the Wacissa River, a river east of US 319. Local residents went ballistic, and with good reason. Not only do the springs and rivers sparkling underneath the pine-studded wilderness remain the brightest of the area's gems, but the inequity of a government agency imposing draconian restrictions on citizens and then allowing a multinational corporation to swoop in and take what it wanted was all too obvious. The Florida Department of Environmental Protection pointed out in one interview that municipal users take far more water from the aquifer than Nestlé, but that municipal water went for things like cooking dinner and bathing children, while Nestlé's water went for profit. Nestlé ultimately withdrew its permit in the summer of 2011, although some hand-lettered protest signs still pepper the lower portion of the road.

Despite the environmental consequences of business decisions made by its namesake and the threat of multinational water purveyors draining the springs, Edward Ball Wakulla Springs State Park remains a splendid respite. Hiking trails brim with palms, slash pines, and wild-flowers, but the water and the 27-room Mediterranean revival lodge Ball built in 1937—complete with marble bathrooms and a thirty-foot-long marble counter—are perhaps the most notable parts of the park.

In the midst of the lodge's grandeur, Old Joe watches over the guests. Old Joe is a taxidermied gator who had a reputation for friend-liness, although an unknown assailant killed him in 1966. The park made a place for him in the lobby, where he oversees the comings and goings from his glass tomb. Old Joe's descendants no doubt live a short walk from his final resting place: Wakulla Springs, which feeds the river that shares its name.

The Wakulla may be Florida's most famous river, although few know its name. Before the magic of computer-generated imagery, Hollywood made films the old-fashioned way: scouts chose locations resembling the studio's vision. MGM filmed several of their Tarzan movies—the ones starring Johnny Weissmuller—at the springs inside the park. The state-operated boat tours take passengers down the same stretch of waterway seen in the movie.

Fans of *Creature from the Black Lagoon* (1954) also know the park as one of the chief locations for the film's underwater scenes. This film has a nifty cult following, especially in the Tallahassee area, and some fans will tell you that Ricou Browning, a diver instrumental in creating the Weeki Wachee mermaid shows, was the "real" Creature, pointing to his underwater work. Other fans claim Ben Chapman, the terrestrial Creature, as the "real" Creature. Until several years ago, the Tallahassee Film Society and the Friends of Wakulla Springs State Park hosted an annual CreatureFest, which included a screening of the film in front of the lodge.

Before the Ape Man or the Creature swooped and swam through the park, though, the park had other legends.

The Wakulla Volcano exists, geologists firmly believe, in the imagination only. A plume of smoke and column of lights would, according to legend, issue forth from somewhere inside the forest. The source, much debated, remained a mystery. One legend posited the smoke came from a den of pirates who hid their gold deep in the swamp; another suggested a volcano caused the smoke and fireworks that periodically issued forth from within the bog. No one, of course, could find the source, though legend has it that many who tried never returned. Any who disappeared in the effort, though, were more likely lost to dehydration, snakebite, or other perils of the 1800s-era Florida swamp than to pirates or the legendary volcano.

What I find so curious about this plume of smoke and column of sparks that more than a few locals witnessed is that it disappeared forever the day of the 1886 Charleston, South Carolina, earthquake, roughly 7.0 on the Richter scale and the first such activity in the area; some geologists speculate that any current seismic adventures in the area are aftershocks of this event.

An earlier legend describes mythical water people who danced in the spring on moonlit nights. The *Guide* describes an "Indian" legend of "water people" no more than four inches tall who held dances in the spring's depths. However, at some point in the evening, a warrior in a stone canoe would show up and spoil the party by scaring them all away.

The next leg of the tour, as US 319 crosses first the Sopchoppy, then the Ochlockonee Rivers, sees jade forests start to collapse under colorful bursts of wildflowers and blossoms on deciduous trees. The salt in the air thickens slightly, and the buildings feel less farmhouse and more fishermen.

Southwest of Ochlockonee Bay, the road runs into the Gulf of Mexico and becomes US 98. West on US 98, longleaf pines create a canopy over bulky, undergrown palm trees. A string of fishing towns usher us west, and seafood shacks, oyster bars, and marinas dot the roadway.

Shrimp boats bob on a blue bay, and weathered wooden homes rest on stilts, propped up like red mangroves. The only homes *not* on stilts are the occasional old ranch-style beach houses. Waterfront homes in the state's more populous areas, such as along Boca Ciega Bay on St. Pete Beach and Treasure Island, are ostentatious declarations of wealth, cookie-cutter McMansions squished into postage-stamp-sized lots. If you've visited the Gulf Coast and taken a boat tour, you've seen them. Homes here look nothing like those. Pine forests, palm thickets, and creamy sand surround these unassuming and somewhat random collections of graying, salty wood slats and steel roofs. So thick are the pines that they completely block many homes from view, the only indication of domicile a mailbox or crushed-shell driveway. All we see for a good long while is a wall of trees, although just beyond the dark mature green of that wall we can peek and see the immature jade of new-growth pine trees. As we pass over the Aucilla River, sunlight dapples the road between the shadows of the leaves. Here and there we see a flash of red, a nod to the autumn in full swing in points north.

At the St. Marks River we commence eating in earnest, kicking off our gastronomic journey at Outzs Too, an oyster bar that looks like nothing most people consider trying.

I learned about Outzs Too on a group road trip. My friend Theresa hailed from this area, and we led a caravan of other Floridaphiles, most of whom followed my candy-apple-red Volkswagen Rabbit in a white Ford van. We stopped first at Natural Bridge just before sunset, and then she swore—swore!—she knew a shortcut south to Outzs Too. We led the way down a road that quickly turned to dirt, gravel, and pine trees. Once our travelers were safely ensconced in the van behind us, Theresa turned to me.

"I don't know for sure that this will get us there, but it should," she confessed.

It *should?* I looked around as I eased my sporty hatchback over ungraded road. Backwoods roads in the Florida panhandle are not made for subcompact German imports. These roads require a truck. Additionally, nothing greeted us at either side of the potholed dirt road. I placed my faith in her—until I saw a group of men ahead sitting upon a cream leather couch, trading beers around a bonfire. Here's the odd thing: there was not another vehicle in sight, nor could we see a house or even a shed. The forest appeared to have one way in—the way we had come. There was zero sign of any way these men could have arrived in the middle of a damn forest. I mean no disrespect to good ol' boys, because I firmly believe that should the zombie apocalypse arrive, these are the men who will save us all, but I did not care to meet them in a candy-apple-red import, armed only with a dachshund, flaxseed crackers, and spotty cell phone reception.

"Don't stop," Theresa said.

"You think I think that's an option?" I asked. "What if we have to turn around and go back past this?"

"Then we drive faster."

Fortunately for Theresa—and myself—the road opened up and there before us lay Outzs Too. Until this moment, no one else knew that she had led us all blind through a James Patterson novel. I forgive her, though, because for these oysters you should be willing to risk both death and humiliation.

Forget about the reviews on TripAdvisor. Forget about your Oysters Rockefeller . . . Outzs Too is a classic roadside dive, and I could not love it more. The oysters taste like the brine of the Gulf, and the staff . . . well, let's just say *they* would not have been deterred by the leather couch/good ol' boy apparition by the side of the road.

Miss Dorothy used to groom dogs. Then one day, the owners of Outzs Too decided to close, and Miss Dorothy decided that she would buy the place. She didn't change anything—at their request but also because, really, why would she?—and she's held onto a piece of local legend. The developers don't have the land, and the legend isn't sitting by the roadside, forgotten. That's a real possibility along US 98, because, while there exist wonderful, glorious pockets of working waterfront and sandy tourist meccas, in between buildings stand, shuttered and empty.

No trip along US 98 feels right without a stop at Outzs Too, and when Barry, Calypso, and I tour the length of US 98, we stop here so he can taste the oysters, too. He, as I expected, is hooked. We stop again farther west, at Tropical Trader's Shrimp along Ochlockonee Bay. Don't let the name fool you: this area isn't tropical. It's pine forests with bluffs of sand that slope into a lime and curaçao sea. Tropical Trader's Shrimp has their own boats. Eat enough up this way and you come away with the definite impression that any restaurant worth its salt has its own boats. Calypso, Barry, and I sit on the wide wooden front porch under a funky shredded blue tarp and paw through mahi and shrimp. Inside, seafood cases and displays of local pickles line the back wall. We tell the waitress our plans to spend the night at St. George Island State Park, and she tells us about the fish she caught there that past weekend. We laze on the porch for just a while longer, satiated on fish and afternoon sunshine, until the anticipation of what lies ahead next trumps the transcendental combination of salt and seafood, and we push farther west.

After Ochlockonee Bay, the water shows itself in unabridged bulk. No more peeks at slivers of turquoise; a yawning gasp of water unfolds before us. So great is the vista that all but the most careful driver may miss an odd preponderance of road signs warning people of bears. The careful driver may also note that the silhouette on these signs looks more like an anteater or, as Barry argues, a rhinoceros.

"I doubt they'd put something out for an anteater," he reasons.

"I don't think we have anteaters," I tell him.

"They should put a caption," he says. "But then we wouldn't need the picture."

In case you're wondering, anteaters are not generally seen in the wilds of Florida. Neither are rhinoceros. Black bears, however, are. At one time, thousands of bear called every corner of Florida home, but development pushed them to the brink of extinction. Today, the Florida black bear has a stronger foothold than it did in the 1970s, but Floridians in most parts of the state are in no danger of stumbling onto a bear in their backyard. Wildlife biologists find black bears mostly in seven areas the state classifies as Bear Management Units. The stretch of US 98 by Ochlockonee Bay runs through one of those areas, hence the somewhat questionably drawn signs.

Ten minutes later we've yet to sight a bear and the waterfront homes start to fade, almost hidden from the road. In some places we see nothing but a driveway fronting a treed lot. This stretch of road feels as though it can go on forever, with nothing but oaks, cypress, and pine trees that part occasionally to show us a sliver of St. George Sound. It is broken only sporadically by a different Florida, not unexpected, but a bit jarring nonetheless. A home with a five-foot-tall Rays baseball peeking out of the undergrowth, its postmodern assertion of fan loyalty standing proud next to the mailbox; the HoHum RV Park; and a sign for Lake Morality, which, by the way, is indeed a lake, not a clever name for a Southern Baptist meeting hall. Although not often used, "surreality" is a word, and that's exactly what I feel as we pass Lake Morality and drive along the edge of Tate's Hell State Forest in Carrabelle.

Immediately adjacent to the Apalachicola National Forest, Tate's Hell State Forest bumps against the edge of the beach. The Florida Forest Service, not the USDA, owns and operates Tate's Hell. To further the sense of surreality, Tate's Hell has its own folklore, as told by *Guide* writers:

> Local legend has it that a farmer by the name of Cebe Tate, armed with only a shotgun and accompanied by his hunting dogs, journeyed into the swamp in search of a panther that was killing his livestock. Although there are several versions of this story, the most common describes Tate as being lost in the swamp for seven days and nights, bitten by a snake, and drinking from the murky waters to curb his thirst. Finally he came to a clearing near Carrabelle, living only long enough to murmur the words, "My name is Cebe Tate, and I just came from Hell!" Cebe Tate's adventure took place in 1875 and ever since, the area has been known as Tate's Hell, the legendary and forbidden swamp.

Even a glimpse into Tate's Hell reveals a paradise of prairie, swamp, and forest. I do question, however, the logic of putting the hiking trail entrance right next to the entrance to the Wildlife Management Area, a sanitized name for hunting grounds.

Farther west still, coastal dunes and the road contour the state's edge, just off the shallow aquamarine trench of St. George Sound that lies between the mainland and the pale, sandy barrier islands guarding the Gulf coast. At Eastpoint, a town that proudly proclaims "Oysters Since 1898," we turn left and cross the water on a long, low bridge out to St. George Island. At the water we turn left again and head into Dr. Julian G. Bruce St. George Island State Park, which wins the dubious honor of "most punctuation used in a Florida state park name." The entire island, including the present park, is partly responsible for the Florida Dream. During World War II, troops trained on St. George Island before shipping overseas. The last vestiges of freedom they saw before fighting a war, perhaps never to return home, were framed by biscuit-colored bluffs, sugar sand, and the blue-green Gulf of Mexico. That's quite an image to carry with you as you go to war; when I consider Florida's population explosion through those lenses, I wonder why we don't have more retirees living here than we do.

I'm a camper. I mean, believe me, I love a good motel/hotel room, but I've slept in a jungle hammock, on boats, in a Volkswagen Vanagon, and tents of varying shapes and sizes. The first time we drove the panhandle in its entirety, we slept in the RoadTrek, which, really, is camping only in the sense that one parks it at a campground. It had a refrigerator bigger than the one I had in my first beach apartment and a queen-size bed.

On the second trip, we sacrificed comfort for simplicity—a tent, a box of cooking supplies, and a cooler in the back of our X-Terra—and found what we missed the first time: stars and waves. Our tent had a screened top, and the island is far enough from the mainland—which, in the panhandle, isn't exactly a major source of light pollution anyway—that every time we opened our eyes we saw a sky pincushioned by stars. Add to that the way St. George wedges its tent sites between sets of sand dunes, and you have a soundtrack of wind and waves to lull you to sleep underneath the starry sky.

That night, lying on an inflatable mattress and dozing under the watchful September sky, I felt a serene euphoria at every path that led me to that moment. Florida, I thought to myself, may pave itself over and constantly reinvent itself to lure people to its beaches, but this, indeed, is the paradise people sought from the state's beginning. Not so far south that heat and humidity overwhelms, but not so far north that sleeping outdoors in September necessitates blankets. Not so crowded that we cannot abide the people, but not so remote that we can't access the island. Perfect.

The next day we left perfection in search of more. This, I s
note, became a recurring theme throughout the panhandle. Every
we landed, I thought to myself, "This place. *This* is paradise." Whe
left, it would be with deep, searing regret . . . until we found the next
scrap of paradise.

So Florida goes, and this, I think, is what draws people here over
and over again: the promise of Eden in bits and pieces. We don't offer
a singular type of paradise as one grand entrée; instead, you can find it
in bite-size portions, discover it in slivers and slices around the state,
each one situated so that the traveler feels they've discovered something new and unique, waiting only for them. The panhandle proves
this with a different Zion every so many miles.

Next up? Oyster nirvana. Apalachicola, a working waterfront with
the bulk of the state's oysters lying just beneath its surface, welcomes us.

A word about working waterfronts: These small towns with sea-
based industry and sometimes a bay beach sit counter to Florida tourism board advertisements. Picture instead a beach with sand that
doesn't exactly look, well, clean. It looks mucky, or maybe it's a tidal
mud flat rather than a beach proper. It's a different type of Florida than
the trope of a sparkling sandy beach, and Apalachicola exemplifies this
point. Walk to the water and you'll see the gritty reality of a working
waterfront, and while it has a charm I adore, it lacks beauty in the con-
ventional sense. Oh, the nets are colorful—as are the fishermen—and
the oysters are felicity on the half shell, but the ideal working waterfront is much like the notion of the pastoral—you might picture a few
cows ready to be milked and ears of corn and beans growing in tidy
rows, but you're forgetting about the cow manure, fertilizer, and mud.

Apalachicola has the best oysters in Florida. All the stuff in the
downtown—the shops, the historic markers, the rustic charm—pale
in comparison to the oysters, because the sweet salty water, shallow
bay, and slightly cooler temperatures offer the trifecta of tasty for
these delightfully slimy bivalves.

Florida fishermen, the *Guide* explains, come in two varieties: net
fishermen and sportsmen. This is still mostly true, although the state
banned net fishing in 1994. In this area of Florida, though, there is a

third type of fisherman: the tonger. Tongers, or oystermen, use scis-sor-like tongs to bring the oysters to the surface. From there, they are sorted by size—oysters have to be at least three inches long for tongers to harvest them—and brought to shore for sale.

Although some of the neighboring towns may look more like aban-doned fishing towns, don't let the bare-bones appearance fool you. This area provides 90 percent of Florida's oysters and 10 percent of the country's. Late in the day, the docks are clear and the boats rock silently on the Apalachicola, with not a soul in sight. Beyond the docks and beneath the boats, however, pulses the beat of an oyster town. The Franklin County oyster industry accounts for one thousand jobs and roughly $1 million. East of Apalachicola, Eastpoint may look deserted, and the town does offer less to land-loving tourists than Apalachicola across the bay, but docks run the length of the waterfront, and fish-ing charters here include an abundance of sportfishing, oystering, and kayaking trips.

Apalachicola has a quaint collection of shops just off the waterfront. We tasted rich handmade chocolates made with tupelo honey at the Apalachicola Chocolate Company, ate salty oysters that would have still looked back if oysters had eyes, drank the nearly local dark Pen-sacola Porter, and perused rusty tin seafaring items in an "antiques" (which is to say anything remotely old-looking that could have conceiv-ably had something to do with a boat, boat captain, or crew) shop.

These diversions, however charming, do not support the town. The town's lifeblood lies just under the surface of the waters surrounding it. The waterfront supports the town, and that waterfront is littered with peeling paint on no-nonsense concrete buildings, not artfully let-tered signs and carefully arranged window displays. Apalachicola men make their living off the briny realities of the sea, and working oyster boats look as though they've put in a full, salty day, because they have. Aesthetics is not a priority, nor should it be, which is not to say those workhorse boats and salty men are not beautiful; it depends, I sup-pose, on how you define beauty. In this part of the state, beauty is shaped by the gritty reality of tonger culture.

On April 20, 2010, the Deepwater Horizon drilling rig licensed to British Petroleum exploded, killing eleven workers and creating a

5-mile-long oil slick in the northern Gulf of Mexico. Oil gushed into the Gulf at an estimated rate of 210,000 barrels per day, and while BP scrambled to control the oil, the Florida oyster and tourism industry held its breath, waiting to see how far into Florida the oil would seep.

Although the disaster did not, as feared, completely decimate north Florida's fisheries and oyster beds, BP paid claims in 2010 to fishermen, tongers, and others potentially impacted by the spill across Florida. Restaurants temporarily had to look elsewhere for their oysters and, in some instances, raise prices. Diners who assumed this stemmed from the oil spill in the Gulf had it half-right. In 2010, Gulf oysters suffered no damage from oil, but some tongers, blinded by oil payoffs, took an extended holiday, leaving few to work the beds.

At Boss Oyster, the manager explains that the restaurant has its own boats certified by the state Department of Agriculture for collection and selling. She also tells us yes, the tongers who decided not to work hurt not only their business, but much of the industry.

"If someone didn't work last year," she tells us "we didn't hire them this year."

Boss Oyster, one of several oyster bars along the bay, doesn't truck in fancy. We sit outside along the water, in view of oyster and shrimp boats, commercial fishing vessels, and, in the distance, more boats. Everything smells of oyster and fish and salt: welcome to a working waterfront. Many Florida towns boast sand and beaches and oyster bars; few can claim oyster boats.

If you tire of oysters, you can also visit John Gorrie Museum, named in honor of the Florida doctor who lived here and pioneered the idea of refrigeration and, subsequently, changed the state's future with the forerunner to air conditioning.

The next stop on our gastronomic dining adventure is Indian Pass Raw Bar, but to get there you have to abandon US 98 for 30A, which is fine, because along this stretch of US 98, I start to feel as though the road's just a touch too well-traveled for the beach-shack vibe so prominent along much of this route. The Raw Bar started as a turpentine company store in 1903. Turpentine, not tourism, once supported northern Florida—pine gum makes turpentine, but not without help from humans who chipped at the tree's bark and tapped it for the sticky gold. The *Guide* repeatedly refers to "naval stores." This phrase does not refer to places where the US Navy buys things; it refers to the industry and products revolving around pine trees, another tie between this part of the state and its neighbors Mississippi and Alabama. In north Florida, at least before DuPont interests and Edward Ball came to town, that meant longleaf pine. In 1939 Florida, over 3 million acres of pine forest yielded 7 million gallons of turpentine.

The Indian Pass Raw Bar catered to the workers, then later travelers and locals. Jim McNeill, the current owner, who is not averse to shooting a meandering hog and serving free pork, came by the business honestly: his grandma, Gypsie, cooked lunch for the turpentine workers in the 1930s. The Raw Bar portion of the business didn't come to fruition until Hurricane Kate ruined the family's oyster business in 1986.

"Having more oysters than we could eat ourselves, and not enough to continue wholesaling, the decision was made to open the establishment as it is today," the restaurant's website reads.

Still feeling my Boss Oyster high, I order the gumbo. Okra, shrimp, tomato, and heat explode into a lowcountry dance in my mouth.

And "lowcountry" well describes some of what we see here. For the next 25 miles or so, the vistas alternate between tidal marsh and steel roofs painted with a coral-reef palette; pine and saw palmetto alternate with sea oats. These two styles blend into a panhandle chic I've yet to find anywhere else in Florida.

Next stop: St. Joseph Peninsula State Park. The careful observer will notice this isn't far at all from St. George Island State Park. Florida's Department of Environmental Protection runs the parks program, which seems odd until you realize it's actually a brilliant strategy for protecting vulnerable lands. At press time, Florida maintained 171 state parks, and that number grows every day. The parks range from the Skyway Fishing Pier State Park, which turned the twisted metal from the Skyway Bridge disaster into a public spot for landing tarpon, grunts, and shark, to the soft rolling sand dunes that stretch for miles across the panhandle. Across the panhandle, twelve beaches fall under the auspices of the state park system. No one can say for sure, but it's a more-than-educated guess that had the state not snapped up all these beaches—100 miles of sandy coastline in all—instead of sand dunes, bathhouses, and covered shelters, we'd be driving past condo canyons, three-for-ten-dollar T-shirt shops, and high-rise hotels.

Just past our campground at St. Joseph Peninsula State Park, we pick up even more seafood at Triple Tails, a seafood market/liquor store with Ziploc baggies of fish in shallow gray Rubbermaid bins packed with ice. Each basin has something different: red snapper filets, ivory scallops, pink shrimp, and an assortment of other fish.

We leave with shrimp, snapper, and rum. As we're paying for the rum, a golden retriever brings me a stick of driftwood. I pet him and throw the stick. That was not what he wanted; he looks at me like a child who has just lost a toy to the neighborhood bully. The girl going into work apologizes; no need, I tell her. As far as I can tell, the dog amuses himself, unleashed, with his stick and a ball in the sand lot, dozes under the palms, and greets the odd customer while his human completes her shift. This does not happen back home. This is still Florida, but everything I see along the highway reminds me of a Florida I thought existed only in a Florida history I imagined.

Even the homes. The road to the campsite, Cape San Blas Road, is lined with dots of colorful houses teetering on stilt legs planted in the sand. Every one seems to have a for-sale sign in front of it. Rish Park, available only to disabled Florida residents, boasts a collection of round, blue-roofed cottages interconnected by boardwalks. Farther down the road, the state park is at the western edge of the barrier island, a thin scrap of sand and trees. Our campsite is no farther away from the beach than a sand dune, covered in beach sunflowers, sea oats, and general Florida scrub vegetation.

....

The sand, too, is unlike that in the rest of Florida. People describe panhandle sand as sugar sand, which is true enough if you try to brush it off your legs. It looks like white powder but feels like a body scrub. Walking through it is another experience entirely; it feels like you're walking through baking powder, or Bisquick. Of course, the state tourism board can't promote that—"Come bake on our Bisquick sand!" doesn't have the same come-hither ring. But indeed, as the surf washes over the creamy sand and retreats again, it leaves perfect pin-sized circular holes and makes the sand look like pancakes forming on a huge griddle.

More than one park ranger calls September the off season, but our campground seems filled to capacity. Despite the crowds, it hurts to leave. The park office warned us about bobcats, promised us the area had plenty of deer, and cautioned us to beware of skunks. I saw none of those things in this perfect slice of Florida's wild beaches. At the edge of the state park, however, the developers wait, ready to do battle for every speck of sand they can turn into concrete. The road is under construction; the park ranger shakes his head when we ask about development—a slow, sad shake that seems to say, "What can you do?"

We push west, and I marvel that the marinas on this strip of water are nothing like the ones in southwest Florida. Fish and oysters and shrimp and scallops pay the bills here, not dolphin watches and sunset sails. Here we see tongers and fishmongers; down south we have charter boat captains and tourists. We look at the same body of water and the same state but see entirely different things.

Panama City Beach is another set of delights altogether, summed up easily in two words: Goofy Golf.

I spent about twenty minutes taking pictures at the Goofy Golf: octopus, dinosaur, Easter Island head, and the gamut of the sorts of things you would expect to find at a mini-golf establishment along Florida's coast.

Panama City Beach offers untold riches of touristana. They did it first, and they did it best. Before them, we offered gator wrestling and mermaids. "Come on, Florida, you can do better than *that!*" Panama City Beach must have said.

Unlike the newer, glitzy flavors of tourism, the schmaltzy syrups that drizzle throughout the city are more traditional ones: wooden roller coasters, Ripley's, and a more authentic version of Orlando's International Drive.

Goofy Golf, too, remains. Established in 1959, it stands in tropical tones of purple, gold, and lamé. You do not feed live gators here (as you may at some of the chain mini-golf establishments Florida supports); you do not see a plane crashed into a faux mountain (as you do at others). It is glorious tourism for tourism's sake, and the faded Technicolor icons of the mini-golf course sum up this pastel tourist life. If surrounding towns want to head down the road to "Anytown, USA," they can, but Panama City Beach keeps its quirky sense of self.

Towns here either run into one another or remain separated by expanses of saw palmetto topped with pines towering above them. Seaside distances itself from these towns with its indistinguishability.

If you watched the Jim Carrey film *The Truman Show*, you know Seaside. Carrey plays the titular role of a man in a pretend life. Location scouts settled on Seaside as the perfect setting for a movie set designed to fool the lead character into believing in a false reality. They chose auspiciously, because Seaside itself is a scripted town. Developers built it to represent an idyllic beach town of yesteryear, and while no one's arguing they didn't succeed, something in this tiny town feels simultaneously lovely and altogether out of place.

Building on the principles of New Urbanism, Seaside is a walkable town—you need a car to get there, and you need one to leave, but once you arrive at one of the fanciful beach cottages designed using choices from a sampler palette of good taste and money, you can park that car and walk—to the doctor, to the food trucks (that actually don't move; they're always there), to school, to the beach, to Bud and Alley's pizza place that serves one of the best Margherita pizzas along 30A, or to the bike trail. Everything is Disney-clean, and Disney-priced. Still, it's utterly charming.

For years proponents of the New Urbanist movement (which favors walkable towns, a sense of community, and a move away from suburbs) held up the watercolor homes of Seaside as an example of what New Urbanism should be. They forgot to mention that few really lived there, at least not all the time. Seaside is a resort town that looks small town, which is why people come to visit. Our waiter tells us that only two people live here twelve months out of the year. Ever heard the phrase, "a nice place to visit but I wouldn't want to live there?" Welcome to Seaside. It evokes images of a 1940s Florida beach town, and I fall in love, but as it turns out, it's just infatuation. At our next stop, I find the real thing: Grayton Beach State Park.

We have no reason to stop other than the sea pines and sand and forgotten beachside feel of this reach of panhandle. It seduces me; I cannot bear to see this stretch of road end. We take our time getting to the park, and when we pull in after dark, I walk the campsite loop with a flashlight. There are so few lights here that, despite plastic palm tree lights strung across the occasional camper or a sturdy campfire in park-sanctioned grills, the inky blackness is punctuated only by starlight and the smell of the Gulf. The next morning we take a long lazy walk to the beach—the campsite is easily a bike ride away, but we have no bikes with us—and I spend the day trying to figure out why I don't live here.

I haven't been so in love with a beach since I first laid eyes on the shimmering waters of the Florida Keys, what seems like a million years ago. I was in college, and we were on a field trip to Islamorada. As soon as we broke clear of the mangroves and I saw the sparkle on transparent emerald water, I felt a sigh in my soul.

Years pass. Things change. I married someone who hated the beach. We only went to the Keys once. We divorced. These two things, while not the whole story, are more than tangentially related. No matter; before the judge decreed the divorce final I had packed my kayak and bike and headed for the Keys. I still loved it. The water still took my breath away as I came over the bridge. But there was so much . . . junk. Key Largo had started to take on the familiar chain-store patina; Islamorada was still a respite, but clearly giving up the ghost. Marathon was nice, but K-Mart and Publix? No, thank you.

The water, though. Man, that water remained the same utopia in a thousand prisms of a glassy, aquamarine rainbow. It's the kind of water that makes you yearn for better adjectives.

The Keys will always, always have that place in my heart, but the placid thrill of finding a slice of paradise where I didn't expect it flows through me when the sea forest opens up and I see the beaches just south of US 98 along the panhandle. Glass meets pale, luminous green, which meets penetrating windswept sand dunes with sand fences. I find sand dollars no bigger than my pinkie. The water is clear, like it isn't there at all, and it feels so good to be surrounded by all these glassy-green prisms sparkling back up at the sky that I laugh when the waves catch me unaware.

Grayton Beach was, for a moment, the Florida Keys dream that I held for so long until I realized the dream has vanished under the weight of chain stores and chemical runoff. Will the panhandle meet the same fate? We are but two hours gone and already I am planning my return, wondering about rental prices, dreaming about a life there.

Florida is fickle. She will give you your dream and then change it on you.

But still . . . that green. That perfect, undulating sea of green.

In the shadow of Panama City Beach and Grayton Beach, Destin seems homogenized. Certainly it has amusement centers—it appears to be the law that every city between Pensacola and Port St. Joe have at least one—boasting mini golf and bumper boats, but more of what you see here is franchise land. The sand becomes even more achingly powder white, taking on the appearance of snow. Still, after Panama City Beach's prismed tropical patina, Destin seems a snowy specter, all the colors of the town shadowed in white.

After Destin the towns come faster and are less distinctive, although there is always, always the powdered sand and emerald shore. At the edge of the state, we make two last stops. First we head to Gulf Islands National Seashore, taking Pensacola Beach Boulevard over the water and to the spit of white sandy island. Santa Rosa Island, where the National Seashore lives at its western edge, is half-dressed in lazy shacks dotted in every color, half-dressed in the windswept wilderness of a sandy national park. Navarre Beach, the part of the island adorned with the coral- and sunset-colored homes, comes first, then the island dizzies you with white sand dunes. As they do so often along this stretch of Florida's coastline, the sand and the water eclipse all else.

Our last stop on the tour is west of Pensacola at the Flora-Bama Bar. This bar, as one may surmise from its name, is at the Florida/Alabama state line. It has had its share of hard knocks. The day before it was scheduled to open in the spring of 1964, it caught fire. Forty years later, Hurricane Ivan ripped through the main building. Both times, the bar rallied, opening for real in October 1964 and hosting a "No

Tears in Our Beer" demolition party in April 2005.[8] The bar patrons insist that Jimmy Buffett wrote "Bama Breeze" about the Flora-Bama, and the fictional bar in the video has a sign reminiscent of the old Flora-Bama sign, and several Internet sites quote Buffett's sister, Lulu, as attributing the song to the Flora-Bama.

The Flora-Bama, like so much of Florida, can't be neatly summed up in a paragraph or a page or a postcard. Robin, one of the managers who has called Flora-Bama home for almost three decades, has a dark pixie haircut and a soft, gravelly voice. She walks me through the bar, touching the felt-tip names written in wood with reverence. It's the First Church of the Dive Bar, and yes, this is a religious experience. The Flora-Bama is a phoenix rising from ashes or, in this case, the sand. On the first floor, you can bang on the rough-hewn wood walls and sand will sift down and mound itself in a diminutive pile between the floorboards and the carpet.

"That's from Ivan," she says with a sad, proud smile. When the 2004 hurricane pushed water and sand from the Gulf into the bar, the staff repaired what it could, replaced what needed it, and opened for business as soon as possible. But the first time they walked back into the Flora-Bama they had no clue what to expect. They found sand dunes in the bar. Nothing will get the sand out of the walls. Storms etch themselves in the memories of those who survive them, and this building, it seems, is a living, breathing thing, a relic of a Florida that survives and rebuilds.

The sand isn't the only thing that remains from 2004. Using her index finger, Robin traces a name on a low rafter and points out that the faded black names all have dates of 2004 or older. The sand, she says, blasted the ink away, adding a premature patina to the signatures.

That was 2004. When we first visit the bar, it is 2011 and the place still has blue tarps and Tyvek covering parts of it. By 2013, its renovation is complete. The new Flora-Bama is still a two-story affair, more so than before. That's courtesy not only of Ivan but the coastal construction line that mandates any rebuild be higher above sea level than most original buildings. Some photos on the wall—and every available space is covered in memorabilia that pays homage to southern rock—are visibly waterlogged.

I grow fascinated with Robin the more she talks, walking through the bar lost in a place I can't get to without her. She traces the old footprint of the bar as she moves, can tell me where some musician or another went through the glass, and about the night Jimmy Buffett showed up, walked onstage, and started playing unannounced. Bartenders didn't immediately recognize him and thought the idea that this guy would grab a guitar that was not his as kind of a jerk move. Of course, they soon realized he was Jimmy Buffett, and, I can imagine, the guitar then sold on eBay for several tens of thousands of dollars.

The bar also hosts an annual mullet toss, where competitors attempt to throw a mullet from one state to the other. Since the bar abuts the Alabama state line, this is not a Herculean task. It is, however, perhaps the state's best-known mullet toss, featured in the *New York Times* and known to mullet aficionados throughout the Sunshine State.

The Flora-Bama only tosses mullet; it does not prepare the shallow-water fish. We feast instead on royal reds, deepwater Gulf shrimp found only along this stretch of the nation. They cost slightly more than other shrimp at eighteen dollars a dozen, but they are worth every extra penny. Each meaty, succulent royal red tastes like buttered lobster. We order these and something called a Bushwacker, which is one part milk, two parts rum, many parts amaretto, and some more parts rum. Calypso, for the record, is wholly and completely bored by the entire affair. She does not eat shrimp, cannot abide liquor, and does not care about hurricanes. She curls up under the table and sleeps while we soak in Robin's stories about the storms, the bar fights, Jimmy Buffett, and the will to rebuild.

Remember, this is a dive bar, nothing more—at least, not when you drive by. But stop by and go inside. Place your order at the food counter, then go get a drink at the bar while the Bushwacker machine spins in the corner. Sit down and feel this place; let the music thrum through you as you watch the sand and the people and the water in the distance. The Flora-Bama, at the end of the line for us, tells you everything about the panhandle I've been trying to explain. It's trendy without trying. It's on the beach without really needing to be on the beach. It's unassuming and unpretentious and wonderful and sun-soaked and a million hues of green and blue and brown and yellow and pink.

Our food arrives. Each red is easily the size of a half-lobster tail, and as we dip every bite in drawn butter while watching the sapphire waters from our brown picnic table on the ivory sand, I am struck by how every moment of our coastline sojourn has leaked color into the black-and-white pages of the *Guide to the Southernmost State.*

Jacksonville

Punta Gorda

2

....

Rainforest Gardens, Blue Springs, and the Loss of Here (US 17)

On being expelled from the Georgia Territorial Assembly for seditious utterances in 1755, Edmund Grey fled to the banks of the St. Marys and founded a colony of outlaws and malcontents, later dispersed by British forces. When Spain ceded Florida to England in 1763, the boundary between Georgia and Florida was in part established along the river. Many Revolutionary War skirmishes were fought nearby, and in 1783 when the American Colonies achieved independence, the St. Mary's was confirmed as the southeastern boundary of the new Nation . . . A railroad trestle (R) parallels the bridge over the St. Mary's; sandy pine flats stretch back from the marshy banks.

A Guide to the Southernmost State

The *Guide* fails to mention the sheer brown beauty of the river and surrounding frontier. Even today it appears a wild land, save for the trestle still perched over the river, right where the *Guide* promises.

Alongside that trestle, US 17 enters Florida over the Saint Marys River.

As the *Guide* notes, the St. Marys once marked the southeastern border of the newly formed United States of America, because Florida came late to the party, remaining loyal to the British Crown during the Revolutionary War. As a reward, Great Britain turned the state over to

Spain in 1784, and they divested themselves of the territory in 1821. Until then, ownership of Florida had ping-ponged across Europe since the sixteenth century, with even the French getting into the game for a time at Fort Caroline. Today, the St. Marys marks the edge of the state, not the country, and while less-savvy travelers bravely ford the river on I-95, US 17 offers those in the know a back door entrance to paradise.

The trestle once carried Seaboard Air Line railcars between Georgia and Florida; trains still use it today. The trestle pivots to allow tall boats to navigate the skinny, twisted river. The bright-blue modernity of our bridge clashes with the vintage trestle, which sinks into the background of the swamp and the sandy pine flatlands reaching back from the marsh.

Florida has more swamp than beach, although Florida marketers tend to lure people to our blond, sunny shores, not our cypress water mazes. Where US 17 enters the state, it seems nothing lies farther from the promise of paradise than this place, although within an hour of this rusted trestle you can find surfers and sun bunnies.

Today we shall not surf. Today we shall slice down Florida's eastern edge and the lesser-seen interior. Two signs herald the entrance: an ash-colored 1950s-era cinder-block wall with stately concrete letters that spell "Florida" and the state-issued blue "Welcome to Florida!" sign. Skinny palm trees frame the vintage sign; nothing frames the other.

Those official-looking signs announce the state's governor. This would be fine if Florida had a habit of keeping its governors off the news, or even electing governors that more than a small percentage of the populace admit supporting. People driving to Florida over the holidays in 2011 would have been most likely to know Governor Rick Scott because, three weeks before Christmas, a correspondent for a late-night talk show made national news when he presented a urine specimen collection cup at a press conference and asked the governor for a drug test. When Scott spent money to add his name to the signs—thirty-five in total, and no other Florida governor had done this—adversaries criticized him for diverting almost ten thousand dollars that had been budgeted for road projects.

Welcome to Florida, indeed!

Leaving the governor behind, we find a less political Florida, re-vealed in a thousand nuances of green, interspersed with the occa-sional shuttered old-school motel, the forgotten rooms forming a half moon around the parking lot and abandoned, empty pools. Ten min-utes down the road, the towering canopy of thick vegetation parts to reveal Yulee, the junction of A1A, but we continue inland toward Jack-sonville, which lines both shores of the St. Johns River, which emp-ties into the Atlantic 20 miles to the east. The city's deepwater port receives cargo from around the globe; it also has countless oil tanks, a nuclear power plant, and a bevy of parks.

Not far from the ultramodern nuclear plant, the Kingsley Plan-tation reminds us our history is every bit as tangled as our present. Zephaniah Kingsley, a slave-trader, used his own ships to bring slaves from Africa to Florida. He also freed one of his slaves when she turned eighteen—after she'd given him three children—and then promptly married her. Hard to tell if they truly loved each other, but he did al-low his bride, Anna, to own land. When Kingsley married Anna, Spain ruled Florida, and Spain liked the idea of people freeing their slaves. Spaniards bought slaves—as did, it is significant to note, the Senega-lese Mrs. Kingsley—but didn't espouse the "slavery is forever" school of thought. It makes sense, then, that Spanish Florida had a high num-ber of free black people, and that when the United States assumed responsibility for Florida, the Kingsleys had some cause for concern. Mr. Kingsley, who had no shortage of wealth and influence, champi-oned the idea of manumission—the freeing of one's slaves—even as he and his wife pragmatically used slaves to work their lands. Today, the nineteenth-century plantation lives on as part of the National Park System.

From there we head into Clay County. The Clay County Chamber of Commerce boasts that it caters to small businesses and offers a "wide array of programs" to help new and small businesses. That sounds bor-ing to me, but I know the real story of the Chamber building: Chimps.

In 1929 the Yale University Laboratory of Primate Biology estab-lished the Yale Anthropoid Experimental Station. Although not open to the public, *Guide* authors determined the station housed "about 30 chimpanzees used for the study of primate reproduction, genetics, behavioral adaptation, hygiene, and pathology."

This was fifty-one years before the founding of People for Ethical Treatment of Animals. Locals called the building the Monkey Farm. Dr. Robert Yerkes studied the chimps for three decades; today, his work continues in an Atlanta zoo under the auspices of the Yerkes National Primate Research Center. The Anthropoid Experimental Station today houses the Clay County Chamber. No chimpanzees are readily apparent.

Disappointed at the Chamber's paucity of monkeys, we stop for lunch at Green Cove Springs, the Clay County seat. The town has a Mayberry-esque aura. Green Cove Springs borders the banks of the St. Johns River, and, true to its name, a spring burbles up . . . into a cement-walled hole. After that it flows through concrete channels into the municipal swimming pool and continues, at roughly 3,000 gallons a minute, to the St. Johns River.

The spring, today gleaming with only a minimum of plastic Aquafina water bottles and Coke cans resting on limestone rocks rising up from its crystal depths, allegedly enchanted Ponce de León, who supposedly presumed it the Fountain of Youth. This is a neat story, except Ponce de León was too embroiled in a long-distance political battle to care about a Fountain of Youth.

....

According to Michael Francis, a USF St. Petersburg professor specializing in Spanish Florida, Ponce de León never mentioned a fountain of youth while he was alive. That connection came after his death, by one of his detractors.

Here's how it happened: Gonzalo Fernández de Oviedo y Valdés, a Spanish court chronicler, didn't much care for Ponce de León, characterizing him as not very bright, too easily taken in by stories, and self-centered. This harsh assessment of Ponce de León's personality may have had something to do with Oviedo's allegiance to Christopher Columbus's son, Diego. You see, Ponce de León was, at one time, governor of Puerto Rico, but Diego, as part of the sort of politics we still see today, wanted him out of Puerto Rico. It was a messy affair and not easily forgotten. Years later, as a way to poke at Ponce de León posthumously, Oviedo wrote *Historia general y natural de las Indias*, which included a bit of satire about Ponce de León getting tricked by the Indians into charging through the underbrush in search of eternal life.

Here's the thing: People knew it was satire. They understood the convention. Even back in the sixteenth century, when doctors opted for hitting patients in the head with a hammer to knock them out for surgery, even *then*, people laughed at the notion of a fountain of youth. And yet, less than one hundred years after it was printed, that satire became history.

....

As do many sulfur springs, Green Cove—despite its ultimate failure to provide eternal life—attracted its share of hobnobbers, back when people hobnobbed. Whether or not the fearless Spaniard actually saw this spring mattered not to tourist bureaus; President Grover Cleveland visited annually, and both J. C. Penney and Gail Borden (of Borden milk fame) owned property here.

J. C. Penney took his love of the area so far as to build a farm colony just outside of town, which morphed into a retirement community for Christian ministers. Today the community accepts residents who practice Christianity; it no longer requires a career in Christian service. Borden bought property near the springs and turned into a cornucopia of parks and courts.

As we walk through the town center, city hall employees enjoy lunch along the riverbank, and while some people stroll along the creek leading from the swimming pool to the river, the town shows scant evidence of tourists, chain-store magnates, or milk queens.

....

Farther down US 17 we pass through Etoniah Creek State Forest. Florida manages more than 1 million acres comprising thirty-five state forests, not including three national forests. These forests are not tree sanctuaries; the pines we see as we poke along Florida's backroads and byroads will fulfill their tree destinies as pencils, diapers, and tables.

The Florida Forest Service makes it clear they're about managing re-
sources, not making sure each tree reaches its full forest potential:
"Through sound forest management practices, the Florida Forest Service is able to maintain the integrity of the forest environment while
providing for the state's future natural resource needs."

Part of that management includes wood cultivation as well as keeping lands open for Bambi and friends. And why not? Florida has a lot
of land and a lot of trees. Lacking state oversight, we'd likely have just
a lot of strip malls along US 17, but as we travel it now we can see a
road not that changed from the *Guide's* "heavily traveled route . . . lined
with billboards, filling stations, roadside eating places, fruit and pecan stands, and tourist cabin camps." These trees will become pencils,
yes, but they will do so at a measured pace, with replacement saplings
shooting up all the time, reverse ramrod soldiers, waiting if not willing
to fall into service.

Etoniah Creek State Forest, in addition to keeping Florida's trees
safe, provides habitat for the scrub jay, a not-so-distant relative to the
more common and not-so-endangered blue jay. Scrub jays get their
name from their homes, the Florida scrub. If you've never seen a scrub,
think of it as a Florida desert, meaning dry and sandy, yet vegetated.
If you've never seen a scrub jay, picture a blue jay after a hard night of
drinking. Duller and more disheveled than their common cousin, these
sweet birds perpetually appear to have just come off a bender. Scrub
jays find sanctuary throughout Florida, although as we add concrete
strip malls and theme parks smack-dab in the middle of the scrub,
the jay packs up and moves into ever-winnowing snatches of habitat.
Today, the US Fish and Wildlife Service (FWS) considers the scrub jay
a "threatened" species. Despite our insistence on trading scrub for cement, the friendly, nondescript scrub jay perseveres. In 1999, the state
legislature briefly considered making the scrub jay, not the mockingbird, the state bird. It made sense: five states use the mockingbird as
their state bird, but no state uses any sort of jay as its symbol. School-
children around the state signed a petition, citing the gentle nature of
the bird—including its propensity for eating out of people's hands—as
one reason. Marion Hammer, an NRA lobbyist, shot down the choice,
calling the scrub jay a "welfare bird."

"Begging for food isn't sweet," she argued. "It's lazy and it's welfare mentality." She also expressed righteous indignation over their feeding habits—the scrub jay, like other jays, eats anything, and that often includes eggs.

"That's robbery and murder. I don't think scrub jays can even sing," she said.

Scrub jays do indeed whistle a quiet song.

The scrub jay lost its bid for becoming the state bird, much as it lost its bid for habitat across the state.

While we don't see many scrub jays left in Florida, we do, apparently, have a burgeoning goat industry. The stretch of US 17 south of Etoniah is absolutely lousy with goat farms. The proliferation of what appeared to be pygmy goats sent me scrambling for the Internet, where I learned about scabies, a disease more common in sheep than goats, and that if you let your male goats hang out with your female goats all year, the kids will have a higher mortality rate. I also found a borderline racist Florida Department of Agriculture brochure that suggested Florida's affinity for goats lies with all our immigrants. Florida, I learned, is one of the top-five meat goat producers. So, uh, thank a Cuban? Perhaps the DOA meant Puerto Rico, although I'm not certain Puerto Ricans qualify as immigrants. Also, I only think this because Puerto Rico made the Chupacabra famous.

Toward the end of the last century, Puerto Rican goat farmers and some people who had goats for whatever other reason people have goats in south Florida reported their goats victimized by the chupacabra, which means "goat sucker." The chupacabra is one of Florida's three cryptids—mythological creatures who stealthily avoid scientific detection—and it reportedly sucks all the blood out of goats and leaves the carcasses, tidy monster that it is. The goats here appear alive and full of blood, but as we continue on, we see signs for a town that claims one of the other of Florida's cryptids: Bardin.

The rest of the world has Bigfoot, yetis, and abominable snowmen. In addition to the chupacabra, Florida has the Bardin booger in north Florida's Putnam County and the skunk ape in south Florida's Collier County. The Bardin booger and the skunk ape differ only in habitat and the skunk ape's alleged propensity for legumes (more on that in a bit).

The Bardin booger lives among the pine flatwoods and swamps; the skunk ape makes his home in the Everglades. Like Bigfoot, those who have seen the man-ape have yet to capture its furry human likeness on a clearly focused length of celluloid. Like Bigfoot, those who claim the Florida versions' existence do so with a passion. Lest you think this sort of passion confines itself to backwoods rednecks, rest assured that even in Florida's legislature, beliefs hold strong. In 1977, representative Paul Nuckolls (R-Fort Myers) sponsored a bill that would have made it a misdemeanor to possess, harm, or molest "any anthropoid or humanoid animal which is native to Florida, popularly known as the Skunk Ape."

"It's an important piece of legislation," Nuckolls told reporters. "They're very important, but I can't get them to the polls."

The bill did not pass, perhaps because of the poor skunk ape voter turnout.

The Bardin booger lives in the unincorporated town of Bardin. Putnam County contains only five cities: Interlachen, Crescent City, Pomona Park, Welaka, and Palatka, the county seat. Of these, Palatka is perhaps the best-known.

Palatka started as a trading post on the St. Johns River in 1821, taking its name from an Indian word—pilaklikaha—that means "crossing over." The *Guide* also says one of the area's fashionable hotels served "adolescent chicken[8]." Further research indicates the writer had dined at the St. John's Inn, which, as late as the 1960s, still served "adolescent chicken" alongside lamb, wild turkey, and sweetbread.

While it offers no adolescent chicken today, Angel's Diner makes my list of don't-miss Florida history. A converted train car that's seen better days, Angel's lays claim to "oldest diner in Florida." Angel's opened in 1932 and has triumphed as the premier greasy spoon along the St. Johns River.

The food critic's take on Angel's? The food is greasy, the seats are few, and the decor is sparse. My take on Angel's? Their food is classic "diner," which is exactly what you should want and expect if you intend to pass under its mint-and-Pepto-Bismol-colored awning. This is not fancy food; it isn't even Florida food—you'll find no frogs' legs, mullet, or wild hog on this menu. You will find burgers that taste like burgers, fries crisp and leggy rather than fat and mushy, and milkshakes called pusalows, made with chocolate milk, vanilla syrup, and crushed ice.

Angel's is remarkable in its unremarkability. It has survived eighty years on the strength of diner-osity alone. There is nothing especially Florida about it, at least not markedly more so than any other Florida diner; nonetheless, a stopover at Angel's makes a road trip to or from the northeast corner of the state feel a little more authentic.

Still full on rich chocolate pusalows, we stop at Ravine Gardens for a stroll.

People don't praise Florida for its mountains. Along that line of thinking, they don't much mention ravines and valleys, either. The highest point in the state, Britton Hill, reaches only 345 feet. To put this in perspective, sixteen states have lowest points *higher* Britton Hill. This makes the 120-foot plunge at Ravine Gardens something of a Florida anomaly.

While *Guide* writers like Hurston and Kennedy worked tirelessly to document the state, other New Dealers participated in the relief as part of the Civilian Conservation Corps. Young men performed manual labor as part of a massive conservation effort. In Florida, the most visible evidence of the CCC lies in the state's extensive state parks system.

Throughout our travels, we stayed almost exclusively in state parks. I've slept in tents along the beach, in a camper among the pines and minihills of north Florida, and in cabins that put most hotel rooms to shame. The CCC played a not-insignificant role in creating this infrastructure, building everything at eight of the state parks. At Ravine Gardens, they converted a rough ravine into a manicured state park, although the park didn't receive its status until 1970. It took the St. Johns River thousands of years to carve the ravine, the state park's website says, but it took workers roughly one year to cover the ravine in one hundred thousand azaleas. They didn't stop there, adding thousands of subtropical trees, vines, and plants. By the end of the twentieth century, the Department of the Interior added the park to the National Register of Historic Places, and the American Society of Landscape Architects designated it a National Landmark for Outstanding Landscape Architecture.

We drive the almost-2-mile weathered brick loop circling the ravine, and the sun pales. In this light, Ravine Gardens looks more like a rainforest than manicured garden. Palms and oaks shoot up from the belly of the ravine; vines twine themselves around cypress trees. Epiphytes, ferns, and wildflowers do as they please in the soil, with no apparent regard for the ordered whims and proper wishes of those federal gardeners. Ravine Gardens, from the top, shows us an orgy of pistils and stamens, a hedonistic floral assault on the senses.

As we make our way down the ravine, the gardens come more into focus. At the bottom of the ravine, a wonderland of ordered verdigris stands in quiet contrast to the blazing disorder above. A footbridge joins patches of society garlic and St. Augustine grass; cypress trees wait patiently at the water's edge as water lilies line up behind them. The water itself moves through a brick-lined aquifer. I can squint and picture the gardens in their azalea-tended glory. I open my eyes, and the order and effort is replaced instantly by the reality of nature in Florida: it heeds no one, pleases only itself, and overtakes any gardener's design.

The wildness poking through the manicured veneer does not diminish the order and sensibility of the area; DeLand's tree-lined streets and marked old-town feel date back to the town's founder, Henry DeLand. DeLand, a baking powder manufacturer, planted water oaks along the town's infant streets in 1876. A decade later the city council offered property owners a fifty-cent tax rebate for every planted tree at least two inches in diameter. So amenable to trees were the landowners that "the response threatened to bankrupt the town, and the ordinance was repealed less than two years later," according to the *Guide*.

Stetson University, founded in 1883 and Florida's oldest private university, makes its home here. The town feels like a college town, with elegant buildings spread along US 17, kind of a stately extension of Ravine Gardens State Park. The *Guide* tells us that in 1939, the town's activities centered on campus, and this remains true today. Campus buildings line the town, as do oaks. Houses reminiscent of southern farmhouses and cracker houses add to the town's dignified feel.

Not far from the painted white wood homes and black shutters are the teal and jade colors of Blue Springs. Blue Springs offers refuge to manatees. The constant 72-degree water makes the state park a safe haven when the rest of the St. Johns River grows colder. Campers can stay all year-round, with winter months filling up faster, both for manatees and people. A typical January afternoon at the park will find visitors crowded around the observation deck, staring down at the West Indian manatees, who, in turn, stare back, supremely disinterested in anything except the green river plants that make up their diets. Visitors may snorkel, kayak, and dive the springs, though not during peak manatee times. When manatees flock to the springhead, they're so thick in the water it is unlikely a snorkeler could wend his way between their lumpy, rough, gray bodies, anyway.

Back on US 17, the stately oaks and blue springs cave in under the weight of Florida's popularity. Sanford skirts Lake Monroe, and today, just as in the 1930s, US 17 contours the lakeshore.

If you travel Florida's backroads long enough, you'll notice that most cities have an ostensibly unique claim to fame. At one time Jackie Gleason called Miami the "Sun and Fun Capital of the World"; St. Pete Beach boasts "Sunset Capital of Florida"; Key Largo honors itself as "Dive Capital of the World."

Sanford, according to the *Guide*, holds a similar honor: the capital of Florida's celery belt, which not many Floridians realized we even had, so that's impressive right there. In 1939, Sanford shipped most of the state's 3.3 million crates of celery to market. Today, Sanford celebrates its crunchy green heritage in a myriad of ways. The city holds an annual Celery Masquerade Ball (complete with the crowning of the Celery Queen). The purpose of the ball? To raise money for *Celery Soup*, a play celebrating the city's history.

Not everything about celery has such altruistic roots: Lennar Homes built Celery Estates, mid-priced, cookie-cutter suburban homes; Celery Estates competes with nearby Celery Key, another boilerplate housing development offering the Florida dream for moderate prices.

The only celery-related items missing from Sanford? Celery. For all its celery-themed events and what I'm sure is celery-related debauchery at the celery after-parties, modern Sanford has no celery farms. It has, in fact, no farms at all. It does, however, have a zoo, an airport, and no shortage of lakes and fishing. Its biggest claim to fame—at least until 2012—was the Senator, a 3,500-year-old bald cypress tree that reached heights of almost 120 feet. The *Guide* refers to it as the Big Tree, "more than 3,000 years old, 47 feet in circumference at the base and 125 feet high."

The Senator got his name when M. O. Overstreet, a state senator from 1920 to 1924, donated the land on which the tree stood to the county. Seminole County used the land to create Big Tree Park, and until January 16, 2012, the Senator was the park's flagship attraction at the park. In the early-morning hours of Monday, January 16, the tree burned. In a matter of hours, 3,500 years of nature, thriving a stone's throw from the congested tangle of Orlando, succumbed to fire.

It does seem apropos foreshadowing, however, to discuss the death of a historically and environmentally significant piece of Floridana as we head farther south together on US 17. As the cities open up, the road closes in, hemmed with the increasingly ever-present Dollar General store, Tire Kingdoms, and KFC franchises.

Here we find our first hints along this tour that, as Florida historian Dr. Gary Mormino paraphrases Gertrude Stein in his lectures, "there is no here, here." The road starts to resemble Anytown, USA: gone are the ravines filled with azaleas and palm trees; gone are the hometown streets of DeLand with oaks rubbing leafy shoulders with one another. This stretch of road offers evidence in the case against globalization, because here, US 17 morphs from a delightful tour to a neon and plastic midway, with strip malls and stoplights rides that strap you in against your will. Except, wait: has it essentially changed at all in nature? I think again of the *Guide*'s first words, both descriptive and prophetic, about US 17: A road not yet wholly paved with asphalt but blanketed with billboards, gas stations, diners, and tourist attractions.

When we pull off the road for Wekiwa Springs State Park, I breathe a sigh of relief. Snuggled against the pressing weight of Orlando's outlying development is a spring, a park, and a wooded campsite. The skies are growing dark with an afternoon summer storm as we slip into the spring.

When I say the encroaching development snugs up against the park, I mean right up against it. Along the wooded trail to our campsite I glimpse yellow stucco homes with bird-caged pools and manicured lawns abutting the park. I wonder how many hapless black garter snakes and not-so-hapless-but-not-as-vicious-as-you'd-think coral snakes receive a death sentence because homeowners didn't really understand what it means to live surrounded by nature.

Wekiwa Springs pushes 42 million gallons of water down the Wekiva River every day. The different spellings of the spring and the river are neither a misprint nor a charming Florida mistake; in Creek language—pre-Seminole—Wekiwa means "spring of water" and Wekiva means "flowing water." In English, we spell them differently but pronounce them identically.

I move to the edge of the springhead on concrete stairs coated with bright-green algae, and Barry climbs down and turns to me after a long moment, wide-eyed.

"I had no idea," he says quietly and not without excitement lining his voice. I realize he means the spring. He's never seen a spring before and always assumed "springs" meant tiny holes in the ground, not dazzling blue-green holes in the limestone that let you peer toward the center of the earth. Florida has fifteen state parks with "springs" in their name; many more include part of a network of springs. Geologically fascinating, yes, he figured, but worth creating a park for? He didn't get it until just this moment.

That's when I understand we see the *Guide*'s tours from two places, Barry and I. I see the roads as something sandwiched between Florida's overdevelopment—chain stores and congested roads and ever-present real estate advertisements—while he sees them as new things to be discovered, a way to peel back the franchised veneer of paradise and peek at why we suffer through the political scandals and overpopulation and hurricanes. In my eyes, Old Florida is about to disappear, but these tours show Barry a new Florida to explore. I consider this as Barry takes a lazy lap across the springhead, emerging from the water as thunder booms overhead. We reach the campsite as the skies open up, recharging the spring and our batteries as we prepare for the next day's drive through Orlando.

Winter Park offers an almost small-town feel, with a main street, train station, and a true walkable district of shops at the town's core. Laid out by New Englanders with a plan for a six-hundred-acre town,

Winter Park still radiates hints of the pastoral. The private, expensive, and old Rollins College bookends the main street. The other end morphs into somewhat less unique housing communities. Trees and shrubbery abound, some of the last greenery we will see until we trade road for swamp in Kissimmee.

Much writing exists on Orlando, and I shall not add to the canon of literature here. Anything you wish to know of the tourist mecca you can learn from a bevy of guidebooks. As we drive through Orlando, I keep hearing Mormino's voice, preaching the paraphrased gospel of Stein: *There is no here, here.* Except for the ever-present knowledge that we are never far from Mickey Mouse, we could be anywhere. Nothing here looks exclusively like Florida.

Everything that follows draws us closer to the Everglades, although in spots it feels we somehow move farther away. At Winter Haven, I am both shocked and not at all surprised to find no vestiges of the Winter Haven described in the *Guide,* where mountain-ebony trees line the main streets in a city surrounded by citrus groves. This town used to host the Orange Festival every January, with permanent displays in concrete houses. The heart of citrus once beat here, but now only a few period signs remain. It seems to me this whole tour is peppered with an on-again, off-again relationship with Florida's swampy reality, and Lake Wales is definitely "off again." My depression while passing through this Florida-less Florida starts to lift as we eke our way farther south along US 17. In Arcadia, I feel my muscles start to ease. The *Guide* describes Arcadia as an "oasis in a vast Florida prairie" surrounded by treeless flatland, and this slow, rambling countryside grabs back for me the Florida triumphing over vacant storefronts with abundant vines, grasses, and palms. To another person, these things may signify a failing economy. To me, it is unquestionable proof that, as Dr. Ian Malcolm says in *Jurassic Park*, life finds a way.

DeLand is a study in the proper care and feeding of Florida farmhouses while Arcadia is its rebellious twin. The architecture in these two towns is not dissimilar: you can find white frame homes with shutters, wraparound porches, and shingled roofs. But DeLand is a true small town; Arcadia has land that spreads out from the town. Arcadia is the surrounding cattle country's downtown. Cattle ranchers and farmers live here, as well as antiques dealers, mechanics, and government workers who head to a stately brick courthouse—probably one of the best-kept buildings in town and also one of the most manicured lawns. The town has an easy looseness not allowed in strip-mall-regimented towns; I see no apparent order as to what store goes where.

Farther south, US 17 meets its end when it joins up with US 41. By this time no question remains that this road is unquestionably Florida, from the dulling sameness of Orlando to the beautiful decay just north and south of Arcadia. The commerce served by the road may not be identical, but it hasn't strayed far from the *Guide*'s prophetic description: It still "serves thriving resort centers, large citrus- and vegetable-growing areas, cattle ranges, and phosphate-mining regions. Leaving the pine woods of north Florida, it parallels the western bank of the lakes and hills. Through the broad valley of Peace River it continues southwest to Charlotte Harbor, an arm of the Gulf of Mexico."

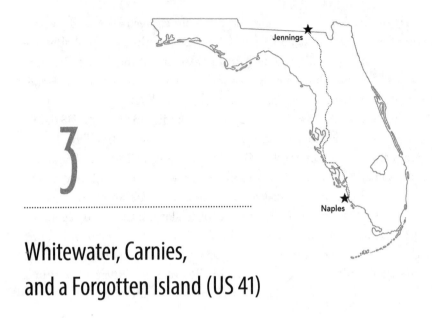

3

Whitewater, Carnies,
and a Forgotten Island (US 41)

Throughout our great Florida adventure, I never quite made sense of
US 41. I finally concluded it should not be one road: it's too different at
each end. So disparate are the north and south ends that attempting to
make it in one run could land you with a severe case of culture shock.

Guide editors apparently agreed, splitting the road into several tours:
from the Florida/Georgia line to Williston; from Williston to Tampa;
from Tampa to Fort Myers; and from Fort Myers to Naples. They also
added a short separate tour that took drivers on a 40-mile trip from
Tampa to Palmetto via Ruskin. Clearly, even before the state's postwar
development boom, US 41's chameleon-like properties posed problems
for travel writers, who described a dizzying array of lifestyles in four
succinct sentences:

> Proceeding down the peninsula, it [US 41] crosses a gently rolling
> area of good-sized farms, and through the sandy pine woods of west
> central Florida to industrial Tampa. Curving around Tampa Bay, the
> highway passes fertile farm lands in the vicinity of Bradenton and

reaches the Gulf at Sarasota, a town of art activities, circus quarters, and game fishing. Turning inland to tropical Fort Myers, on the Caloosahatchee River, it traverses a region of flatwoods, palms, and occasional marshland on the western edge of the Everglades. The route returns to the Gulf at Naples, where it joins US 94, a section of the Tamiami Trail leading across the Everglades. (*A Guide to the Southernmost State*)

It's not just topography that changes the road, not a simple case of hills over flatland. It's culture and demographics and commerce. The road by the Georgia state line, in Jennings, has few of the chain stores populating the roadway's lower parts. Jennings, a sylvan town of about 838 people, has an average household income of just under $40,000. At the southern end, Naples, a suburb of the Everglades and, somehow, Westchester County, New York, has just under 20,000 people and an average household income of over $163,000.

At the Georgia border, US 41 runs a ribbon of hills southeast through fields glimpsed through mossy oaks. Naples, where the tour ends, beats back the swamp with an endless maze of pavement and planned communities. Between the two roads lie some of Florida's finest jewels.

At the top, Hamilton County has the state's only Class III whitewater rapids, at Big Shoals State Park. During conditions that meet the region's water needs, the Suwannee River rises about sixty feet above sea level. I have big plans to shoot the rapids, but the ranger tells us not to bother because today we could cross the riverbed at a leisurely pace without wetting our knees. The water is less than fifty-nine feet above sea level which, the park ranger tells us, makes the river non-navigable. While the southern end of Florida has no elevation worth mentioning, the north end does, with Hamilton County's whopping one-hundred-plus-foot elevation. That's Florida mountain country.

Since I moved to Florida in 1980, I've seen mountains exactly three times. I didn't understand how water levels affected rapids here; I had to have Barry explain it to me. When the state gets not enough rain, the water level drops, and there isn't enough water for rapids. But when the state gets too much rain, too, the rapids disappear, because a flooded river means flat water. As soon as the water drops to less than fifty-nine feet above sea level, the rapids disappear. When that water rises, they reappear, but when the water rises to more than sixty-one feet above sea level, the river once again goes flat. It's a narrow window.

Rangers record the levels daily and can tell you with a phone call what type of water—if any—you'll find at the park. This matters greatly, because you can't bring your car to Big Shoals. You have a mile hike from the parking area to the put-in. No big deal if you have one of those neat wheely deals for your kayak. I don't. We instead head to Stephen Foster Folk Culture Center State Park in White Springs, where we make camp. The *Guide* reports that the springs boast legendary medicinal qualities. Locals capitalized on these alleged healing qualities. This included building a three-story underground springhouse and staffing treatment rooms with doctors so people could take a health vacation to White Springs, also called White Sulphur Springs.

By the 1930s, the appeal of mineral springs as a tourist health destination started to fade, perhaps in part due to many potential tourists standing in breadlines instead of boarding trains south to Florida. Two decades later, the Stephen Foster Memorial Museum (now the state park) opened. Stephen Foster wrote the state song, "Old Folks at Home," commonly known as "Way Down upon the Swanee River," and yes, the misspelling of the Suwannee River was intentional.

While the Florida legislature made this our state song in 1935, the song does not mention Florida at all; the Suwannee starts in the Okefenokee Swamp and flows through Georgia, into Florida, and out to the Gulf of Mexico. Foster could have intended any part of the river as the subject of his stanzas. I say "could have" because he never actually *saw* Florida, no evidence suggests he saw the Suwannee in Georgia, and, in fact, he only chose the river for the song because it fit with the meter of his song. Furthermore, Foster wrote the song for a blackface minstrel group, an unfortunate but accepted art form of the day. But in 1935—some eighty years after the end of the Civil War—the legislature thought this delightful tune, designed to make black people sound like they pined for the bad ol' days of plantation life, better represented the southernmost state than "Florida, My Florida," the not-at-all-racially-charged and spells-places-properly state song ad-opted in 1913. It gets better. It was only in 1978 that we replaced "dar-kies" with "brothers" in the second verse of the song, which a vocalist would sing at every gubernatorial inauguration. Only when Governor Charlie Crist took office did these performances stop; he challenged the notion of using the song, and under his leadership Florida legisla-tors held a contest for a new state song. Although ultimately the leg-islature adopted "Florida (Where the Sawgrass Meets the Sky)" as the state anthem, Florida retained "Old Folks at Home" as the state song, albeit a Stephen-Foster-scholar-approved version with less offensive lyrics.

The difference between a state anthem and a state song? That is an excellent question, one the legislature isn't explaining. Our darlings die hard, I suppose. Nevertheless, we maintain—at taxpayer expense—a lovely culture center honoring Mr. Foster.

Throughout these tours, we attempted to stay at state parks when-ever feasible. Without exception, every park ranger loved his or her park and the whole of the state as much as I did and never hesitated to share local anecdotes. These enthusiastic men and women are per-haps the state's finest (albeit grossly underpaid—new rangers make about twelve dollars an hour, before taxes) representatives. The bath-houses, however, varied greatly, and without question I found the Ste-phen Foster bathhouses some of Florida's most well-apportioned. The park offers modern amenities and bathhouses that border on cushy, although they appear a modest, one-story affair. Each shower stall has heat lamps, benches, and plenty of hot water. The park offers a host of folk-related activities, including daily quilting, blacksmithing, and other crafting activities, and a folk festival the final weekend in May.

Each night when we stopped the camper, we had a routine. While Barry hooked up the water and electric and did other "man things," I found my shoes, clipped a leash on Calypso, and stretched her stubby legs and mine in a brisk walk around the grounds. From one campsite to the next, we often saw the same faces and campers. End-of-the-day dog walks are a necessity for many couples traveling the state together. It is on these walks that I hear tales of snakes, because while many of my camping brethren enjoy the outdoors, snakes have the worst

PR of any animal except for, perhaps, the spider. Calypso is paying a downed tree trunk great interest when a woman with a dog of her own stops to tell me about a rattlesnake by the split-rail fence about forty feet away. Now, I don't expect everyone to know how to identify venomous snakes. People often mistake the nonvenomous king snake for the deadly coral snake. Incidentally, the coral snake has the most toxic venom of any Florida snake but is not as deadly as you might believe. Oh, it's a member of the mamba family, and its venom is nasty, wicked stuff, but—and try not to giggle here—the coral snake is a nibbler. Instead of striking, injecting venom, and pulling out her fangs to strike again, like a respectable rattlesnake or copperhead will, the coral snake latches on and ruminates on whatever she's got in her mouth, like a baby with a Zwieback cracker. If that's the tender spot between your toes, you're in a world of trouble. Get to a hospital—a good one—soon. If she tries to nosh on your elbow, though, chances are you're going to get away with a nasty bite. Nevertheless, people tend to react strongly when they see a coral snake—or when they think they have. Coral and king snakes have mostly the same color bands but in different order. Rhymes *should* help you remember: "red touch yellow, kill a fellow" and "red touch black, friend to Jack." But the one time I saw a coral snake, in my thrill and panic I couldn't recall if it was "red touch black, friend to Jack" or "if his nose is black, he's a friend to Jack," so I can understand how people might get confused. Rattlesnakes aren't confusing snakes, though: the rattle tends to make them easy to pick out in a crowd. I believe my fellow camper, and poor Calypso—bred to go into holes and pull out badgers—doesn't understand why we complete our nightly walk on the paved portion of the path.

The next morning we head south. The Santa Fe River, a tributary of the Suwannee, loops around the state in this area, disappearing at one point. For 3 miles the river travels underground, disappearing northeast of O'Leno State Park by Interstate 75 and poking its head up for air at River Rise Preserve State Park. O'Leno State Park offers the typical extraordinary experiences for this area of the state: birds ranging from tiny sparrow-shaped things to owls, mammals like deer and otter, and a plethora of leafy things. The park once ran through the town of Leno, founded in 1800, but when the railroad went around the town instead of through it, the town withered. By 1896 it was a ghost town, although people from nearby towns gathered at "Old Leno" for swimming and picnics. In 1935 the Florida Forest Service bought the land on which the town once stood, and while Stetson Kennedy and Zora Neale Hurston toured the state for the Federal Writers' Project, the Works Project Administration hired the unemployed workers of High Springs, 6 miles away, to build a training camp. The camp included a dining hall, tower, and suspension bridge and was intended to train people who wanted to go into the forestry industry. This lasted for two summers, until the Forestry Service turned the park over to the state park system, making O'Leno one of the first parks in the state. Today the suspension bridge still creaks and groans as I move across it, the river far below me.

Past Williston and before we get to Tampa, bumps and hills begin to flatten themselves into level roads. This is horse country; the telltale double fence signals the four-footed treasures contained within. Williston and surrounding areas boast more than 1,100 horse farms. South of Williston we find Romeo, the counterpart to the slightly-farther-south Juliette, both essentially ghost towns. A local legend involving a pair of star-crossed lovers inspired both town names, the *Guide* tells us, adding in its deadpan fashion that "the misspelling of the name was not intentional."

Maps still show the town of Romeo as well as Juliette, and between the two, Rainbow Springs State Park, a mecca for kayakers, tubers, snorkelers, and flower fans.

First a phosphate pit and later a privately owned attraction that included glass-bottom-boat tours, a zoo, and treetop monorail tours, the park closed after traffic repeatedly chose the interstate over US 41. From the mid-1970s until 1990, the park succumbed to nature, native plants overtaking the manicured gardens, paths, and zoo cages. In 1990 the state park service officially took over the park.

A self-guided walk along sloping, flower-fringed brick paths takes guests past a man-made waterfall, the springhead, and a set of eerily overgrown zoo cages. The almost Victorian feel of some of the volunteer-maintained gardens falls into wildflower-lined trails at the park's edges.

Farther down the road, Brooksville awaits, as, at one time, did a lovely bar called Miss Kitty's. By "lovely" I mean "gritty." I visited Miss Kitty's exactly once, a graduate student enjoying a retreat at a manor house called Chinsegut in Brooksville. After dinner, Ray Arsenault, one of the program leaders, announced he needed to watch the baseball game and would like to go to Miss Kitty's to do so. My fellow Florida scholar Jon looked at me, and we both raised our eyebrows. Uncle Ray (as we called him) wrote *Freedom Riders*, a powerful history about black and white young men and women who boarded buses and rode them into the segregated South. The bumper stickers on his late-model Volvo leave no ambiguity as to his left-leaning political inclinations. He is a gifted man who has spent his entire life in academia and should not be allowed unattended in country bars. We followed in Jon's pickup truck and watched Uncle Ray wedge his Obama-bedazzled car in between two trucks with rebel flags and gun racks and walk toward the front door.

"He's going to get killed, isn't he?" I said to Jon. Jon laughed, then nodded, and together we went to absorb the bleached neon wonder that was Miss Kitty's, a Hank Williams song viewed from the inside out. I loved it instantly. Uncle Ray looked like the academic version of Joe Pesci in *My Cousin Vinny* and asked our waitress, in tight white jeans, a moussed mess of unnaturally blonde kinky curls, and bright-pink lipstick that in no way eased into the fine lines assaulting her upper lip, what the women at the next table were drinking. The waitress glanced at the fuchsia drinks held in buxom hurricane glasses.

"That's a Knock-Me-Down-And-Fuck-Me," she replied without an ounce of humor.

"Ah." Uncle Ray paused, but just barely, then nodded his head and said with great dignity, "I believe I shall have one of those."

Jon, who clearly took his graduate assistantship more seriously than I ever did, ordered the same. I ordered a rum and Coke. We watched the women line-dance and flirt with the much younger band. Our drinks arrived. I looked at the two men at the table and raised my squat rocks glass and clinked it against their taffy-colored hurricane glasses in a toast.

South of Brooksville the road slants toward the west, angling for Tampa. While the *Guide* tells motorists to expect a "long stretch of cypress ponds and cut-over pine lands," within miles the road loses the wooded feel and takes on a more suburban tone, with chain grocers, planned housing communities, and shopping centers.

This stretch of US 41 runs nowhere near the Gulf of Mexico, although the road offers the occasional view of tributaries that feed Tampa Bay and, on a clear day, the Bay itself. South of Tampa the road runs closer to the Gulf, but marinas and barrier islands block the view.

As the road crosses the Hillsborough River and runs through Ybor City's history-and-nightclub mecca, urbanism awakes. The *Guide* describes an Ybor City where Cubans planned a revolution just before the Spanish-American War and where, in 1936, cigar factories produced over 2.5 billion cigars. Now, the Columbia Restaurant still serves Spanish dishes in its original building, but visitors to the city are more likely to take in a movie than hear a lector read aloud to the cigar workers.

And yet history holds its grasp.

"From Cuba, Spain, and Italy, the Latin-Americans of Ybor City and Tampa have imported their own customs and traditions which survive mostly in annual festivals. The Cubans found good political use for voodoo beliefs brought by slaves from Africa to the West Indies and there called *Carabali Apapa Abacua*," the *Guide* tells us, describing a cultish marriage between voodoo and Cuban revolutionaries, the resultant group called Naningoes. Naningo societies, found only in Tampa and Key West, the *Guide* continues, had elaborate initiation ceremonies that included "street dances of voodoo origin."

Ybor City has a National Historic Landmark District, which means that entire blocks, not just one or two buildings, have history deemed worthy of preservation. The Ybor City Museum Society works to safeguard the city's heritage, but the architecture, roadways, and signs all signify that, despite the appearance of upper-middle-class condominiums that cater to working professionals, Ybor City intends to retain the character described in the *Guide*, that of a city separate from but equal to Tampa. Both cities, the *Guide* says, "retain their native customs, their squalor and beauty, their picturesque festivals, and contribute to the city's gayety and color."

In parts of Hillsborough County, the road abuts the Alafia River. In the 1960s and 1970s, the landscape was forever altered with draglines and heavy equipment from the burgeoning phosphate extraction at Lonesome Mine. Cytec Industries donated the husk of what the *Guide* describes as formerly an area "wooded with magnolia and bay" to the state in 1996. The state re-created a "second nature," or a re-created wild area, for the park, and mountain bikers now use the steeply graded trails created by mining.

The park has a smattering of lakes, also a by-product of mining, but the Alafia River runs its course through the park. I saw my first-ever manatee while paddling the river in the 1990s and screamed when his powerful gray fluke slapped the black water of the river not two feet from my canoe. I'd never paddled on a blackwater river, and not being able to see what lurked beneath, coupled with the stern paddler's—a future ex-boyfriend—inability to keep me from nosing into the spider-lined riverbanks, had me on edge. I did not expect to find a manatee on a freshwater river, but since the Alafia drains to Tampa Bay, I should not have been surprised.

Geographically, the river runs close to the Hillsborough River, and for years it played second fiddle to the Hillsborough, at least in terms of size. In the early part of the new millennium, though, Tampa Bay Water, an agency created to settle the water wars raging in the Tampa Bay area, started combining Hillsborough River water with groundwater, or water pumped from the Floridan Aquifer well beneath the spongy limestone.

Those water wars centered around groundwater and wells near burgeoning suburbs; homeowners complained that groundwater withdrawals from those wellfields caused their own private wells and lakes to run dry and sinkholes to suck the ground into the earth. As the debate raged, the West Coast Regional Water Supply Authority—which would later become Tampa Bay Water—tried to help. The agency coordinated water supply and delivery for three counties (Pinellas, Pasco, and Hillsborough) and three cities (New Port Richey, St. Petersburg, and Tampa) while reportedly calming tensions. The solution was a compromise—the area still gets drinking water from the Floridan Aquifer, but Tampa Bay Water, which runs the facilities, also uses an often-functioning, allegedly state-of-the-art desalination plant and surface water from the Hillsborough River. When you consider that the area depended wholly on groundwater for drinking water in 1998 but used the Hillsborough River for 28 percent of the drinking water supply in 2008 and used it for about half of the region's drinking water supplies in 2012, it makes sense that the Alafia River now exceeds the neighboring Hillsborough in the amount of water it pushes to Tampa Bay.

South of the Hillsborough River another Florida awaits: Gibsonton and the International Independent Showmen's Association, or IISA. For those of you not familiar with Gibsonton, I have one word: carnies.

Gibsonton didn't always serve, as it does now, as a winter home for carnies, called showmen in polite company. The larger-than-life boot, the breakfast eatery called "Giant's Camp," the midget mayor . . . in a state surrounded by the bizarre, the extreme, the freakish, Gibsonton wasn't just another carnival roadside stop. It was where the carnies went—and still do—to get a break from the circus, be it a Florida circus or any number of Greatest Shows on Earth across the country.

Of course, before the carnies came, there were pirates. From the *Guide*:

> Residents have often searched for buried pirate gold in the vicinity. One group, in possession of an old chart, unearthed a skeleton sitting upright, and below it a metal disk with the points of the compass and a needle marked on its face; in the excitement one of the party snatched up the compass without noting the direction indicated by the needle. Although many days were spent in excavating the premises, no treasure was found.

This sounds wonderful, although I approach this tale with reluctant skepticism. These are the same writers who tell us "Tampa has adopted Jose Gaspar, the infamous Gasparilla" and then assure readers that he, along with Black Caesar, "were real enough pirates." Although the book references Gaspar and his treasure multiple times, no Florida historian has yet been able to prove Gaspar existed anywhere but in the minds of a marketing department wishing to bring people to Tampa for the annual Gasparilla Festival.

Gibsonton has no pirates today, and the town, an unincorporated affair, now lacks the carnival splendor described by former *Tampa Bay Times* columnist Jeff Klinkenberg in the fall of 2005:

> Everything is larger than life at Giant's Camp, an otherwise modest eatery on the Tamiami Trail in southern Hillsborough County. There's the size 22 sneaker allegedly worn by the late Al Tomaini. Then there are those biscuits, twice the size of hockey pucks but tasting more of the divine . . . The dour carnival sideshow attraction known as the Lobster Boy, born with pincers instead of hands, was no stranger to Miss Margaret's cooking. Percilla the Monkey Girl, and her husband, Emmitt the Alligator Man, also were regulars at the lunch counter. Same goes for Melvin Burkhardt, the Human Blockhead, who pounded nails up his nose without damaging his taste buds.

Today, Gibsonton has a collection of homes on par with any Hillsborough County subdivision. Pockets unlike the rest of the world remain, of course, but you can easily find a three-bedroom, two-bath gray concrete block home with an attached garage, complete with a manicured lawn and immature oak trees.

Every year, though, IISA meets for its annual convention, and more than four thousand members descend on the unincorporated town. For that week, they, not the soccer moms and bank tellers who live down the street, own the town.

Not far away another anomaly makes an annual pilgrimage, this one to the warm waters of the Apollo Beach power plant: manatees. The Apollo Beach power plant, run by Tampa Energy Company (TECO), burns coal for energy and uses salt water for cooling, then discharges the water into Tampa Bay. When the rest of the water in Tampa Bay drops below 68 degrees, the manatees head for the Apollo Beach hot tub. The waters grow thick with manatees, and so many people come to see them that TECO built a boardwalk and manatee-viewing station for the people who showed up clamoring to see them.

"Well, that's not very interesting!" one man exclaims as I peer down at a herd of manatees basking in Tampa Bay. He has a point—they don't flip in the air like dolphins, or sit up and beg for mackerel like walruses, but whether or not a group of manatees are interesting, I suppose, depends on how you look at it.

Manatees are warm-blooded marine mammals that look a bit like gray or brown blobs with tiny heads and even tinier eyes. They have all but useless front flippers, a semicircular tail fluke that does the real work of moving them through the water, and a substantial amount of body fat. They remain chunky despite a steady diet of aquatic plants, and to get those plants they graze in shallow salt or brackish water. Given their drastic body composition and their rather inefficient mobility systems, they are notorious for their lack of maneuverability, and they cannot quickly avoid a boat. Most adult manatees have propeller scars on their backs; the less lucky ones don't survive a tangle with a prop. Not surprisingly, manatees are on the endangered species list.

Florida first started trying to protect manatees in 1893, but not until 1967 did the creatures receive federal protection. The Marine Mammal Protection Act made it illegal to interfere with the behavior of a marine mammal. In Florida, that list includes dolphins, whales, and manatees. The Endangered Species Act, another federal law, offered further protection in 1973, and in 1978 the state passed the Florida Manatee Sanctuary Act. These protections could not have prevented the deaths in the winter of 2010, which saw record-breaking cold air and water temperatures in the state. Manatees, who prefer their water a comfy 72 degrees or better, did not fare well. Of the 500-plus manatees reported dead in 2010, the Florida Fish and Wildlife Conservation Commission (FWC) reported that almost half of those manatees—244—died from hypothermia. Yes, they flocked to warmer waters, such as the Apollo Beach power plant, but to get food, they had to venture into colder waters. Because the water was colder, they apparently waited until they were really, really hungry—and, consequently, had less insulating body fat—which made them prime candidates for hypothermia. These numbers, by the way, are five times the average annual manatee deaths.

Although the manatee-viewing center draws locals and tourists alike, this coastal stretch of tour—from Tampa where it becomes Gibsonton to Palmetto and rejoins the southern edge of the tour—allows, as it did in the 1930s, more for agriculture than it does tourism.

Ruskin started life in 1910 as a tomato cooperative with a twist: Chicago lawyer George Miller founded the town, the *Guide* tells us, as a socialist colony. Miller bought six thousand acres and set six hundred aside for Ruskin College, proposed as an Oxford-like education with a twist: "Students were to have four hours of schooling and, quite unlike Oxford, four hours of farm work a day," the *Guide* says. This fell apart with the onset of World War I.

Ruskin remained a tomato town until recently, complete with an annual tomato festival where, the *Guide* proclaims, the "town's most popular girl" gets crowned Tomato Queen. In the latter part of the twentieth century, the town stopped holding the festival, although after a three-decade hiatus, locals resumed crowning a Tomato King and Queen in the early part of this millennium.

Keep driving to Sun City, which, in 1939, was a ghost town with eighty-five residents, founded during one of Florida's many land booms to attract Hollywood to the Sunshine State. The "city" had a painting of what it would look like once it had triumphed over Hollywood as a moviemaking nirvana. That never came to pass, and I can't say what happened to the painting, but *Guide* writers reported the town as having run-down shacks, a railroad station, and a warehouse turning to dust.

The ghost town moved slightly down the road and metamorphosed into an "active adult living area" where "volunteer hosts" escort potential buyers around Sun City's "amenities campus." Sun City rivals only the Villages in central Florida for middle-class organized retirement living, golf carts, and farmland turned suburbs. Sun City Center has a team of volunteers who run the community association and have permission from Hillsborough County to drive unlicensed golf carts on the streets. Those who love it say Sun City Center offers them a new lease on life, far from snow tires and overwatchful adult children. Those who hate it say it's Viagra and Stepford disguised as Paradise.

Our 40-mile detour, started just south of State Road 50, rejoins the main road in Palmetto, but we double back to the main tour to visit Terra Ceia, an island just south of Tampa Bay isolated from the mainland by a mangrove thicket and Terra Ceia Bay. Here you'll find the Citrus Place, one of a handful of remaining citrus soldiers. Ben Tillett opened the Citrus Place in the 1970s as a "You Pick" grapefruit business. When citrus canker struck his groves a few years later, he could only allow workers to go into the groves. Soon after, the Citrus Place became a packinghouse and ultimately progressed to a packing and shipping business. Today, the Tillett family still owns the grove and the shop in front that sells citrus, juice, jams, jellies, and fruit sections, although Mr. Tillett's business is a dying industry. He sells bushels of honeybells and Valencias as he watches the Florida citrus industry cough its death rattle, despite what the Florida Department of Citrus's marketing says. Tropicana and Minute Maid get much of their juice from Brazil. Tasting fresh Florida juice, much less unpasteurized and locally grown and squeezed juice, will be something people tell their grandchildren about, not something they do with their grandchildren.

Because he wants to protect his business through any means necessary, Tillett started selling clams raised by a local clam farmer, Curtis Hemmel, who harvests an average of 300 million clams (including clam seeds) every year. Tillett displays the clams proudly in the Citrus Place, pulling out a newspaper article about the clam farmer and talking about how the farmer grew them "right here, in Terra Ceia Bay." He assures customers that if there are any left at the end of the week—although he is quick to say there never are—Hemmel takes them back to the bay so they don't die.

They're not oranges, but clams pay the bills.

As US 41 moves south, the density of box stores, chain stores, and drive-through windows increases inversely with the latitude. The road also moves closer to the coast.

I am unapologetically a fan of Florida's Gulf coast.

The route crosses the Manatee River at Palmetto. On the other side of the river the road intersects with State Road 64, which leads you away from the detritus of US 41 toward Anna Maria Island, a "resort at the northern extremity of Anna Maria Key, (which) consists of many cottages in a jungle setting," according to the *Guide*. It's not exactly a jungle anymore, but you will find more explosions of foliated color here than you will in any point north. Much has changed on Anna Maria Island since 1939. Palm savannas surrendered to beach cottages, and while the island herself rises but a few feet above the warm, turquoise Gulf, bungalows at Anna Maria's edge prop themselves like mangroves, resting just out of reach of salt and waves.

The spirit of the island remains untouched. Sand and shells abound, bursts of blazing pink bougainvillea cascade over fences, and dazzling orange birds of paradise stand guard along walkways. While the other side of Tampa Bay boasts the most densely populated county in the state, that county's bright-pink Don CeSar across the water fades against the tropical landscape of colors and the ever-permeating salt air.

You can trace the silhouette of much of Florida's coast with condominium- and hotel-colored crayons. Not so here; everything on this 7-mile strip of paradise—even its stilt homes—is short. The island draws tourists without needing tall hotels and convention centers; visitors can make their way around the island's shell-lined streets and paths using foot or pedal power. The island has no chain restaurants, and while you can get milk at a small store, you'll need to head to the next town over for a supermarket.

The towns along the barrier island here run parallel to the coast and US 41. Holmes Beach, Siesta Key, Longboat Key—all these towns are a study in understatement, especially as compared with the McMansions and condominiums scoring the barrier islands to their north. The beaches here are tropical tints of aqua and ultramarine, the cream sand tanned by the sun.

West of US 41 on State Road 684, Cortez is not quite the tourist beach paradise lying east of it. Cortez is a fishing village, littered with docks, wood boats, and fishing boat captains. Fish nets spread themselves across yards; the area has an annual seafood festival to celebrate its heritage as a seafood mecca.

Back on the mainland, the road cleaves Sarasota, pulling along the now-expected collection of franchises. Off the main road, Sarasota

Jungle Gardens lets people scratch a Moluccan cockatoo on its neck and then watch an exotic animal show, complete with the time-honored Florida tradition of a bird on a bicycle (and one on roller skates) and Madagascar hissing cockroaches. The park has a flamboyance of flamingos, a reptile show, and a wooded park. Sarasota also has the John and Mabel Ringling Museum of Art, the Ringling mansion (called the Ca' d'Zan), Clown College, and a circus museum (Sarasota once hosted Barnum and Bailey every winter.)

....

Venice Beach, west of the town's small airport, attracts beachcombers and divers looking for sharks' teeth. Fossilized sharks' teeth wash up on the shore of the beach. Scuba divers also find larger teeth just off the beach, although a walk during an ebbing high tide will reveal the black triangular gems. Sophisticated teeth seekers may use a wood frame with a piece of screen stapled across to sift the sand for the prehistoric treasures.

....

US 41 turns east here, crossing the Peace River, cutting through Port Charlotte, and traveling over Charlotte Harbor. To the west, Rotonda sits, an odd, almost-populated wagon-wheel-shaped town. In the 1960s, developers planned a circular community. They cleared the land, installed underground utilities, set up water and sewer infrastructure, and named streets. If you build it, they seemed to believe, they will come. Which people did, mostly. Anecdotal history suggests that 75 percent of Rotonda became populated with higher-end homes and vacation rentals.

But the other 25 percent—all spatially concentrated in an area called Rotonda Sands—did not. Rows of platted lots and streets transformed from neatly manicured lots to overgrown parcels of Florida wilderness. Locals suggested the streets lining the barren lots made excellent landing strips for those looking to bring drugs into the country. The town never had a heyday before it became a ghost town.

Rotonda Sands had another chance in the housing boom in the early part of the new millennium, and people started building homes on the wild empty lots. Hurricane Charley in 2004 and the housing market crash a few years later halted the development, isolating those who had finished building and moved into their homes, making them unintentional caretakers of a wild and aborted Florida dream in a brand-new ghost town. In 2012, Rotonda Sands finally started to finish development as people started turning the abandoned husks of concrete and roof tresses into homes.

Port Charlotte—new since *Guide* times—rests on the edge of Charlotte Harbor. The *Guide* calls Charlotte Harbor a fishing village; today, it attracts sunseekers, anglers, and snowbirds.

Through this area US 41 alternates stretches of green-lined roadway, swirling lower into the swamp, and blocks of shops and parking lots. Not far off US 41, we turn west to an almost-forgotten island, connected to the mainland by the Matlacha Bridge. The mangroves fall away to reveal a Gulf coast fishing village peopled with fishermen, artists, and locals enchanted with Old Florida. To the south, Sanibel is the prom queen of Gulf coast islands, but here Pine Island is her mangrove-encrusted, tomboy little sister. Instead of beaches, walls of state-protected red mangroves surround and prop the 34-square-mile island up on green water, preserving the calm, slow lifestyle of the nine thousand folks who call the island home.

Pine Island supports a thriving arts community, most evident along Pine Island Road with its loose groups of art galleries and restaurants, housed in shacks splashed in coral, yellow, and pink and topped with corrugated tin roofs.

To many of Florida's visitors seeking the theme park and beach experience, there is nothing to see here. Nothing on Pine Island calls to mind other Florida coastal towns; those root-heavy trees protect, too, the island's roots from developers and droves of tourists.

This is the Florida that once permeated the lower parts of the state but now lies forgotten, buried deep in the muck of shopping malls, time-shares, and miniature golf courses. The people? They are rednecks, good ol' boys mocked by those with Yankee heritage. They treasure the land Florida forgot to love and then just forgot.

Nothing to see here, really. Instead of "cuisine," folks serve platters of hearty food—grits instead of escargot, pork in lieu of tofu. Visitors can take fishing trips or cast a line at the Matlacha Bridge, known for almost a century as the "World's Fishingest Bridge," but don't even think about asking for sushi.

People come here and find solace as the salty, muddy water calms and quenches. The entire island, including Bokeelia, Pineland, and St. James City as well as Matlacha, is a dolorous souvenir of yesteryear's Florida. Developers either forgot or couldn't sell this nugget of land to the highest bidder before the government hit the brakes on the dredge-and-sell dream.

Nothing to see here, unless you care to travel south for Sanibel's rich yet quaint lifestyle, head east to Fort Myers for the beach, or farther south to Naples for the suburban swamp. Take a boat west to Cabbage Key. Go east to Palm Beach for glitz, but know that Pine Island's too far off the interstate to travel, especially since it foolishly lacks shopping malls, Holiday Inns, and putt-putt or other golf courses. Just a bunch of crusty fishermen and shopkeepers, not much else to see here.

Nothing to see here, nothing at all. Just the present that the rest of Florida's beaches traded for the future, and the past it sold before the state even knew it had it. Green and red and aquamarine and silver explode around the island as the sunset lights the streets, palm groves, and trailers. Shrimp nets draped across the boats behind homes remind islanders of their heritage and, hopefully, their future.

Nope, nothing to see here.

Before the state passed a ban on net fishing, Pine Island was a thriving fisherman's town. Today the island has changed.

"I moved to Pine Island in 1990," says Charlie Williams, a career fishermen once crowned a mullet king in his hometown of Gulfport, Florida. "There were eight fish houses and over 350 fishing families. Then came the gill net ban in '95. Now there is one fish house and 90 percent of all those families are gone . . . divorced, foreclosed, and dead . . . really sad. Multiple generations of true Floridians wiped out by lies and the ignorance of voters in the state of Florida!"

Like other mullet fishermen, Charlie—CW to his friends—is still angry about the net ban. They argue that it wasn't the small-time fishermen like themselves—one-man operations in small skiffs—that hurt fish populations, but the big fishing machines. Small-time mullet fishermen like CW had to resort to cast netting for mullet, which yielded far less fish than the banned gill nets.

North Fort Myers is on the banks of the Caloosahatchee River, a river with origins almost 70 miles east in Lake Okeechobee. The Caloosahatchee marks the northwestern edge of the remaining Everglades. Boat captains who wish to cut across the state rather than around its southern tip run through Redfish Pass, into the Caloosahatchee, and through a series of three locks before they reach the lake. Captains reach the first lock, the Franklin, 9 miles from the Fort Myers Marina. The next lock, Ortuna, is 22 miles east, and the final lock before the Big Water is yet another 16 miles. The locks help keep water in the Okeechobee; the water levels get progressively higher as the river gets closer to the lake. Without the locks, both to the east and west, the surrounding towns would flood. The locks also allow the water to flow south to the Everglades; without that flow the Glades would dry out.

In Fort Myers, US 41 explodes into splashes of neon and paint, with the road expanding from two lanes to four and the shops growing larger and more national in nature. Here Thomas Edison and Henry Ford both built winter estates. Edison came to the area believing that bamboo would offer up a filament perfect for his incandescent bulb. It didn't, but he did get a lovely resort home as a consolation prize. Allegedly, once he did invent the perfect bulb, he offered Fort Myers free lamps. The town declined, fearing the lights might give the cows insomnia.

Henry Ford and Harvey Firestone funded Edison's work, along with the federal government; defeated by bamboo but enervated by his light bulb invention, Edison believed he could find a way to produce rubber. He did, but nothing came of it.

South of Fort Myers in Estero, the Koreshan State Park is where we make camp for the night. The Koreshans were, to put it objectively, irregular—even for Florida. When the *Guide* was published, Estero was the capital for the Koreshan Unity, established in 1894. The Unity believed that humans lived not on but inside the earth and that we could achieve immortality. The path to immortality involved celibacy—for everyone but its leader, Cyrus Reed Teed, who apparently romanced anything that moved. Followers may have accepted this because they believed Teed immortal. It must have been a great shock, then, when Teed actually died, although, as the *Guide* maintains, a true believer can surmount any challenge:

> Because Teed had convinced his followers that he was immortal, on his death his body was placed on a cypress plank and laid on the banks of the Estero River. For several weeks his disciples awaited a triumphal reincarnation. It finally became necessary to place the remains in a bathtub. Soon a hurricane swept the bathtub away, and no trace of it or the body was ever found. The plank, however, was found unmoved on the spot where it had served as a bier, and this was enough to restore the faith of the sect.

"True up to and including the bathtub," Koreshan historian Daun Fletcher agrees, but adds: "The county stepped in when they found out they had him on ice and told them they had to do something proper with the body, so they then put him on a pyre-type thing and the hurricane swept that out. The result of him not coming back 'in 6' (which is what he said—but didn't clarify six what: Minutes? Hours? Days? Months? Years?) was a loss of faith and members. It was the slow beginning of the end."

Believers died out at the end of the twentieth century. In the 1960s, the last four believers deeded the property to the state.

While the state park has done a remarkable job of preserving the history of the cult, what stands out for me is the gopher tortoise.

After Calypso's twilight walk, Barry and I headed to the bathhouse and its shiny white washer to put in a load of shorts and grubby T-shirts. When we beat our way back through a barely cleared path of palms and berries, we see a gopher tortoise lazing about at our campsite. Calypso is both excited and perplexed by this bit of Florida wildlife; she circles and barks at the tortoise, to no avail: it continues its steady but not-so-fast trek back into the palm thicket.

Later, we sit and enjoy a sunset drink as we watch the palms. After the sometimes-hellish globalized path of US 41, the palm thickets and heavy Florida air make a nice, Florida-centric break from the reality of the state's south urban centers. As we discuss the underbrush and gopher tortoise, a green snake appears on a saw palmetto frond. He stares at us, and we at him, then disappears as quickly as he arrived. As night falls, the stars are easily more abundant than the chain and box stores we passed on our trek toward this bizarre New Jerusalem.

At the end of the road, the dramatic changes not unlike those described in the *Guide* exhaust me. As described in the original tours, we saw hills, farms, pinewoods, industry, farms, and ended in the subtropics, at the edge of the Everglades.

Tomorrow we will drive into the drained Everglades known today as Naples, where wealthy-enough retirees remade the western edge of the swamp into a sparkling suburban dystopia, with the mire and muck of the Glades creeping toward the city but so far losing the battle.

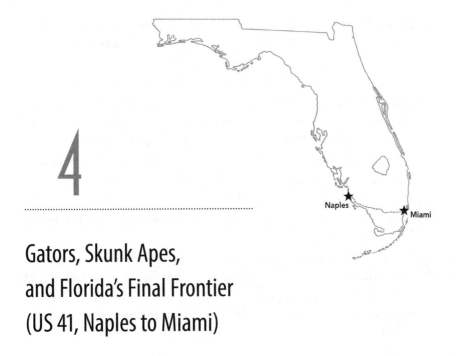

4

Gators, Skunk Apes, and Florida's Final Frontier (US 41, Naples to Miami)

The highway connects the Atlantic with the Gulf, proceeding in long straight stretches across the Everglades, a primeval swampland.

A Guide to the Southernmost State

Most drivers heading to the Keys take I-75 for the west-to-east leg of the journey; this stretch, known as Alligator Alley, offers a speedy and, since the state fenced the gators in on either side, relatively safe route. I say "relatively" because one of my closest friends drives an otherwise perfectly fine Toyota sedan that has a few bullet holes in it from a trek across Alligator Alley. Beyond that, though? Totally safe. Adventure seekers, back-roads fanatics, and Floridaphiles, however, take their chances on the east-west stretch of US 41 across the Everglades. The narrow, two-lane Tamiami Trail that cuts its way bravely across Florida's final frontier offers up the spirit and soul of Old Florida.

"The Tamiami Trail was conceived by Captain J. F. Jaudon of Ochopee, who in 1916 completed surveys of the route," the *Guide* explains. The Everglades comprised much of this area of the state then—and now. In Carl Hiaasen's *Skinny Dip*, the failed murderer/antagonist makes the acerbic yet not wholly untrue comment, "River of grass, my ass." When Marjory Stoneman Douglas wrote *Everglades: River of Grass* in 1947, certainly she had a reverence for the Glades. She knew damn well there was no river, but she also knew the Rivers of America series needed writers. When she approached publishers Rinehart and Company, she knew she had the skills and the reputation. The problem was, she did not have a river, so she took a bit of poetic license to make the Everglades into one.

See, the Everglades are a floodplain, although that description doesn't do the unique ecosystem justice. They're a muddy mixture of green rainbows of grass and trees, mixed into and sprouting from rich, mucky soil, textured in layers down to the state's very limestone. The water blankets the muck with a thin, tea-colored veil only a few inches thick but miles across, more mud flat than river.

People operate under all sorts of misconceptions about the Everglades. The worst of these describe the Everglades as a river, with banks on either side, which could not be further from the truth. The Everglades is wet land, bordered on its south by the aquamarine shallows of Florida Bay, on its east by the cool, deep-cobalt Atlantic, on its west by the placid green Gulf of Mexico, and on the north by the "dinner and show" motif of central Florida's performing killer whales and short, fabulous, gay men dressed as the world's most famous mouse.

Inside those boundaries, the Everglades provides a shocking, glorious example of what most of the Sunshine State looked like centuries before we called it that. Think of the Everglades as Robert Frost did the woods: lovely, dark, and deep, although not deep in the traditional sense. The spongy limestone aquifer teeters dangerously close to the surface.

The Everglades, before we called them such, attracted explorers searching for another type of green: money. Orchid hunters braved the swamp, filling railcars with the blossoms; plume hunters slaughtered blushing pink roseate spoonbills, soft white egrets, and sleek, stylish terns, pushing them toward extinction. Only after plume hunters destroyed roughly 95 percent of the state's wading shorebird population did state and federal government get involved, passing various laws to protect nongame birds at the turn of the twentieth century. They did this with varying success; Guy Bradley, a plume-hunting guide turned Everglades game warden, died when an outraged local shot him in the line of duty. The shift from bird feathers to ecotourism took a century; in between, the world decided it needed a better way to cross south Florida. Despite some local support for an east-west passageway across the Everglades, most of Florida remained skeptical, so much so that boosters crafted a public relations stint to show the world how safely it could cross the future Tamiami Trail (then identified as US 94).

"Lee County citizens organized and dispatched a motorcade over the proposed route to arouse public interest and show the feasibility of the undertaking," *Guide* writers explain. Take note of the word "proposed." I don't understand—and the *Guide* does not at all demystify—how the motorcade intended to safely cross this *proposed* route. While the water ran only a few inches deep and, perhaps, disappeared almost entirely in the dry season (the trailblazers left Fort Myers on April 4, 1923, when the water would have been nice and low), the water doesn't present the true problem in slogging across the Everglades. The muck does, because most years, it does not dry out.

Nevertheless, in a blind fit of almost wholly misguided optimism, intrepid explorers left in a convoy of ten cars and twenty-three men, led by two Indian guides (we can assume the *Guide* meant local Miccosukee or Seminole men). They headed east, undeterred, we can assume, by threats of malaria, wild animals, or perishing in Florida's outback.

"After a perilous three-week trip, during which they were reported lost several times, seven cars reached Miami, and the trail became the most discussed highway project in America," *Guide* writers note. I would think so; they make no mention of what may have happened to the other three cars, although in her book, Ms. Douglas insisted that when men died working on the Trail, workers buried the bodies as they went. Think about that for a moment: when you drive over the Tamiami Trail, you travel across a road constructed literally on the blood, sweat, and tears of the men who built it. Oh, and the bodies. You're driving over their bodies. Don't let that stop you.

Nonetheless—perhaps *because* of these things—this is my favorite stretch of south Florida road.

Heading east on US 41, drivers can lose themselves anew in Florida's wilderness. The businesses and development, after a spell, fade, and the bright-green darkness of the Glades takes over. It is a physical and spiritual transition. As the buildings surrender to the swamps and strands, so does the illusion that our state contains nothing more than three-for-ten-dollar T-shirt shops, theme parks, and beach bars.

Under the midmorning sun, we pass the last of the national minimarts and see a man and a woman sitting outside a gas station. What catches my eye first is a sign announcing, "Hold and Hug a Baby Gator!" Every roadside wildlife exhibit worth its salt allows pale tourists to hold a hatchling or stroke the bumpy smooth inky-green head of a juvenile so long as a rubber band holds its prehistoric pointy maw closed, but what I find curious about these attractions is that gators do not cuddle. They don't understand the concept of loyalty. Feed a gator every day of its life, a wrangler at Gatorland once told me, and, given the chance, it will still attack and, if possible, kill you. Gators are prehistoric remnants and still retain a superannuated genetic survival instinct paralleled by no other. Florida daily newspapers and "News of the Weird" columns across the country regularly run pieces about gators appearing everywhere from swamps to shopping malls and snatching the unsuspecting dachshund, golden retriever, or horticulturist and killing it, hobbling it, or eating its arm.

Hugging, rubber band or not, therefore, is ill-advised.

The couple sitting outside the "exhibit" is clearly doing their best to tempt passersby. They look exceptionally comfortable, they and their twin gators, ensconced in once-lovely dining room chairs. In their laps, each holds a gator. Not a baby gator, either, but more of a teenager. I do understand that rubber bands or a good-quality tape will hold a gator's jaws closed indefinitely, and in all probability, the couple used tape to keep the gators' jaws shut. Nonetheless, we do not stop to check.

When I first took my parents to the Florida Keys, I insisted we travel along the Trail. As a young girl we would take Sunday drives; my father would steer our 1976 maroon Buick and, later, our 1983 jasper-green Volkswagen Rabbit, down every backroad in Florida. He would head out of the city. We had no destination on these sojourns; the journey rewarded us in green vistas and father-daughter time.

On our first family Keys trip I helped my dad discover a new slice of Florida along this, one of the state's least-altered roads. West of Ochopee, I spy a frigate bird that doesn't look right: it has a forked tail like a frigate but a white body and shorter wing span. I have never seen a swallow-tailed kite, but I very much want to, and I hold my breath and grab the somewhat limited *Audubon Field Guide to Florida*. I find the page I need and let my breath out. It is indeed a swallow-tailed kite. Before I can say anything, I see another, and I can hardly believe it; when I turn in my seat to alert my parents, my mother tells us she sees others. As my mother often identifies ospreys as eagles and catbirds as mockingbirds, I don't quite believe her until I turn my head back to the skies above the Everglades and see a flock of at least fifteen, perhaps more.

My mother compares these graceful white arcs of avian beauty to stealth bombers. While I tend to see beauty in anything arising from the Glades, her comparison probably has a truer ring to it. Everything about the Glades, from the political rape of the land to the less meta-phorical struggles between the creatures who live there, is war.

The sawgrass, trees, and sheets of water covering the Everglades hide incredibly fertile muck. Couple subtropical temperatures with air that, on a dry day, you would still call "moist," and you have two immediate results: things decompose at an alarming rate, and when they do, things grow out of the decomposed soil at yet another alarming rate. Under precisely these conditions, delicate orchids, sturdy oaks, and scores of bird colonies thrive.

Sugarcane, philodendrons, and every vegetable from acorn squash to zucchini thrive in this rich black mire, too, and farmers wasted no time hitching their wagons to these conditions. The only problem, really, was the water. Either farmers lacked enough when they needed it, because it kept moving off the edge of the continent, or they had too much where and when they didn't want it.

In a move strikingly lacking in environmental vision or even the most rudimentary understanding of that whole "cause and effect" thing, we dammed the Everglades, straightened the river that fed it, and drained what land we thought we needed.

The Everglades you see today is a sliver of its former self. Consider this: Shingle Creek, which starts just south of Orlando's SeaWorld, is one of the Everglades' northernmost feeders. This tiny creek starkly contrasts with the Kissimmee floodplain and relatively flat banks. It flows south to Lake Tohopekaliga and drains to Cypress Lake, where it will rendezvous with other tiny blackwater creeks as it pushes south. It used to feed into a twisting and knotted expanse of river that slid its way south to Lake Okeechobee, then meandered on, in its own time, toward the lower third of the state. Most think of that lower third as the Everglades, but at one time, "the Everglades" meant everything south of southern Orlando. Suffice it to say that today the Glades suffers from a marked lack of water. The South Florida Water Management District, one of five state boards, hand-picked by the governor and created to control flooding, now dictates to whom and where the water flows. Most often, the cypress, birds, and gators lose to sugarcane, cattle ranchers, and cul-de-sacs.

This division of natural properties resulted not from greed—at first—but ignorance; initially, people blamed the swamp for malaria and other mosquito-borne disease. The land was hostile, untenable, and, as the *Guide* describes it, "a half-submerged waste of sawgrass studded with cypress hammocks and oasis-like palm islands."

This, of course, describes the Everglades south of Lake Okeechobee, because by the time the WPA reached the Everglades, most of the Glades had already succumbed to agriculture.

The bulk of the Everglades' entry in the *Guide*'s "Natural Setting and Conservation" chapter reads as follows: "The Everglades—until 1842 an unexplored, mysterious region known only to the Seminole who found sanctuary there from invading whites—form a vast area, much of which is underwater throughout the year, and nearly all during the rainy summer season." The Everglades, in their unaltered state, may have stretched to present-day SeaWorld, but in the

1930s, development and agriculture had so diminished them that the Tamiami Trail bisected them, according to the *Guide*.

That division was more than a road; life south of the Trail differs from life north of it, because to the north the water management district dams the water and damns the Everglades in one swift motion. When there's not enough water to go around, the dammed water supplies irrigation and other industrial uses north of the national park. When there's too much, the floodgates open—literally—and the parched reaches of the Everglades get an abundance.

The problem with this is that fish and birds and gators and trees need water all the time, not just when corporate agriculture doesn't. The other problem with this is that the water flowing into the Everglades has passed over a great deal of fertilizer and cow manure, which isn't exactly the healthiest combination for an ecosystem. Fertilizer contains, among other things, phosphorous. While the Everglades historically contained low levels of phosphorous, thanks to fertilizer runoff from farms in areas draining into the Glades, the Everglades struggles now with too much. Phosphorous promotes plant growth, but not the types of plants indigenous to the Everglades. Nitrogen-loving plants crowd out the local flora, growing so rapidly and effectively that they cover the surface of the water. This, in turn, lowers oxygen levels in the water, effectively suffocating fish, crabs, and any other living thing in the water. With no living things in the water, mammals on land have no ready food source.

Think of it as a circle of death, one that repeats. Part of the problem in finding a solution (although some agencies do make a concerted effort) comes from the sheer number of agencies responsible for the well-being of the Everglades: the Army Corps of Engineers (ACOE), Florida Department of Environmental Protection (FDEP), South Florida Water Management District (SFWMD), Florida Fish and Wildlife Conservation Commission (FWC), National Park Service (NPS), the Council on Environmental Quality (CEQ), and the United States Geological Survey (USGS). Craig Pittman, an environmental reporter who covers statewide issues, refers to the Everglades as the "River of Alphabet Soup."

....

On the west edge of the Glades, Ochopee, Chokoloskee, and Everglades City breed a different strain of Floridian, one unconcerned with beaches and Disney and busy working the oyster beds, giving airboat tours, and crabbing. Do they lament the way the state has punished them in favor of sugar, citrus, and cattle? Not really, except to snort derisively when I ask about the water management district.

To the east, Naples far outpaced this limestone-and-oyster-bed town, and it, not the now-named Everglades City, became the county seat after Hurricane Donna in 1961. It's just as well. The Everglades Rod and Gun Club (a de facto men's club for rich guys) remains, but so do the people of Everglades City and neighboring Chokoloskee, and it is unlikely that the Yonkers and Cleveland transplants of Naples would find much in common with the folks in Everglades City, whose families migrated years before Naples grew into the asphalt jungle teeming with retirees just a few miles away.

Say the name "Totch" in Everglades City and everyone knows who you mean. Loren "Totch" Brown, a sort of Floridian Robin Hood–meets–Davy Crockett, is the folk hero of these parts. He lived the whole of his life in Everglades City, carving a living out of the Glades as opportunity presented itself. He hunted until it was illegal; after that, he poached what he once hunted legally. He fished until running drugs became both more lucrative and prevalent; he went to jail for this but came home a hero, and, he points out in his book, *Totch: A Life in the Everglades*, he supported his family as he coexisted alongside the looming wet Florida frontier.

Before his death in 1996, Totch explained his life in two paragraphs:

I am Loren G. "Totch" Brown, a lifetime native of the Florida Everglades. My great-grandfather, John J. Brown and grandfather C. G. McKinney were among the very first to settle in the southwest Everglades, in 1880. My mother Alice Jane McKinney and father John J. Brown, Jr. were born here in 1892. I was born here in 1920.

At times my life in the Everglades was sustained by no more than what the Glades had to offer and the Everglades have never really let me down. Despite many hardships while bogging across the

Everglades for food or hides to sell, they always gave me a warm campfire and a place to lie my tired body down. This makes the Everglades a very special and dear place to me.

The Brown family still runs airboat tours of the area.

My friend Stacey works in a law office in an area of St. Petersburg that feels about as far from Chokoloskee as you can get. You rarely see Stacey without makeup and classy shoes, and yet she has direct ties to Totch Brown. Her grandmother Nellie was Totch's cousin, and although Nellie lived in St. Petersburg, when she died her family brought her back to Chokoloskee Island. I thought it would be nice to pass Stacey's well wishes onto family when I stop in for a Totch Brown airboat tour. I ask the ladies behind the desk if they were related to Totch.

"Oh, are you kin?" a hefty blonde woman snaps her gum and asks me. Surprised, I say no, I am not. I mention Nellie and her relation to Totch, and soon the ladies at the front counter are retracing the Brown family genealogy with both a rapidity and skill I admire. In less than five seconds they've placed Nellie and packed me off to an airboat captain. As I climb aboard a lavender-hulled airboat I jokingly ask the captain if he's related to Totch.

"No, ma'am," the boy says. "My fiancée is, though." He then relates his genealogy as well as hers, causing me to suspect that only two families people the whole of Everglades City and Chokoloskee. Conversation quickly ceases over the sound of the airboat, and he takes us out to Chokoloskee Bay for a thrill ride over the flats, coming to rest in front of a small island with an even smaller cottage at its center: Totch's cottage. He fished here, slept here, and died here, and the Brown family left it essentially intact; it has remained remarkably undecayed for the climate. Totch lived sparsely: a bed, a stove, plywood walls, and peel-and-stick floor squares are framed in odd juxtaposition to modern windows, a storm door, and steel green roof. Dead and live bugs adorn odd spots in the shack. The building remains dry, elevated slightly off the land with blocks. We walk quietly around the island, the drone of airboats the only sound in the distance and the breeze lessening the August heat and drying our damp skin.

Back on the airboat our young captain zooms over the bay and heads for a wall of red mangroves. When it appears we will slam into a tangle of salty trees, the captain turns the boat ever so slightly and the crooked roots part to reveal a tunnel. Within seconds we leave the blue, clear bay for the bistered dark underpaths weaving water around and through the island. He spirals us through a maze of channels until we see another airboat heading straight for us; the burrows allow room for a lone boat. As we drone toward the approaching boat, the mangroves open up and both boats swing starboard, passing easily before the tunnel hunkers down around us once again.

Red mangroves have roots that appear to prop up the rest of the tree. In more developed areas with newer mangroves, these roots rise a foot, maybe two above sea level. Here they look more like wooden cages from a fantasy novel than a sophisticated root system, and from my seat in the airboat I must look up to see the top of the roots. Through the roots I see even more roots in an ever-reaching intricate spider web of trees. I see nothing but mangroves and hear only the buzz of the airboat. This, I think to myself, would not be a bad place to dump a body.

Of course, that's not a new idea. The Ten Thousand Islands, of which Chokoloskee and Everglades City are but two, are anecdotally known for such things. The most famous "stasher of bodies?" Edgar Watson. Marjory Stoneman Douglas wrote of the murders in *River of Grass*.

"At Chokoloskee they found several men talking to a Negro in McKinney's store. The story the Negro told was that he'd worked for Watson for a long time and had seen him shoot a couple of men. The Negro said he'd buried a lot of people on his place, or knocked them overboard when they asked him for their money.

"Watson was away, the Negro said. His overseer, named Cox, killed another man and the old woman and forced the Negro to help him cut them open and throw them in the river. He said he would kill him last, but when the Negro got down on his knees and begged to be spared Cox said he would if he'd promise to go to Key West and get out of the country. The Negro came up to Chokoloskee instead and told everything.

"A posse went down to Watson's place and found plenty of bones and skulls. The overseer got away and has never been seen there since.

"The next day Watson came back in his boat from Marco and stopped in McKinney's store in Chokoloskee. He came walking along the plank, quiet and pleasant, carrying his gun. And here were all the men of Chokoloskee standing quietly around with their guns.

"Mr. McKinney walked up to Watson slowly and said, 'Watson, give me your gun.'

"Watson said 'I give my gun to no man,' and fired point blank at McKinney, wounding him slightly. As if it was the same shot, every man standing there in that posse fired. Watson fell dead. Every man claimed he killed him, and nobody ever knew because there were so many bullets in him."

No one ever went to jail for killing Mr. Watson.

Our airboat continues, searching. Coastal Florida towns often offer dolphin-watching tours in abundance, but on an airboat ride the captain will comb the Glades for gator. I've worked on several dolphin tour operators in Pinellas County; gator tours excite me far more. These airboats, by the way, never search long. Researchers estimate Florida has 1.3 million alligators, each one pulling a primeval chord in us, connecting us to both the swamp and our own soupy origins.

Continuing down the road a bit, one man has devoted his life to a wild animal of a different sort: the skunk ape. Ochopee has three claims to fame: Joanie's Blue Crab restaurant, the smallest post office in the United States, and the Skunk Ape Research Headquarters.

The smallest post office is just that—a diminutive building on the side of the Trail about a quarter mile east of Joanie's Blue Crab. Joanie's Blue Crab maintains somewhat capricious hours and costs more than you might expect, but it serves non–gas station cuisine, and the crab comes from local water. They also serve gator, frogs' legs, shrimp, and, for the less-than-adventurous, chicken wings, hot dogs, burgers, and beer. The live music—often provided by Raiford Starke, a band named for the state prison—adds to the local "watering hole" vibe.

The final and perhaps most curious stop in Ochopee honors the skunk ape—south Florida's version of the Bardin booger—a hairy, hulking man-ape with, as skunk ape aficionado Dave Shealy claims, a propensity for lima beans.

Big Cypress National Preserve surrounds Dave Shealy's Skunk Ape

Research Headquarters. The only spits of privately owned land remaining belong to the Seminole Tribe of Florida and the few lucky landowners who made rudimentary improvements that precluded the government from taking their land for use as a preserve.

Dave Shealy has devoted his life to studying the skunk ape; he believes they exist and says he has seen them. He says they live in the Everglades close to alligator holes; he says they eat both animals and vegetables; he says you can attract a skunk ape with lima beans.

Crossing south Florida via US 41 instead of Alligator Alley, you can't miss the Skunk Ape Research Headquarters. For those of us who remember Florida roads patchworked together with bush-league tourist traps, the lure of the Skunk Ape Research Headquarters may be too strong to resist. For those of you who don't remember that Florida, the Skunk Ape Research Headquarters offers a taste of vintage Florida kitsch.

If you've popped in hoping to learn more about the skunk ape, you'll find the bounty of information in the gift shop; no need to pay the admission fee. Here Shealy sells field guides and DVDs about his quest; they'll tell you about the skunk ape's habits as well as some things to expect if you're daring enough to venture off the well-traveled paths in the Glades.

Inside the attraction proper you won't learn anything else about the skunk ape. Instead you'll see exotic birds and reptiles as well as a paddock of alligators. You can hold a small gator and let a cockatoo snuggle against your neck. Do not expect the bird show from the sixty-dollar-a-day places, but in its stead you can drape yourself in a (hopefully) docile yellow albino Burmese python.

Since 2002, python hunters have removed more than two thousand Burmese pythons from Everglades National Park. Overwhelmed owners free their pets into the swampy morass of the Everglades, where the snakes meet other freed Burmese pythons, fall in love, and do what comes naturally to snakes: reproduce and eat alligators, rabbits, and other wildlife upon which the already-fragile Everglades ecosystems depends. The state issues permits for people to remove pythons and allows them to sell the meats and hides, although on its website the Florida Fish and Wildlife Conservation Commission notes that pythons found in the Everglades may have mercury levels so high that eating them is ill-advised.

The pythons in the Skunk Ape Research Headquarters are not for eating. Here they enjoy a kind, if somewhat confined, existence. While the building has a somewhat dog-eared appearance, animal curator Rick Scholle keeps the animal pens clean and the parrots, social creatures that crave interaction, get more here than in many homes. Florida may be rife with "exotic invasive" snakes devouring local snakes, with bounties placed on every reticulated reptilian head, but at the Skunk Ape Research Headquarters, the snakes live happily in enclosures, the outside world protected from them and they, protected from the outside world. The albino Burmese we get to touch came from the surrounding swamp, rescued from the state's python hunters and, in turn, the Everglades rescued from it.

That night, as we bed down at a hunting camp a few miles north of the Skunk Ape Research Headquarters, nothing else will do but catching sight of the elusive cryptid. At 5:00 a.m. I wait, wide-eyed and sleepless in a dark hunting shanty that belonged to a man who dug out a pond and elevated a piece of his property. When the government turned the surrounding swamp into a preserve, he held onto his boggy piece of paradise. I wait; if the skunk ape exists, I have a better chance of seeing him here than most other places.

Last night's fire has rumbled down to embers. The wood cabin's screen-covered openings, ideal for hot summer nights in Big Cypress, offer no shelter from the morning's cold murk. As the moon begins its final descent and the sun readies itself for rise, I blink and squint at a shadow by the lake. A deer? Too tall. A person? Too tall. A skunk ape?

Perhaps.

The concept of wilderness perplexes me. I've read that humans cannot see wilderness; the concept of "wild" omits human interaction. But in the rustle of the still winter morning, far from electricity or plumbing, no other word describes this place. Everything outside this wood cabin remains untamed; if I step off the camp, into the swamp, I have left civilization. This world tolerates humans without welcoming us.

If you don't want that level of seclusion but you want to spend the night in the Glades, Shealy owns a campground next to the Center. It has more amenities than the cabin where I kept vigil, but odds are the campfires still smell as good and you're still close to Florida's wilderness and, with some luck, the skunk ape.

As for what I saw that morning? I can't swear I saw one. Then again, I can't swear that I didn't.

We push east, and I watch out my window, counting gators in the roadside drainage ditch. When road workers built the Tamiami Trail they used the nearest available land to create the elevated roadway. What resulted was a canal stretching the length of the Trail on its north side: a thin stream of inky canvas painted with air plants, gators, and orchids. Every now and then a green highway sign will announce you have entered Gum Slough or the Fakahatchee Strand. What it really means is that you're in the swamp, you've been the swamp, and, for at least an hour or two, you're going to stay in the swamp. Once you accept or embrace your situation, you can sit back and enjoy the scenery.

And what scenery it is. Here you will find an abundance of La Florida; the wildlife horn of plenty filled to overflowing with kingfishers and their Don King haircuts, alligators and their sleepy, flirty, murdering eyes, and vultures feasting on everything in between. If you have a choice as to when you drive east on this stretch of road, drive it at or near sunrise. The sun lights up the trees, and a humming orange glow rises like fire in the Everglades. Birds take flight from every tree, starting their day with hope for swamp bugs, carrion, and fish. Seeing flock after flock take flight from the Glades is a perspective adjustment ordered up by the universe; it is impossible to believe your problems matter after you see what certainly must be millions of birds going about survival with graceful indifference.

As you edge closer to Miami you have ample opportunity to take one of many airboat rides, and soon after you pass the large Miccosukee Casino at Krome Avenue you find the reassuringly benign assortment of gas stations, Subways, and other proofs of civilization.

Fewer birds, but you're out of the swamp. Of that there is no doubt.

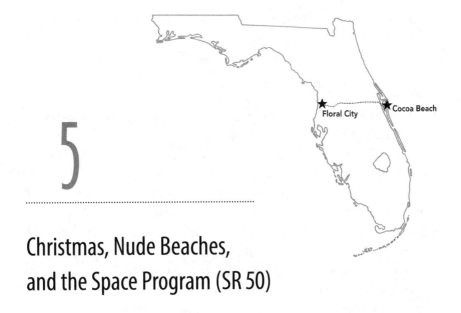

Floral City

Cocoa Beach

5

Christmas, Nude Beaches, and the Space Program (SR 50)

Along State Road 50—then State Road 22—*Guide* writers saw varied plant communities "from flat pine forests to marshland and scrub palmetto thickets" and described a road that "traverses a country of vineyards and citrus groves, and reaches its highest elevation near Oakland." The *Guide* describes the route's eastern beginnings as a "broad expanse of marsh and swamp, dotted with clusters of tall cabbage palms."

That same stretch of road makes me think of nude beaches.

Farther east along the road and slightly to north, the University of Central Florida teems with college students. When I attended as an undergrad, Colonial Drive—which is what they call State Road 50 by UCF—offered us a heavily trafficked escape from Orlando to Cocoa Beach. At the road's eastern terminus a host of diversions tempted us, but we only had eyes for Playalinda Beach, an almost legally acceptable nude beach. By "almost legally acceptable" I mean that officials would tell you they didn't allow nudity, but they wouldn't ticket you for being naked. The logic escaped me, but I didn't care—I was all grown up and by god, I was going to sunbathe nude.

Because it was incredibly close to NASA—it's part of the Canaveral National Seashore at the south end of the charmingly named Mosquito Lagoon—officials closed Playalinda during shuttle launches. Other times, we'd head down to sunbathe and the shuttle would be on the launch pad, an orange-and-white phallic symbol casting its intimidating shadow over the sunbathers, the symbolism not lost on us.

Heading west from the Atlantic on this trip, light-years after sunbathing in such a shadow, the road between Port Canaveral and UCF blissfully lacks the commercialism so apparently necessary in Orlando proper. If you visit the town of Christmas during the season of the same name, you'll see quite a line at the post office with people queuing for a clever postmark, but beyond that, some of these towns give the appearance of being settled by folks whose cars broke down on their way to somewhere else.

Blame Orlando. It kind of absorbs everything in its path. It's depressing to dwell on it; even more so if you take the time to look around and wonder what we've lost.

Today central Florida residents know this road well, although they would likely not recognize it by the *Guide*'s description, which reminds its readers that until 1925, much of this section of the countryside consisted not of surfaced roadbed but of sand trails. At one point the hard black slab skims the edge of Florida's theme park industry. Although the world's most prosperous mouse may seem light-years away from roadside trailers selling pulled-pork sandwiches advertised on hand-lettered cardboard, which you will find slightly west of here, the same road that passes these of-the-moment eateries also puts you within thirty minutes of the back door to the Happiest Place on Earth.

Orlando oozes out into the wooded areas, much like, on a stormy day, the swamp will ooze on into the city proper, but if you travel far enough west, the forest takes over once more. First it peeps through, then it consumes.

As we approach the madness of the mouse, I wonder when the supernova will collapse upon itself, leaving only a nebulous cacophony of platted houses and Targets, along with specialty shops that propose an odd union of products, such as the mattress and gun shop. Those aren't two separate stores. Orlovista, once known for cock fighting, now offers only a string of homes. Farther west, Ocoee once boasted large oaks; today, it lies roughly 14 miles due north of Cinderella's Castle. The "Stepford Suburbs" and this stretch of road seem engulfed by Tire Kingdoms, KFCs, and other chain stores, all virtually indistinguishable from one another, and all engaged in some tacit serfdom to Disney. Oakland, found just west of a dense web of highways, spans a narrow bit of land between the expansive Lake Apopka to the north and the much smaller Johns Lake to the south. Clermont lies just outside of the hustle and bustle. Once travelers saw oranges perched atop mounds of sand dunes, but the mouse has taken this land, too, replacing the groves with more suburbs.

It's an odd corner of the state, the smack-dab middle, but as we push west, things really get interesting. It will ultimately open onto lovely expanses of vegetation and roadside food stands and those roadside pulled-pork sandwiches I mentioned. Leafy trees, carefree palms, and stately pines replace popular franchises. Between Clermont and Brooksville, towns offer no tourist attractions but plenty to attract fans of a Florida more filled with greenery than theme parks. This lovely stretch of Florida appears unaltered by citrus, cows, or vegetables. Of course, we are too close to Pasco and Hernando Counties to be completely untouched, but the land feels pristine.

At the Withlacoochee River the tour ends, and I am happy to find today something that is remarkably similar to the beauty seen eight decades ago by *Guide* writers: "There are no settlements, no filling stations, and few signs of human habitation. Small garden patches cleared in the wilderness support isolated settlers; now and again an old seedling grove is passed, hemmed in by towering oaks, gums, and a matted tangle of jungle creepers which threaten to smother the scraggy trees. This primitive region is much as it was in 1539 when de Soto and his army, 'sore vexed with hunger and evill waies,' floundered northward through a land 'barren of maize, low and full of water, bogs, and thicke woods.'"

Whereas everything 40 miles either side of Orlando on this road seems irrevocably ruffled by the Disney influence, here, Mickey seems irrelevant. This is a tenuous Florida, caught between the grasp of two realities: the one I see in front of me, a wild Florida, claimed by green palm fronds and black rivers and spoken of in the *Guide*'s rhapsodic imagery, and the one I know is knocking at wilderness's door—suburbia and the promise of a three-bedroom, two-bath paradise near the happiest place on earth.

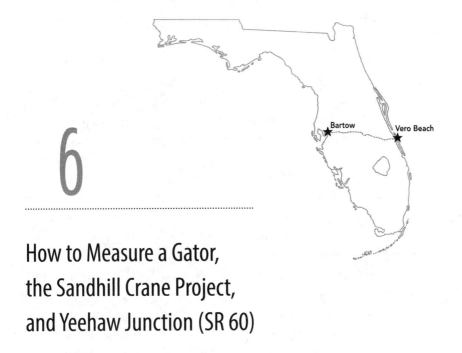

6

How to Measure a Gator, the Sandhill Crane Project, and Yeehaw Junction (SR 60)

Growing up, we didn't call it 60; only tourists did that. We called it Gulf-to-Bay, because that's what it was, both in name and function. West of Bartow, State Road 60 connected Tampa Bay with the Gulf of Mexico. Only as we packed ourselves off to college did we, too, start to call it 60. We joked that you could tell who stayed in Clearwater and who left home by what they called the road.

For all that discussion I can count on my fingers the number of times I took 60 east of Bartow before I graduated college: twice. Once all the way to Vero Beach and once again quite by accident. I never once in all those times saw it as it was, as the *Guide* describes it, a "coast-to-highlands route," one that required travelers to carry axes as they crossed the dense Florida jungle. We have since tamed the land where "inundated lowlands proved especially formidable."

The *Guide* gives its tacit stamp of approval to the conquering of nature but cautions travelers that the road remained "sparsely settled between Vero Beach and Lake Wales," which is not the case where I start the route, in Pinellas County.

Pinellas County, the western terminus of State Road 60, has more people per square mile than any other Florida county. We pack nearly 1 million people into a quite small space, and three main ways of getting from the airport in Tampa to north, mid-, or south county. State Road 60 offers the northern exodus from Tampa International Airport to our sought-after beaches. Today commuters travel that stretch of 60 daily, but in 1939, the tour started and ended at Bartow. The Courtney Campbell Causeway (now part of 60), then referred to as the Davis Causeway, existed only as a side trip into the brand-new Pinellas County (prior to 1912, Pinellas was part of Hillsborough County). Back then, people drove US 19 to get into Pinellas County.

We start in Bartow, just as the 1939 *Guide* did, and head east. Neighboring Brandon and Bartow share one thing: a vast cultural wasteland of self-storage facilities and strip malls. At this point I can only hope things will improve. The *Guide*'s description of the area starts east of here, at the phosphate pits, which I take as an inauspicious sign. We push on and, thankfully, the buildings grow sparser and the landscape grows increasingly verdant, greenery broken only by phosphate pits. This is the first thing the *Guide* notes about this area: "The highway passes large excavations dug to obtain pebble phosphate, deposits of which were discovered along the Peace River in 1884 . . . It is found embedded in a matrix of sand and orange-red clay, which is also rich in fossils of land and sea animals."

Today large companies, not locals, profit from the mines, the detritus of mining leaving "mountains" that evoke images of the South Dakota Badlands.

The Peace River had a more appropriate name in the first version of the *Guide*: Peace Creek. "River" calls to mind a wide expanse of moving water, and at the route's start we see not a river but an exquisite yet narrow tea-colored slip of water passing beneath the road.

As the road winds its way out of Hillsborough, through Polk, and into Osceola County, suburban living falls away all but completely, replaced instead with cattle, streams, and ever more varieties of green: stringy, piney green; heavy, waxy, oak green; and grassy, easy green.

Longleaf pines tower over mature live oaks with shorter limbs draped with silvery, almost yellow, gray moss.

Here we travel the only scrap of pavement, save the occasional bar and grill, feed store, or agribusiness-related building. Because no houses sprouted along the roadside—it looks like mostly grazing land, at least from the road—trees grow not just up, but out, and the foliage overtakes the landscape in a wild, yet calmly pastoral, way.

Citrus trees grow in groves, and although they arrived with the Spanish, their ordered, bulbous blossoms mesh in mathematical perfection with the wild nature of the landscape. Cows graze, and each Bessie seems to have her personal mottled brown-and-white cattle egret. Everything appears to live large off the bounty of the land here.

Juxtaposed with the cows and phosphate, homes in the Lake Wales Historic District tend toward the traditional, rather than the traditional Florida ranch: these homes have columns. The town has an art center not far from the Y'all Come Back Saloon and, only slightly farther away, Bok Tower Gardens. East of town the smell of burning citrus hangs heavy in the air.

Florida oranges sometimes fall prey to an Asian bug, citrus psyllid. The bug feeds on citrus trees and, as it does, spreads a bacteria that works its way through the tree's vascular system. One effective yet devastating way to stop the bug? Burn the trees.

Before we pass through the historic district, out the van window I see a different shape, something too large for a great heron or egret: sandhill cranes—one fledgling "teenager" who already reaches three or four feet high. It calls to mind a lesson I learned years ago about the power of the Florida nightscape, and I learned it at the next stop on the route: Lake Kissimmee State Park.

Years ago I took myself camping at Lake Kissimmee State Park. I packed my tent, my kayak, and my camping supplies and headed out. I was not new to Florida but had limited experience with the state's interior, especially solo camping. Inside the park perimeter, I marveled at large—quite large—gray squirrels, and when I saw deer I tried to take their picture, capturing only their backsides adorably scampering away.

When soon thereafter I happened upon a trio of sandhill cranes,

I reveled in how they seemed reluctant to leave their spot simply because a human stopped by. I snapped a few photos of the taller-than-me, leggy birds with piercing eyes and scarlet-blazed heads but thought nothing more as I made my way to my campsite, pitched my tent, and took my kayak down to the lake.

I paddled the edges, watching the reeds and water lilies, and noticed a pair of eyes watching me carefully. Gator. I started to feel distinctly "tracked" as opposed to "watched." I noticed that no matter where I paddled, the eyes and I remained roughly the same distance apart. I was either hallucinating, or the gator was keeping up with me and keeping his eye on me.

You can tell a gator's length by measuring the distance between its eyes. I took some measure of comfort in noting that his eyes *seemed* fairly close together. Nevertheless, I gave my saurian friend a wide berth and a small wave, hoisted my lonesome kayak up on bank, and made my way back to camp and dinner.

I had fallen restlessly asleep when I heard a hard-edged rustling. I tried to shake it off; in the woods, in the dark, a toad hopping sounds like a hog crashing through the underbrush.

Years ago, I mocked the movie *The Blair Witch Project*, taunting co-workers scared by the film, leaving bundles of sticks on piles of rocks in front of their office doors. On this night, scenes from the movie played in my head, and, in my head, they played out just beyond my tent.

When it's dark in the middle of Florida, it isn't just "lights out in the bedroom" dark. It's swamp black. Before I could talk myself down from the ledge, I grabbed my cell phone, pillow, blanket, and car keys and sprinted to the car. I turned on the headlights.

I saw nothing.

I toyed with leaving, but that meant getting out of the car and packing up, and the Blair Witch was *out there*. I thought about driving to a hotel, but the park lies several miles off 60, and the road isn't exactly lined with Holiday Inns. I recalled a Walmart several miles back, but, really, I probably stood a better chance of getting killed while sleeping in a Walmart parking lot than I did from the Blair Witch.

Finally, I dozed, albeit fitfully, in the car. In the morning, I stretched my aching neck, cooked breakfast, then started to pack up, convincing myself I'd only heard the horrible crashing noises in my head when, with my back to the trees, I heard the same awful sound. I stiffened; I could feel its presence right behind me. Whatever logic remained after a night spent waiting for death in the front seat of a car fled with its tail between its cowardly legs. Slowly, heart pounding, hands shaking, I turned.

I came face-to-beak with a sandhill crane and two of his compatriots. He leveled his gaze, then looked imperiously *down* at me. We were inches apart. I tried to breathe and found no air. My mind flew furiously through its memory bank of strange Florida headlines. I had no recollection of "Death by Bird"; this gave me almost immeasurable relief.

The great beast tilted his tiny, pointed head to the right, then stretched it to look around me. My brain whooshed as air rushed in once I realized he was eyeballing my food.

"Shoo! Scat! Go on now!" I said. He pulled his head back. He and the other two birds moved to the edge of the campground, watching me thoughtfully as I packed and departed. I finished packing my car, took a shaky breath, and went looking for another put-in to paddle the much-abused Kissimmee River.

....

Years ago, humans decided we would fix the flooding issues brought about by the seasonal, dependable, essential rainstorms that soaked into the aquifer. These rains proved necessary for maintaining stable supplies of drinking water, providing sustenance for countless ecosystems, and generally keeping things plugging along in paradise. Cattle ranchers, however, especially those who purchased land at a steal close to the river, found the seasonal flooding something of a nuisance, and, much to their delight, the local water management district fixed the problem, redesigning an intricate network of slippery, twisty waterways into an orderly, flume-like affair.

As with so many environmental fixes, these engineers knew only what they were doing, not whether doing it would cause devastating changes to the entire lower half of the state. To quote *Jurassic Park*'s Dr. Ian Malcolm, they "were so preoccupied with whether or not they could that they didn't stop to think if they should."

Straightening the Kissimmee, as you may surmise, failed spectacularly. It turns out that rivers tend to go where they please, and no math problem or hydrologic model in the world exists that can predict with 100 percent accuracy where that might be. The only way to know for sure where water might go comes from looking at where it has gone before.

All things considered, perhaps the engineers tasked with working on the Kissimmee should have done this. The Kissimmee River used to run from the southern edge of what is now SeaWorld into Lake Okeechobee, which drained, pre–water management hijinks, into the Everglades. With the same deference to beauty they offered the river itself, engineers named the thirty-foot deep canal "C-38." Changing the rate of flow and volume of flow caused, in layman's terms, a load of problems. Put more scientifically by the South Florida Water Management District, "Before channelization was complete, biologists suspected the project would have devastating ecological consequences."

The project controlled flooding but destroyed life as birds and fish dependent on the river knew it. The straightened, deeper river became a canal that rushed over the bottom rather than meandered. By increasing the rate of flow, nitrogen-rich fertilizer, pesticides, and animal waste from farms and ranches lining the river swirled into the Everglades with every rainstorm, crippling the future of life downstream. Before that, though, the Kissimmee River itself grew oxygen-poor and unable to sustain the life that depended upon it, threatening wildlife in and around it.

In a rushing charge of backward motion, civil engineers have started fixing the Kissimmee once again, which, everyone agrees, would be a lot easier had they not tried to fix it in the first place.

Along the fixed parts of the Kissimmee—and by this I mean the stretches that engineers have now fixed twice and, hopefully, for good—the river winds and twists, verdant and lovely and alive with snakes and hyacinth and gators and bass. The parts fixed only once—which is to say broken—play out a boring, straight, and dead nightmare. But those living parts, and the lakes that feed them, evoke prehistoric beauty.

....

You will read about the Kissimmee River and the fishing it offers—at least, in its wildest parts—in many tour brochures. If you want to immerse yourself in your fishing vacation, though, seek out a fish camp. Fish camps may be the area's true jewel. Like most of Florida with water nearby, people fish here. The difference between this area and the coastal fishing areas comes in the how and why. Along the coast, sure, some people come to fish, but more likely than not, some of those people fish incidentally—perhaps they're visiting and they find themselves with an afternoon or day free, so they locate a charter boat, pay their money, and bring home some bright-red grouper or sleek gray mackerel.

Not so here, along Florida's inland. Here, people don't fish because there's not much else to do; fish camps attract people who are here for one thing: freshwater fish. These people espouse a different culture. The men here—and they are largely men, although not only men— want fish. And perhaps beer, but mostly fish.

Anglers love Lake Kissimmee; outside the state park exists a constellation of fish camps run by divinely hardened women. They sell beer; not dark beer, not craft beer, but Beer with a capital *B*, because all that matters is that it's cold, fermented, and hoppy. Beer and Bass: Welcome to Lake Kissimmee. Welcome to the middle of the state, actually.

Moving east, the road meets the edge of Lake Wales State Forest, indicated by a sign and much taller pines. The *Guide* doesn't mention the forest, describing instead a chain of lakes dotting citrus groves, palms, and "purple and red bougainvillea and golden flame vines [that] cover gateways to the groves; driveways are landscaped with gay-colored petunias, phlox, and zinnias."

East of the forest Westgate River Ranch offers an "authentic ranch experience," if such an experience includes a full-service marina, airport, and neatly manicured grounds. The ranch offers rodeos, skeet shooting, hayrides, airboat rides, and a petting zoo, but for those truly wishing to get a bead on the local scene, the ranch offers water access to the Kissimmee River.

Lake Kissimmee narrows to a river at State Road 60, feeding directly into the straightened, "fixed" run of river. Cows, water hyacinths, and cattle egrets fringe the water. From time to time the original curls and kinks of the river overlap the dredged and boring canal with scraps of wildlife. The river stays straight and, like the River Ranch, sanitized and almost nonthreatening, until the southern edge of Kissimmee Prairie Preserve State Park. After the park, it writhes and crunches up on itself before it returns to the static, precise right angles near Chandler Ranch Road. Even then, a squiggle of river defies the ordered plane of water, crossing back and forth over the river, teasing it with its organic path, all the way to Lake Okeechobee.

Back on the route, away from the golf course/dude ranch and the Kissimmee River, Yeehaw Junction graces the crossroads at US 441, not far from the Florida Turnpike. Once a town center for cattle ranch-ers, downtown Yeehaw Junction now boasts the Desert Inn motel and restaurant, a Stuckeys gas station, and a blinking stoplight. Built in the 1800s, the Desert Inn's bar gives scant indication, save for the televi-sions, that much time has passed since the grand opening. The main change? The Desert Inn used to have both hookers and booze. Now they just have booze.

In a collection of his columns, *Dispatches from the Land of Flowers*, Florida columnist Jeff Klinkenberg rhapsodizes about the food at the Desert Inn, praising the meatloaf and chili and extolling the virtues of the owner's frogs' legs.

Since that 1994 piece the owner handed over the cooking end of the business to others. Her pies, breaded-right-there onion rings, and aforementioned frogs' legs gave way to less individualized food, but the drinks remain strong and the atmosphere unchanged. George, a defaced male mannequin adorned with customer signatures, still lurks in the ladies room. The polished wood of the bar still evokes images of cowboys and crackers ending a day in town with a shot of whiskey. The waitresses will still try to scare you with ghost stories about the "museum" upstairs.

East of Yeehaw the road sprawls into four lanes, divided in half by a metal guardrail. After a few miles, the guardrail yields to a grass median. The south side of the road here seems one long orange grove, while the north side is nothing but green between the Desert Inn and Interstate 95 almost 30 miles away.

The road ends at Indian River Boulevard at Vero Beach. In town, a citrus museum pays homage to the once-fertile orange and grapefruit trees and packing plants that formerly played a starring role in the center of the state but now make only cameo appearances. Farther west, the orange, grapefruit, and pine trees give way to the Intracoastal Waterway, and either north or south leads you to causeways that will free you from gators, things that go bump in the night, and ghosts, delivering you to Vero Beach, where I fail to see the *Guide*-promised road leading up to it, one "bordered with tall clumps of bamboo, brilliant scarlet hibiscus, graceful cocos plumosa palms, and symmetrical Australian pines," but instead find the sweet smell of citrus and a more gentle, low-lying development than what I left at the route's western end.

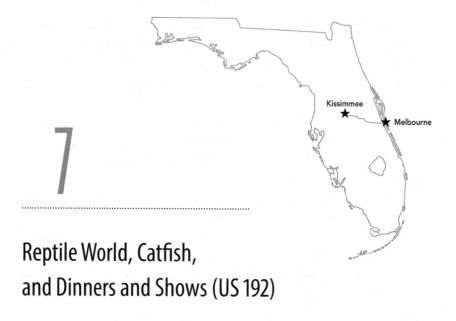

7

Reptile World, Catfish,
and Dinners and Shows (US 192)

A Guide to the Southernmost State tells us that US 192 offers "limited accommodations." Today, this road, at its western terminus, has every type of lodging you could imagine, from camping to luxury resorts featuring daily duck parades. By comparison, the middle segment and eastern end may as well be the far side of the world.

When I say "middle" and "eastern," don't let me kid you: US 192 is a stub of a road, especially compared to the seemingly endless streamers of road comprising some of the longer tours. It doesn't go far, its 74 miles bisecting the state from Melbourne on the east to Kissimmee in the center. It's so short that I travel it alone in my candy-apple-red Volkswagen Rabbit rather than the camper. After visiting friends in Cocoa Beach I decided to return home via 192; it's an easy turnoff, and in no time at all I abandon the beachside palm thickets, trading them for a jungle of box stores, lawyers' offices, and drive-throughs. This is hell, suburban-style. The strip of road between the beach and I-95— the one the *Guide* called "underwater" and "unexplored"—fell first to naval stores and then to homogeny. The Dollar Generals of the state once again triumph, however briefly, in this cultural wasteland of low quality at marginally lower prices.

But—and this is a refreshing "but"—west of the interstate you see only green. Pastures remain, although the lumpy Brahman cows of *Guide* times have muddied their bloodline sufficiently enough that most of the cows here have the sleek shoulders of a shampoo model. Pine trees of all sorts, including the much-hated, "non-native," gracefully leaved Australian pine—dot the roadways, with cows and palm trees thrown into the mix to keep it interesting. Sandhill cranes, with their crimson-kissed heads, and wild turkeys with ugly throats and beautiful plumage wander across the greenscape. Just before we reach Holopaw (which the *Guide* tells us means "place where something is hauled" but doesn't clue us in as to what was hauled to or from there) oaks triumph over pines and cranes. At the intersection of Turn Around Bay Road—and yes, that is its real name—and 192, Holopaw shows up with modest homes and white picket fences. Some of the larger lots are graced with blue tractors and green farm equipment, but the town fades away into the trees, letting the road have its way with the surrounding landscape. The trees open up again briefly for a planned community called Harmony, boasting a population of 1,200 but not on any map. That's because it isn't a real place; it's what developers call a "master planned community," and at first glance I write it off. Now, I don't know how I feel about it, which I suspect may be the developer's plan.

Read the PR: Harmony promotes sustainability and green practices. That's a good thing, right? But there's something intrinsically suspicious to me about a planned community, perhaps because I live in an unplanned community that offers the intangibles Harmony promises. But Harmony's core values posit that "people live better when they live in regular contact with animals and nature," and Harmony apparently has tried to put those words into action with public access to motorboat-free lakes, miles of nature trails, and landscaping guidelines that encourage native plants.

But still, Harmony is not an organic place. It is yet another in a long string of contracted paradises nestled among Florida's less-touched paradise. The developers re-created wild Florida, but they had to clear a goodly bit of wild Florida to do so. They do lots of good things from an environmental perspective, but in the end, Harmony is a planned development. The homes get cut from a mold, and the lawns are not "first nature"—they're re-creations based on what used to exist rather than what used to actually exist.

Something about a planned housing development that cuts down trees to replant things in a more organized manner, all while shielding the streetlights so we can see the stars and encouraging people to produce less waste and recycle their rainwater still makes me uneasy. I want to like it, if only on principle, but cannot, on another principle.

Back on the road, I realize that if people use 192 for commuting, it isn't during normal commuting hours. At almost five o'clock, traffic has not changed measurably. In all likelihood, I-4 or one of the state's east-west toll roads carries any commuters who, for whatever reason, must travel between Melbourne and Kissimmee. Most of the cars here aren't cars, but pickup trucks, and not the pretty kind you buy to occasionally pull your Chris-Craft to and from the boat ramp. No, these trucks haul and tow and push, but don't let the lack of shiny paint fool you. The men driving these trucks—and, for my proximity to Harmony, it seems discordant not to see any other women drivers—take care of their vehicles.

Traffic comes to a dead stop just past Harmony. It's soon clear that the traffic jam is atypical; local boys step out of their cars to see what they can see, although they almost definitely have a higher vantage point from the seat of their D-series pickup. No one lays on their horn. No fights erupt. After a half hour, I get out, too. I'm hungry, I have to use the bathroom, and I want to know why we're not moving.

"Car accident up ahead. Someone died," one of the men tells me. "They've got an air ambulance." I don't know how he knows this until I notice the chain of communication working its way back. One driver passes information to a few trucks, then the last driver gets out and tells a few trucks behind him, and so on until the line knows what's holding up traffic.

This, I think to myself, is what northerners simply don't get about the people they call rednecks. Our "rednecks" practice a basic civility here not often seen in city traffic jams. These folks—these neighbors—know what community means. I felt its presence along that roadway. Stuck in traffic, hungry, desperate for the ladies' room, I saw clearly what the middle of the state gained by not turning itself over to tourists: community. You don't find it as much along the transient beach towns, with tourists and snowbirds and out-of-state landlords, but here, in the state's grounded middle, families, not investors, own land, not just homes. They build community and have each other. It was not a big moment, but it sure was nice.

Once traffic picks up again, St. Cloud comes up quickly. Here I see signs that the magic of Disney grows nigh. I see the first 7-11s and Walgreens since I-95, and, as even more proof that tourists do venture off the mouse-eared reservation, Reptile World Serpentarium.

In 1972 Reptile World started as a venom farm. Handlers milked snakes for venom and sent the venom all over the world. By the end of the decade, though, owners say that the steady stream of people wanting to take a tour prompted them to allow people to watch the snake milkers at work. For under ten dollars, one website boasts, guests can tour the facility and watch "expert snake handlers milk the world's most vicious and deadly snakes live before your very eyes with only the glass separating you from huge angry cobras, rattlesnakes, copperheads, water moccasins and many more."

The attraction also offers a "relaxing" stroll across the grounds, where visitors can see iguanas, turtles, and, of course, an alligator.

Between the legacy of angry cobras, planned communities, and friendly traffic jammers, by the time I reach the edge of Kissimmee I want food and a place to sit that isn't a car. I stop at the Catfish Place, where I must choose between frogs' legs, catfish, and country-fried steak. I choose steak, collards, and beer. I suspect it is the last place I will see along 192 that offers frogs' legs; between here and I-4 a steady stream of Denny's, Pizzeria Unos, and an odd combination of drive-through restaurants and "dinner and show" establishments where tourists can eat spaghetti and meatballs and watch actors play knights and gangsters will dominate the roadside.

The final town on the route, Kissimmee, gets only a sentence in the *Guide*'s tour, noting it is at the junction of US 17. In reality, Kissimmee is a huge part of what most tourists see when they come to worship at the altar of the mouse, but in the 1930s, there was nothing to see here. Which, if you can picture it between the neon signs, corkscrew-shaped water slides, and dinner-and-show venues, is nice, and alive and well just a few miles east on 192.

Kissimmee, Orlando's tourist-swollen cousin with a chain of tourist-supported endeavors, also has another claim to fame. Before the cattle ranching, sugar farming, and Florida Dream dried it up, the Everglades started its slow journey off the edge of North America here. Shingle Creek, one of the initial feeders for the Everglades, ends just behind a gas station across from SeaWorld, but the closest practical kayak put-in is just off US 17/92.

I approach Shingle Creek with a light heart and high hopes.

I welcome the narrow blackwater creek that originates by Discovery Cove and quietly curls south through the theme park capital of the world. In delicious juxtaposition to the dinner-and-show explosion, I find my path to the Everglades' genesis, sandwiched between Pirate's Island mini golf and Gator Alley gift shop. US 192 crosses Shingle Creek, although no sign marks the waterway. At an airboat rental stand boasts a sign touting "Real Florida!" I pay my dollar ramp fee and push off.

This tiny creek starkly contrasts with the Kissimmee floodplain and relatively flat banks. It flows south to Lake Tohopekaliga and drains to Cypress Lake, where it will rendezvous with other tiny blackwater creeks as it pushes south. Paddling Shingle Creek reveals Florida's "scrub," a desert with water, prickly pear cactus, and patches of sand beyond oversized, muddy, emerald leather ferns and reedy, plump pine trees. Here live an estimated two thousand scrub jays. For a half mile I contend with sunburned tourists powering tiny airboats, but at the half-mile mark the creek closes and shallows, and while markers warn power boaters away, I am free to paddle under, over, and into this world. I glide past a submerged tree, wiggling my boat around its wrinkled skin as a hawk lights on one of its arcing branches, a wriggling fish in his beak.

The creek closes in, trying to choke me out, and I grunt and pole my way around deadwood and cloying weeds, bumping over things and hitting my paddle on branches above. I can't paddle; I have no room.

Dry season. The downed trees and underwater obstacles test my agility and maneuvering skills, and I surrender what I know to just keep going. I scooch and pole and sweat and breathe. Oak and pine and I don't even notice what else scrape my head and the tops of my hands. Spider webs tangle in my hair, and glistening blue bugs find my thighs. I can't push myself forward more than a foot or two at a time; I tuck my paddle under my arm and develop a plodding rhythm of lurching forward a couple of feet, then turning my boat by sticking one hand in the loam to curl it around an unseen log and using the other to pivot off the nearest upright branch, then reversing over the underwater obstruction for about a foot, catching my breath, and going forward again. Muck and bark coat my hands, mixing with blood and ragged ripped nails and scraped flaps of skin. I twist around branches and follow the water and almost despair and fight the squishy mud and detritus and huff, and all at once it opens again. I find myself in a patch of water at least a foot deep and clear and moving just enough for me to know it moves. Pea-green specks of pickerel move around the deadwood and caress my hull. I sit for a moment; ahead of me, deadfall blocks the way.

I stop paddling; the water here runs so shallow that it will not take me upstream or down. This is it; the end of the line, the beginning. In higher water I could reach the beginning's end, roughly across the street from Discovery Cove, channelized in proper Florida fashion. It starts behind a Chevron and parallels a tidy apartment community. The end of the beginning looks no different than a drainage ditch lined with the verdigris of St. Augustine grass and ornamental assortments of ecology.

The *Guide* doesn't focus on the Everglades and its ecology but instead brags on land tycoon and developer Hamilton Disston, who bought most of this land for twenty-five cents an acre and installed a system of drainage canals. Since that 1881 purchase, much about the Kissimmee area has also celebrated all things Disston-esque, whereby we set upon conquering the land, making it bend to our will. An unfortunate side effect of what the *Guide* inaccurately calls the "reclaiming" of fields and pastures is the temporary triumph of man over wilderness, and while many of my colleagues decry Walt Disney World for this, it started well before him with Disston's land purchase. Disney, by the way, has set aside no small measure of its property for wilderness to reclaim, which it has, with vigor. As for Shingle Creek? This trickle so rarely seen by tourists in rented canoes or taking an airboat ride assures me that, even in the most populated corners of our state, if left alone, the wilderness seemingly tamed by Disston and others like him, survives and will one day return.

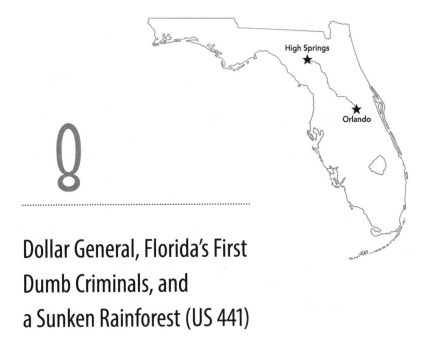

Dollar General, Florida's First
Dumb Criminals, and
a Sunken Rainforest (US 441)

While *Guide* writers admit the Orange County seat—Florida's largest inland city, both then and now—had grown from a cow trading post to a city in the prior forty years, they qualify that sentiment by, in the same sentence, saying Orlando was a city "resembling a cultivated park." They further expound upon the city's citrus, dairy, and poultry farming routes. They toy with the notion of the city being named for Shakespeare's Orlando, the adored if somewhat dim romantic.

Orlando, you have broken my heart. None of this—save the city's population proportions compared to the rest of Florida's landlocked cities—remains true.

In the 1990s I lived on Winter Park's Morse Boulevard, just outside Orlando, and I loved it. Other than buying groceries, I did all my shopping by walking around the corner to Park Avenue. I found birthday gifts at local shops. A local florist made me a Christmas wreath for my front door. I sipped coffee at a non-Seattle-based shop that was neither trendy nor pricey. Friends and neighbors would walk down the street and get sushi at a hole-in-the-wall place; the bookstore next door always had a lively game of checkers at its sidewalk table.

Orlando seemed far away, but it wasn't. Not really. We'd drive downtown to get terrified at Terror on Church Street and marvel at the tourists who'd managed to wander away from the theme parks for an evening. We'd use the parking garage that had flowering bushes on its outside so we didn't have to fight street traffic, but we'd move the car if we wanted to head down Colonial to go dancing at Dekko's.

I worked as a stagehand for Orlando Opera Company, and the company shared space with Southern Ballet in a building donated by Florida Power. Before every matinee my coworker Angi and I would climb a narrow ladder up to the roof and spread dark, heavy, plastic Visqueen over the long, narrow skylight. Lake Ivanhoe curved along the building, and I loved the view.

In case it isn't clear, I loved everything about Orlando and Winter Park. The only thing wrong was that it was way too far from the beach, and I need salt water like beagles need to howl. I moved back home to Clearwater. At first I visited Orlando frequently, but over time the visits have grown less frequent. Every time I visit, however, a piece of me dies, because this is no longer the same Orlando with quirky map shops and Korean restaurants where the servers don't even pretend to care they don't speak English. A few holdouts remain, but the personal feel has disappeared under a cloud of assimilation.

In his book about small-town America, *The Lost Continent*, Bill Bryson writes of his search for Amalgam, the small town of his youth. He does not find it; he instead falls upon what he calls Anywhere, USA—over and over again. In Florida, we're not like Anywhere, USA, but I do notice a trend for our cities to homogenize themselves *with* one another, syncing themselves up to each other like computers mirroring iPods and iPads—anything you can find in one, you can find in another, and even if the screen looks slightly different, all the same things are there. Nowhere more than along US 441 does this haunt Florida's culture, this synchronization of all businesses, people, and self.

Sadly, this is not confined to Orlando. The tours that roam near any towns near Orlando and other population centers—Tampa, Jacksonville, Pensacola—drip with homogenization. This creeps into even the smaller towns, where chambers of commerce find themselves torn between welcoming any new commerce—even a chain store that may hurt local mom-and-pop shops—and casting about desperately for ways to set themselves apart from other small towns. Every small town wants to be unique, but the reality is that if you don't know where to look, it's easy to feel set adrift in a sea of similarity.

In his book *Land of Sunshine, State of Dreams,* Florida guru Dr. Gary Mormino mentions a 1990s postcard of the Orlando skyline. "Welcome to Orlando!" the postcard read. One problem: the skyline didn't belong to Orlando. When polled, area readers thought it might be Halifax.

As I drive down US 17 and US 441 through the Orlando area and a dozen other smaller towns, my heart breaks for Winter Park and every other small town in Florida that lost its "here." Nowhere, though, is this more severe, more pronounced, than in Orlando.

Dollar General stores all look the same, whether they're nestled under live oak trees or set amid palm trees—and in Florida, you see both these things. After seeing the bits of the state that still have a scrap (or more) of "here" remaining, the yellow signs of these stores symbolized the loss of our "here."

But outside Orlando—and there is much worth seeing just outside Orlando—you can find tree-lined streets and deer, as you would do near and in Wekiwa Springs and Blue Springs and DeLeon Springs. The crowds thin as we travel north along US 441, heading away from Orlando and Apopka and into towns like Zellwood and Mount Dora.

Zellwood earned a place in the original *Guide* because it sold Lake Apopka muck for fertilizer. Lake Apopka, unfortunately, is no longer the gem in the city's crown. In 1980, Tower Chemical's questionable disposal practices caused pesticides to contaminate the lake. The EPA designated the lake a Superfund site. At the same time, local farmers were letting phosphorous runoff head straight for the lake, which also did not bode well for the lake's residents or its inhabitants.

Governor Lawton Chiles signed the Lake Apopka Restoration Act, and the state—through the St. Johns Water Management District—started buying corn farms and turning them back to swamp.

While this has been fantastic news for the health of the lake, it has whittled the corn industry down to one lone sweet corn farm—Long and Scott Farms. Every year Zellwood has a sweet corn festival, although twice organizers canceled the festival, once in 2009 citing dwindling numbers, before it died for good in 2012. The lake, however, continues to attempt to survive. The Friends of Lake Apopka (FOLA) continue to fight for lake-related issues, from hydrilla removal to stopping a proposed airport.

North of Zellwood, Mount Dora lures antiquarians. Mount Dora's highest elevation reaches 184 feet, and the chamber of commerce proudly informs people that "some homes have basements." Mount Dora is a small town—just over twelve thousand people—characterized, both in 1939 and today, by its tree cover and older buildings. A drive through the town requires leaving US 441 but reveals a quaint center, with bed-and-breakfasts, tree-lined streets, and small shops selling, among other things, bumper stickers proclaiming, "I climbed Mount Dora!"

In 1981 the town went pink. The filmmakers of *Honky Tonk Freeway* wanted to use Mount Dora as a filming location. The premise of the movie is that the small town of Ticlaw wants an exit on the new freeway, lest its safari theme park lose visitors. The mayor and town will do anything, including painting the town pink, to attract visitors. Mount Dora agreed to paint many of its buildings pink for its turn on the silver screen. *Honky Tonk Freeway*, despite characters that included Ricky the Carnivorous Pony and Bubbles the Waterskiing Elephant, was a failure. The movie cost $24 million; it grossed only $2 million.

Today the town has repainted the majority of the buildings.

Leesburg, the self-proclaimed largest and oldest town in Lake County, greets us with more tree-lined streets and small-town charm. The high school catches my eye on a drive through town; it has an almost-Mediterranean feel. In 1927, the city built the high school on 10 acres donated by Lee Meadows, who used to play pitcher for the Pittsburgh Pirates.

The rest of Leesburg appears to be struggling. It's a designated Main Street Community, and the city employs a full-time manager who tries to improve business in the designated Main Street area. The idea is that the city can help small businesses by marketing them and making improvements to the area where they are located. As we drove Florida's backroads, it seemed we saw more Main Street Communities either clearly failing or (hopefully) just starting their renaissance; the sign "Welcome to X, A Main Street Community!" invariably signaled an upcoming drive through a one- or two-street district with bedraggled shops, cracked pavement, and only some minor improvements. Usually we would spot a Dollar General not far away. Not all Main Street Communities fail: St. Petersburg's Grand Central District breathed new life into a rundown area. Leesburg does not yet reflect overwhelming triumph, but it looks to be trying.

....

Today, local and national news stations alike run stories of less-than-brilliant criminals. With a frequency that many would call statistically improbable, these crimes and criminals have at least a passing connection to Florida. Just outside of Leesburg is evidence of one of the state's first, setting a precedent that continues today.

Most folks have heard of Ma Barker and the Barker-Krespis gang, but they may not know that when she and her sons, along with their gang, fled, they fled to Florida. They felt the need to reinvent themselves in Florida because they had kidnapped bank president Edward Bremer in 1934. After receiving $200,000 ransom, they released him in February, and in early 1935 they remained on the FBI's wish list.

Criminally speaking, fleeing Chicago for Florida well before it was the outlaw "thing to do" should have been a smart move for Ma "Machine Gun" Kate Barker and her grown criminal sons. One problem: when they left their apartment, they neglected to pack the map, on which they had circled "Ocala" in pencil. Florida in February was a bonus for federal agents, who spotted Fred Barker standing by a rowboat at Lake Weir. A shootout followed; agents killed Fred and his mom. This set a precedent to which future criminals would unintentionally aspire.

Something even more curious than escaping the FBI draws people here these days: the Villages.

The Villages, which bills itself "Florida's Friendliest Retirement Town," is a collection of planned neighborhoods, two town squares, and property leased—not sold—to businesses. Touching part of three counties—Sumter, Lake, and Marion—and encompassing 30 square miles, more than fifty-one thousand people live in the Villages. It is not a city; it is a privately owned chunk of land. The residents, not the counties, maintain the roads, utilities, water system, and other parts of the infrastructure. The developers own a newspaper, radio station, and cable channel in the Villages. This is not the strangest thing about this community of active seniors.

The whole of the Villages allows golf carts, with separate lanes and paths for travel. People who cannot see well enough to pass the state-mandated eye exam can still drive golf carts. People who can barely walk can drive golf carts. People who never learned to drive a car can drive golf carts. Many drivers here are perfectly capable of handling a golf cart or a car. Golf carts, however, are so plentiful that many homes come with a garage only big enough for a golf cart, not a car. The carts don't necessarily look like golf carts, either. Many drivers soup up their carts to look like classic Fords, or Corvettes, or any other car they always wanted (or perhaps used to own). This is also not the strangest thing about the Villages.

Florida's Friendliest Retirement Hometown has skyrocketing rates of syphilis and chlamydia; the occurrence of these two diseases increased by 71 percent from 2005 to 2009. Local news reports attributed this rise to women and men no longer having to fear pregnancy, but one resident—who asked to remain nameless—has another explanation:

"There's nothing else to do here," he laughs.

This, perhaps, is the strangest thing about the Villages.

....

US 441 moves along to Juniper Springs. With cool, clear water, it's a kayaking paradise. Need a place to park your camper? Ocala National Forest offers camping and hiking. Outside Ocala, Silver Springs still offers the glass-bottom boat rides they offered in 1939. The *Guide* describes the spring as "a group of 150 natural springs issuing from the porous Ocala limestone and flowing into a common basin." Passengers gliding over the clear-water spring in glass-bottom boats can see to depths of eighty feet.

The theme park was once the home of the Ross Allen Reptile Institute. Today the park has Ross Allen Island, which includes spiders, snakes, and otters as well as some of Allen's archives. The *Guide* describes a different institute. The Florida Reptile Institute displayed snakes, lizards, turtles, gators, and crocs. Mr. Allen also bred various reptiles and amphibians. The *Guide* tells us the Institute sold diamondback rattlers (from one to five dollars, size dependent) and uber-deadly coral snakes (from three to five dollars, again, let's assume that's size-dependent). Looking for more variety in your slithering reptiles? You could have purchased a snake assortment: eight snakes, all at least four feet long, for a scant ten dollars. Looking for something prettier, or perhaps less expensive? Try the $2.50 box of ten tiny, brightly hued snakes, although interestingly the catalogue did stipulate it would not send venomous snakes to people under eighteen. If you were thinking you wanted to give something more . . . impressive . . . at Christmas, consider a crocodile or an alligator. A two-foot baby crocodile sold for three dollars, but a ten-foot croc carried a three-hundred-dollar price tag. Gators started at a quarter, but the luxury model, twelve feet long, cost about one thousand dollars. The Institute also sold less daunting turtles and lizards and "choice" black widow spiders for fifty cents.

The *Guide* fails to describe what makes a black widow "choice." A search of the USDA website revealed no such categorization for arachnids.

....

North of the Villages and Ocala, 441 exhales a sigh of relief. The densely populated road at the edge of Florida's retirement mecca once again spreads out in stands of pine and oak.

The road bisects Paynes Prairie, a flat expanse of wetland. The prairie itself is a collection of tight sinkholes covered in grasses, flowers, and plants; the flora filters the rainwater that recharges the state's main drinking water supply: the Floridan Aquifer. The prairie is home to more than two hundred types of birds, including sandhill cranes and bald eagles. Like so many other undeveloped areas in Florida, here you can easily spot a deer. Unlike so many other undeveloped area, you also must watch for bison, a possibility so real that the park forbids pets on Bolen Bluff, Cone's Dike, and the La Chua Trail "due to potential conflict with alligators, snakes, and bison."

Near Gainesville the road has less green and more concrete, but the green triumphs once again as we drive north. Slash pine and farms, not franchises, line the roadway, as do stands selling produce and shrimp. Sinkholes filled with spring water make for excellent diving and snorkeling; others, like Devil's Millhopper Geological Park, reveal a tiny rainforest in their drier depths, 120 feet below the surface. Just outside High Springs, the *Guide* writers passed through a small turpentine settlement called Paradise. I don't see it on my modern-day map, but I understand the name.

At High Springs the sinkholes and springs tempt divers, swimmers, and nature lovers. This tiny town in Alachua County—just over three thousand people—is alive with a green canopy of trees over iridescent-blue water, and the cacophony of south 441's STDs, traffic jams, and Dollar Generals feels like a hallucination.

And yet we are not so far I forget the echoes of Orlando, and I feel a hollow sadness that I never will see the cultivated gardens and dairy farms catalogued by *Guide* writers. At home I page through *As You Like It*, and when my finger finds these words, I wonder if perhaps the *Guide* writers prophesied the O-town of today: "Thou art not for the fashion of these times/Where none will sweat but for promotion."

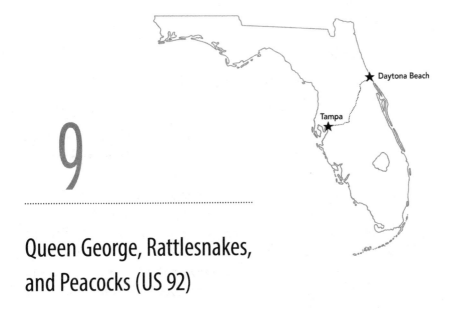

9

Queen George, Rattlesnakes,
and Peacocks (US 92)

From marshlands and tangled cypress hammocks the highway
rises into a rolling prosperous countryside of citrus groves,
truck gardens, poultry farms, and large vineyards.

A Guide to the Southernmost State

As it did then, US 92 crosses some of Florida's less-developed lands,
at least on the east side of the state. Unlike the 1930s, however, this
route today plays the chameleon, taking the form of various roads as it
pushes west and south from Daytona Beach. Two tours comprised US
92: from Daytona Beach to Lakeland; and from Haines City to Clearwater. The astute student of geography will note the overlap between
Haines City and Lakeland. The initial east-end tour of US 92 took a
more direct route south to Lakeland from Groveland; by merging the
two, we meander west before Haines City, then double back east of
Lakeland to make a second pass to the city's south.

After leaving the throngs of sun bunnies on the beach, the quiet
burst of the pastoral west of the I-95 on-ramp offers a pleasant, serene surprise. Only the tiniest patches of development exist between

107

Tomoka Wildlife Management Area and Clark Bay Conservation Area (a tract of land co-owned by the St. Johns River Water Management District and Volusia County). The route turns south just north of De-Land, where small oak-lined streets work themselves into the larger canopy nicely as the route again turns west, crossing the St. Johns River and passing through several different drainage basins. *Guide* writers mentioned that the road divided east and west watersheds, but in reality the route also comes close to the Kissimmee River Basin area. At its terminus in Lakeland, the route meets the edge of the Green Swamp and runs again along the edge of the Kissimmee Basin.

The *Guide* described Eustis as a "pleasing tourist town." Eustis calls itself "America's Hometown." Even with more development than the part of the road we leave immediately behind us in the east, fewer than twenty thousand residents spread over 10 miles. By comparison, New York City has about twenty-six thousand people per square mile.

For more than one hundred years the town has held an annual GeorgeFest, a February festival celebrating George Washington's birthday. The festival crowns a King King George and Queen King George, although to avoid confusion (and many, many jokes), they call them the "Georgefest Orange King and Queen."

The original route follows Bay Street south out of Eustis to 441 and west to Leesburg, twining between Lake Eustis, Lake Harris, and Lake Griffin. At Leesburg, the road intersects with US 27, and the original route follows US 27 for a small south run. We slalom between the two roads—27 and 33—to get to Okahumpka a few miles south.

Today Okahumpka is a tiny stop, perhaps best known for the Oka-humpka Service Plaza along the Florida Turnpike, which crosses south of Okahumpka. Visitors to Cracker Country at the Florida State Fairgrounds can see the Okahumpka Train Depot, built in 1898 and donated to Cracker Country seventy years later when Seaboard Coastline railroad no longer wanted it. The depot marked one of many stops along Henry Plant's railroad. In Florida, Plant's railroad ran from the northeast corner of the state, through central Florida, and southwest to Tampa. Along this route railcars stopped in Okahumpka for lumber and turpentine.

West of the turnpike, we see few buildings, the route alternating verdant citrus trees with rich fields of pale green. We see our first sign of modern-day developments just north of State Road 50 and Lake Jackson. Route 33 joins with 50 southeast to Groveland, where the original driving tour heads south again, passing Erie Lake, Pretty Lake, and more verdure and few homes until it reaches Polk City north of Interstate 4. It swivels west and south under the interstate and, for a fashion, alongside it.

Today I-4 overshadows this leg of the journey, but US 92 runs alongside the interstate for a long stretch of this tour. It starts in Haines City, a former citrus center and a town perched on Florida's ridge. At one time Florida was completely underwater; the peninsula's middle existed only as a series of islands. As inhabitants of these islands, the resident plants and animals evolved and adapted, learning to survive and even thrive on these islands.

Florida's landmass grew, and the islands became the center part of the state, a higher point known as the Lake Wales Ridge. US 27 forms the backbone of the state; from this center point the peninsula fractures in disparate regions.

As one fracture moves west toward the coast, the road runs between lakes. By the time the route reaches Lake Alfred, 7 miles from US 92's branch of US 27, the road has passed a half score of lakes. Today this area feeds the Disney beast; people know the name Haines City because it's emblazoned on a green interstate sign that also leads to a popular gas and restaurant pit stop just west of Walt Disney World.

Haines City has grown around Walt Disney World. It's no longer a citrus center; today, twenty thousand people live in roughly 18 square miles. After traveling relatively emptier parts of the state, it feels suburban and crowded. From the city limits you can see the Walt Disney World fireworks, and a stone's throw away you can find Legoland, the former Cypress Gardens.

Cypress Gardens, although it no longer exists, evokes two sharp memories for career Floridians: water-skiing shows and southern belles. The park opened in 1936, when its flamboyant owner, Dick Pope, converted a swamp into a "proper" garden. It was, perhaps, the earliest incarnation for the masses that proved the wilds of Florida could be tamed.

And so they remained until September 11, 2001. Fewer people traveled as the U.S. air industry regrouped, and within two years the park closed. It reopened in 2004 as an "adventure park" but closed again soon thereafter. In early 2010, Merlin Entertainment—the owners of Legoland—announced they would open a Legoland where southern belles once ambled.

Today the park cordons off a plot of land devoted to Cypress Gardens history. The owners brag on the park's website that they preserved a banyan tree planted in 1939. They talk of historic gardens they restored—camellias, azaleas, and other exotics. The *coup de grâce*? A southern belle, built entirely of Legos.

The route heads next to Lakeland, an odd mix of industry and architecture. The buildings crowd closer together as you approach, a Florida metropolis bursting with shipping centers for supermarkets (including the Publix headquarters), a regional warehouse for Rooms to Go, and a bevy of other distribution centers. Florida Southern College boasts Frank Lloyd Wright architecture. Warehouses populate the land here much like strawberries and tomatoes do in the next town over: the aptly named Plant City.

Tampa's west end once showcased rattlesnakes at the Rattlesnake Emporium. Handlers would sell their meat and put on shows. Guests could taste rattlesnake, buy a can of rattlesnake meat in Supreme Sauce, and watch snake proprietor George End milk a rattlesnake (he sold the venom). Mr. End ran End's Rattlesnake Cannery and Reptilorium (that's apparently a word) from an old gas station. Atop the building he built a neon sign with a coiled rattlesnake beckoning to drivers. Aside from the rattlesnake meat, he sold Snake Snaks, which were smoked and salted rattlesnake slices intended as hors d'oeuvres. The Reptilorium offered samples, and if a visitor ate one, he or she received a seal made of rattlesnake skin. This seal identified them, the attached card read, as a member of the Ancient and Epicurean Order of Reptile Revelers.

End died when a rattlesnake bit him.

The *Guide* lists more than one way to reach Pinellas County: Memorial Highway, a tribute to fallen World War men (in 1939 we had fought only one world war). The Memorial Highway connected Tampa with Oldsmar. Highway improvements and developments have fractured this highway since the *Guide*'s debut, although *Guide* writers naively posited that the road department would not widen the road because it would destroy the trees. The Davis Causeway connected Tampa to Gulf-to-Bay Boulevard and was named for a local businessman who earned his living by dredging the sea bottom and turning it to real estate, because either we *really* understood absurdity or we had no idea what damage we were doing to the environment. Today it's called the Courtney Campbell Memorial Causeway, after a Clearwater beach resident and former U.S. representative. To show Mr. Davis's family he is not forgotten, the Tampa side of the causeway has named part of the shoreline Ben T. Davis Beach.

The *Guide* does not direct us across this causeway, sending us over the Gandy Bridge into Pinellas, then north from St. Petersburg to Clearwater. It lists few facts about Pinellas County: a peacock farm in Clearwater, poultry and squab farms in Pinellas Park, pirate tales of Safety Harbor, and car stories about Oldsmar.

On part of the former peacock farm site in Clearwater, Seville condominiums bear the farm's namesake, now long gone save for the odd peacock screeching from the rooftops of the nearby Morningside housing development. I live in Pinellas County, and I have seen peacocks as far south as the Jungle Prada area of St. Petersburg, a good thirty-five-minute drive southwest from the former farm.

North of Clearwater, Tampa Shores (now Oldsmar) is named for R. E. Olds, who built Oldsmobiles. Safety Harbor has a mineral spring within the tony walls of the Safety Harbor Spa. According to the *Guide*, the town's first settler, Odet Philippe, came upon the town while in the Florida Keys, when an old pirate colleague (who once captured him but ultimately became his business acquaintance, suggesting that pirates, while not compassionate, were often pragmatic) suggested "Espiritu Santo."

The *Guide* retells the legend of the town's naming this way:

The pirate displayed a chart and pointed out Espiritu Santo Bay, as De Soto had named Tampa Bay in 1539. "There is but one other to compare to it—Naples," declared the pirate, who lyrically described the beauties of the place and the mineral springs at the head of the bay.

On the unnamed pirate's advice—and also with no documentation to support this story—Safety Harbor residents today believe Philippe settled their small town, which today boasts a marina, the luxurious aforementioned spa, a shoreline park named after Philippe, and no pirates whatsoever.

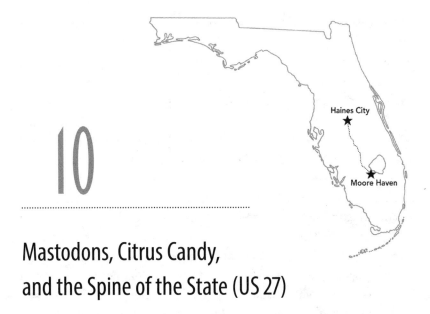

10

....

Mastodons, Citrus Candy,
and the Spine of the State (US 27)

Watch for cattle along the highway.

A Guide to the Southernmost State

The *Guide* included introductions at the start of each tour. These introductions would list some of the cities a motor tourist would see as well as pertinent details, such as whether or not one could find lodging along the roadway and pavement conditions. Also, cows. Florida was—and remains—a big cattle state, and apparently they were like squirrels along Florida's 1930s roadways.

"Watch for cattle along the highway" is a not-uncommon warning. Of the twenty-two original driving tours, only two fail to warn motorists about cattle meandering into the highway. One of those two is the stretch of US 41 that crosses the state west to east, cutting clean through the Everglades. *Guide* writers mention cottonmouths and gators, though as more of something of a photographic challenge than a warning, but no cattle.

The other road, US 27, traveled from Haines City to Moore Haven along the Lake Wales Ridge, an ancient beach that now lies smack-dab in the center of the state. Either the cattle there knew enough not to cross the road, or the land had other uses, like the mounds of citrus planted in that high, sandy soil. We start slightly north of Haines City, in Clermont.

This route, the *Guide* promises, "climbs the rolling hills of the ridge section, circles sparkling blue lakes, and for miles winds through large citrus groves. From the hilltops the land is a changing checkerboard of green trees, sapphire and silver water, and brown tilled fields."

Soil beneath the hilly route has not as much sand as it will in parts south, where "flat fields of cabbages, beans and sugar cane flourish without regard to the calendar," according to the *Guide*. The Lakeridge Winery makes good use of this soil, growing muscadine grapes and making red wine, white wine, and port. This winery makes only grape wine; several Florida wineries market a distinctive but wholly unpalatable variety of berry- or citrus-based wine. While oenophiles wrinkle their noses at muscadine wine—the large southern varietal will never compete with California or Washington vineyards—it is to the winery's credit that it has not capitalized on the area's citrus heritage to make such a wine.

The 2010 Census lists just over twenty-eight thousand Clermont residents; in 2000, it had fewer than ten thousand. The 1980s freezes killed off much of the citrus crops, and while orange bulbs hang from trees dotting the landscape as heralds of yesteryear, they compete with orange harbingers of development: barricades and cones littering US 27.

The Clermont Citrus Tower is the perfect Florida landmark, not tall by Manhattan standards, but plenty tall for central Florida. At 226 feet in the hilly middle of the state, it reaches 500 feet above sea level—think of it as "Florida Tall." Built in 1956, observers could take the elevator to the penthouse observation platform and gaze out over lots and lots of citrus.

Midcentury, oranges ruled the land. Groves rolled out over every hill and escorted travelers up and down the road. Building a tower that touched the sky so people could survey the kingdom must have seemed the natural thing to do.

"Back in those days, it was one of Florida's main tourist attractions," the current Citrus Tower owner, Greg Homan, explains. "The big three [were] Silver Springs, the Citrus Tower, and Cypress Gardens. That was before the turnpike was built and 27—Highway 27—was the main thoroughfare. They'd go to Silver Springs where the Tarzan movies were filmed, then they'd come to the Citrus Tower and go up to the top. It was the center of Lake County; it was the center of the citrus industry. Lake County, at the time, produced more citrus than the state of California."

Homan used to grow oranges, just like his neighbors. In the 1982 freeze, he lost most of his groves to frost, just like his neighbors. He tried to hang on to his livelihood but found he could not. He turned to a different way of living off the land: real estate. However, he never got the oranges out of his blood, and when the Citrus Tower (and surrounding acreage) went up for sale in the mid-1990s, he bought it.

"The Tower has taken three hits over the years. The first hit was when the Turnpike was built—it took a lot of traffic off of the highway. The second hit was the investors that I bought the Tower from; they really kind of milked the Tower. It went downhill, not much maintenance was done. And then the third hit [were] the freezes of the eighties wiped out the citrus industry in this area."

His wife, Suzanne, runs the gift shop.

"We used to grow oranges. Now we grow houses," she jokes. The Homans charge four dollars for a ride to the top. I ride the elevator to the top—not that I have other options, as the Citrus Tower has the ground floor, and elevator shaft, and an observation platform, now walled- and glassed-in for my comfort and, I imagine, insurance purposes. As far as the eye can see, it sees houses. In the 1960s, people could supposedly see 16 million citrus trees from the tower. Today I see only one grove and estimate it contains roughly six thousand trees. I cannot begin to count the houses.

"I wish it could go back to 1982," Suzanne says when I mention the view to her upon my safe return to land. She maintains a pragmatic view of development: "I understand the anti-growth people, but Clermont would now be a ghost town."

As we leave, carillon bells—or, at least, a computer program that plays a recording of them—rings out "Old Folks at Home." We start the van and leave the city, driving past highway traffic cones, barricades, and bulldozers.

Lake Louisa State Park perches atop the state's lumpy center. It sprawls over a gathering of hills and still has some feral citrus trees scattered about. These trees, remnants of orange groves planted in the 1940s, drop kumquats, lemons, and the occasional sour orange along a path ringing Dixie Lake. Surrounding them, the land is a colorful collection of wildflowers and butterflies. Cabins along Lake Dixie offer lakeside retreat, complete with fireplaces and rocking chairs on screened wood porches.

Heading south out of Clermont the sloping land evokes images of roller coasters. Crops of houses stacked on the hillsides give the urgent impression that at any moment they could slide down the hill into one of the area's many lakes. South of Clermont, you still see oranges. The Showcase of Citrus, adjacent to a grove, sells juice, jellies, and jam. For part of the year it feels a bit barren, but when the citrus trees fill with fruit every fall, the air thickens with orangey sweetness.

As we approach the route's junction with I-4, subdivisions with oddly inappropriate and often tragic names ("Eagle Ridge" with a noted lack of eagles perhaps the most obvious example) grow more dense, but once we move past the cluster of McDonald's, gas stations, and Denny's servicing people leaving Walt Disney World, the road changes again, and we find ourselves passing between citrus groves and old buildings.

In Patsy West's 2008 book *Enduring Seminoles*, she points out that alligator wrestling was the first Florida tourist attraction, but while Seminoles wrestled gators for tips near Miami, Florida orange groves drew their share of people, too. People loved to tour groves and watch machines sort oranges by size. When they were done watching, they'd treat themselves to a sample of "liquid gold": fresh-squeezed juice. They'd buy gallons of juice, pay to have gift boxes of oranges and grapefruits sent back up north to their shivering friends and family, and leave with an orange ice cream cone or a box of citrus candy.

In 1939, a Realtor named C. S. Taylor bought a candy factory called the Sun Dial Sunnyland Citrus Candies and Tropical Sweets. Sunnyland Citrus Candies, started by two ladies who made jellied citrus candies for their tearoom, became Taylor's Tropical Sweets. The original candy factory is a House of God "worship center" a half hour away on US 17, but to the west, on US 27, the original machines still churn out citrus candies in Davenport. When Taylor died in 1972, his widow sold it to Paul Webb.

At Webb's Candy Shop the lady behind the glass cases of mahogany fudge and tawny peanut brittle tells us that when Webb bought the business, he did so intending to move the shop. Taylor's widow allowed it with the caveat that the Webb would keep making citrus candy in addition to the planned array of goat's-milk fudge and chocolates. In 1975, Webb's found a new home on US 27, and while the glass cases contain chocolate in every iteration, on every table cellophane boxes display rainbows of jellied citrus candy.

On the counter by the register, a divided dish tempts me with four types of citrus candy. I haven't had these since I was a kid, but once I determined we'd stop by the historic candy factory, I've craved those jellied orange slices and spearmint leaves. This candy looks only the slightest bit like what I remember, but, I tell myself, it's the real deal. I take a sample. I close my eyes in anticipation. I take a bite.

It tastes not exactly as I recall, a mix of sugar with a hint of what must be orange. Intense waves of sugar and not even a hint of orange flood my taste buds. Nonetheless, we buy a box of citrus candy—I'm not sure how it has citrus in it, but it does, the woman behind the counter assures me—and send it back home. It may not be the stuff I remember, but it's part of our history.

The tidy shop that contained Webb's also had a Dunkin' Donuts. I suck down a coffee gratefully as I note more and more construction replacing those rolling orange groves. US 27 quickly turns into something akin to what I saw along parts of 441.

Gary Mormino calls US 27 "the spine of the state," and as we pass through Lake Wales, the road reveals the truth in this title. Here a turn to the east will unfold a wrinkly bump, present alongside the road as we bisect the center of the state.

Today called "The Ridge," this land formed waterfront sand dunes during the Pleistocene era, when sea levels were as much as one hundred feet higher. When elevated, the Gulf of Mexico covered most of western Florida, up to the dunes comprising the ridge line found along US 27. The US Fish and Wildlife Service likens the tips of land protruding from the primordial Florida seas to the Bahamas as we know them. Isolated from the rest of the world, animals and plants evolved on these islands, and when the seas fell away roughly 2.3 million years ago, the scrub hills remaining held a community found nowhere else.

Paddlers along the nearby Peace River can find a treasure trove of sharks' teeth and dolphin fossils as well as the occasional mastodon bone, but these finds, curious only to those who don't know the prehistory of the land, pale compared to the ecological cache found along the sandy hills of central Florida. The soil, low in nutrients but high in sand, drains quickly, which means the rainfall here recharges our aquifers at a healthy rate. Many of the living things here exist nowhere else in the world: forty plants are endemic to the Lake Wales Ridge. One of them, the Florida ziziphus, is a plant botanists believed extinct until its discovery along the ridge. The biodiversity along the ridge includes four rare animals—including the Florida scrub jay—and a host of insects believed to have evolved along the ridge and nowhere else. While a history of citrus farms and ever-encroaching development have decimated an estimated 85 percent of the original scrub, government agencies and nongovernmental organizations have spent more than $75 million to buy parcels of land for preservation.

Lake Wales marks the primeval shoreline of the ridge. The city website brags it has "Vintage Charm—Progressive Vision," but the historic downtown clearly struggles. Beautiful brick architecture lines the main street, but of the few shops among the vacant storefronts, many are inexplicably closed in the middle of the day.

The main street part of Lake Wales—and this town, too, boasts a Main Street Community sign—and the outskirts vacillate between looking utterly beaten down and extremely scary. The grass grows high, reaching out over curbs into the streets, as if trying to escape the desolation; ramshackle homes are in various stages of patchy disrepair.

Back on the route, I grow despondent. US 27 through Clermont revealed a glorious pastoral countryside finding its way among the development. Here I fear the land has surrendered, and I feel the weight of cement on my shoulders as I take one last look at Lake Wales's decaying Hotel Grand; from a distance it looks almost regal, but moments ago I gazed at the crumbling edifice through a locked chain link fence. I looked up at peeling paint, missing fire escapes, and boarded windows and felt a cold fear for the vanishing bits of Florida. The hotel fades into memory as we seek out the lush hammock, protected from a concrete fate by the boundaries of a state park.

Highlands Hammock State Park is a few miles off US 27, but they're country miles, which means the assaulting colors of strip malls and ubiquity have plenty of time to make themselves scarce as we descend into the liquid of the forested palm swamps. We're in palm country well before we reach the entrance to the park, and the only difference between the road before we officially enter one of Florida's oldest parks and the road after it is that the park has more signs. The signs direct us to our campsite, a grassy clearing under tall, stretchy pines. We recline under the pines, listening to the sounds of the forest. In the morning we drive a lazy circle around Loop Drive.

Loop Drive feels like a secret forest trail, with cabbage palms reaching higher than you feel they ought to as pines tower above them, coupled with oaks to close off the sky from the underbrush. It is dark and, even in early September, cool. The boardwalk trail that leads over the swamp is shadowed and breezy. As I make my way along the elevated wood boardwalk, cypress knees rise out of the swamp to greet me. The water is everywhere, it seems, curling around tree trunks and finding ways to run around fallen trees.

I can only describe the swamp here as perfect. I am not speaking hyperbolically; at home, when reviewing my notes and photographs, its magnificence strikes me once again. The water, a clear black mirror, reflects the glorious ruched cypress trunks rising from it. Golden-white sunlight filters down through the leafy canopy and bounces light patterns off the swamp. The trees and the water and the light twist into infinity, vanishing beyond the mist of the swamp.

And it's like that everywhere I turn on the boardwalk. There is no vista I would leave out, no one sight that takes my breath away less. There is a beauty in any wildness, of course, but there's an empirical beauty in the symmetry of a swamp. It may look to the uninitiated like haphazard arrangement of green and brown and wet and light, but if you look closely, you can see that everything has symmetry, a counterpart, and a place. It is science and art and reason and wild.

The boardwalk itself is part of the experience. Tree trunks grow around and through the weathered wood planks, and at one point, the side rail disappears. The water here isn't deep. I know that. But I also know I'm in a swamp, brimming with things unseen just beneath the sheen of dark water. Several hundred feet into the swamp, the rail to the boardwalk disappears, and I pause while trying to identify the purple floating flower and concentrate on grabbing branches and maintaining my balance well above the water. Once my footing feels secure again, I begin to step again along the narrow planks. Emerald bits of duckweed cover the water, and muted amethyst swamp lilies float in their midst. The trees are massive, rough, and strong, and I feel a sense of perspective as I wander along the boardwalk, which now starts to jut out at odd, stiff angles, as if a child had hammered the supports haphazardly into the muck supporting the swamp. Walking ten feet forward takes twenty feet of zigzagging boardwalk, and while it's time-consuming, the backdrop has no parallel.

All too soon the boardwalk leads us to an earthen path carpeted by leaves. Vines twine around palm trunks, and the banana-yellow orb spiders build webs as big as a Volkswagen between them, well off the ground and out of the way of humans. So thick, though, are the spiders that often two or more spiders have used the same tree to anchor one side of their web, giving the impression of a silken treehouse with no roof and no floor.

In the more manicured areas of the park, sour orange trees grow side by side with palms that easily reach one hundred feet into the air. It is the wrong season for sour oranges—or, really, any oranges—but the park was long known for its sour orange pie, sold at the restaurant I am told is temporarily closed.

The Civilian Conservation Corps museum across the courtyard is not closed, however, and I poke my head inside. Highlands Hammock was built in part by CCC workers. These workers may have been the sort of men who believed in the importance of parks and preserving part of the wilderness for people to experience, but it wouldn't have mattered: they were young, unemployed, and broke. They needed money, and if nature and the WPA intended to provide, they would take it. The work included planting trees, putting an elevated deck through a swamp, and building roads. These college-age men received thirty dollars per month for their work in the swamps of Highlands Hammock; of that, twenty-five dollars went to their mom and dad.

The smallish museum here pays homage to those young men. On display are artifacts of CCC work in eight state parks: Highlands Hammock, Myakka River, Hillsborough River, Mike Roess Gold Head Branch, O'Leno, Fort Clinch, Torreya, and Florida Caverns State Parks.

....

South of Sebring the route is sparsely populated, buildings a minority among citrus trees and tributaries of the Okeechobee, which grows ever closer. As we cross out of the heaviest citrus land we will see on these tours, we pass a giant orange pineapple with a sign proclaiming "JUICE" underneath it.

Welcome to Shonda's Souvenirs in Lake Placid. The parking lot is empty, and the landscaping has reclaimed the weaker parts of the pavement. There is no one inside the ranch-style orange building, and the store is dark. I walk to the glass front door, inside of which a small pile of mail has accumulated. I step back and look up at the lettering running around the top of the building: "TEE-SHIRTS—FRUITS— SHONDA'S SOUVENIRS—HONEY—ORANGE JUICE."

Yellow and orange mesh bags of fake oranges and grapefruit hang in front of mostly closed vertical blinds in each of the store's wide glass windows. Inside, the shop looks messy but not abandoned, although the Progress Energy bills yellowing just inside the door belie the notion that perhaps Shonda just called in sick today. A sheet of metal lies in the tall weedy grass against the side of the building; at the roadside, a hand-painted orange sign boasting "Fresh Produce" is fading quickly to the color of a Meyer lemon. Shonda, I fear, will not return.

As we make our way toward the end of US 27, I try not to think of Shonda as foreshadowing the future of citrus in Florida. Instead, I try to understand why she built that huge orange pineapple.

Toward the route's end, the *Guide* no longer speaks of the landscape in rhapsodic verses of sparkling lakes and rolling hills; instead, as the road edges toward the vastness of the Everglades, its tone changes. The *Guide* describes "muck fires" that "cast a heavy pall of smoke over Moore Haven." The last paragraphs are liberally peppered with tales of fires, alligators, and the well-made point that humans have "no effective control" over the forces of nature in the Everglades. The final paragraph, no more than a sentence, encourages people to travel the whole of what we now know as State Road 80, which skims along the underside of Lake Okeechobee and takes drivers out of the swamp and to either coast.

"The fires rob the soil of humus, and the smoke renders automobile driving hazardous," the next-to-last paragraph reads, "although a State fire-control unit has a record of extinguishing more than 600 fires annually, the 'Glades are of such an extent that no thoroughly effective control has been achieved."

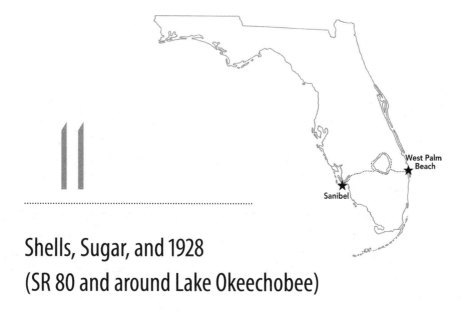

Shells, Sugar, and 1928
(SR 80 and around Lake Okeechobee)

Passing through the open range country of central Florida, reminiscent of the Old West with its cowboys and herds of range cattle, the highway follows the Caloosahatchee River to Fort Myers and the Gulf Coast at Punta Rassa, fringed with sand flats and low-lying keys overgrown with mangroves.

A Guide to the Southernmost State

Florida cowboys. If you don't spend time in Florida's inland areas, that may sound odd. Florida doesn't have cowboys; the *West* has cowboys. Florida, by comparison, has beaches and sand and Disney. Somewhere between those beaches and the mighty mouse, though, Florida has cows. Lots and lots of cows. Since Ponce de León dropped off the first herd in 1521, Florida's cattle industry has kept the interior of the state alive. Today, Florida ranks twelfth in the country for the number of beef cows, with 4 million acres of pasture and another 1 million acres of woodland used for grazing.

Cattle ranching in Florida isn't a new concept; cows and cowboys roamed this route when *Guide* writers traveled it, and if the travelogue's tone in the above quote is any indication, people didn't realize how much ranching factored into the Florida economy back then, either.

The tour in the *Guide* ran a fairly direct line underneath Lake Okeechobee, crossing the northern edge of the remaining Everglades, which writers noted as "America's largest swamp" although today we know the Everglades includes nine disparate ecosystems, several of which are not swamp, and "following the shore of Lake Okeechobee" just as State Road 80 does today. The writers also noted the lake was "encircled with fertile black fields growing great quantities of winter vegetables and sugar cane."

As we plod along the lower swampy third of the state, there's no doubt that Florida's chief land use has more to do with working the land than sunning oneself upon it: this route has pasture and planted fields in abundance. In 1939, this tour ran in a straight line from West Palm Beach to Punta Rassa, but we opt to also circle around Lake Okeechobee. Without stops, this route will take just under four hours. Prior to now, the only way I've seen Lake Okeechobee is from the right seat of a low-wing, four-seater prop plane. The pilot indulged me and treetopped over the lake, swooping down low so I could get a good look at the big water. That day, our single-engine Grumman Traveler followed a series of locks west to the Gulf coast. Beyond that, however, I've only read about the lake, heard stories about the lake, wondered about the lake.

Many of the stories come from Barry, who's a boat captain by trade. When he made boat deliveries he would often cross Lake Okeechobee. If you're trying to get a boat from one side of Florida to the other, you don't go around Florida's southern tip. You cut through the lake, using the channelized St. Lucie River on the east and the Caloosahatchee River on the west. On the east, State Road 76 follows the river; State Road 80 more loosely follows the Caloosahatchee on the west.

A series of locks keeps the water where the state water management districts think it should be, which means they keep the lake from flooding sugarcane fields. For boat deliveries and pleasure cruises, this means captains must time their trips by when they can get through the locks and bridges. Heading toward the lake, the water level rises with each lock. Heading away from the lake, the water level drops. State engineers only allow the lake to touch outside water at roughly twenty fixed points.

Lake Okeechobee drains south into the Everglades, east into the Atlantic, and west into the Gulf of Mexico. On the Caloosahatchee River's western edge, bridges connect Sanibel and Captiva Islands to the mainland. Motorists pay six dollars to cross over into Sanibel, the larger of the two islands at just over 10 miles long. Sanibel is barely a mile wide at most parts, with its widest stretch maybe 3 miles across. The island resembles Fort Myers, Cape Coral, and the mainland cities on the other side of the bridge in much the same way a bulldozer resembles a palm tree. Sanibel has one main road, a two-lane affair lined by a bicycle path that seems more crowded than the road. The highest building on the island is the Sanibel Lighthouse, painted a deep brown that contrasts with the color-washed island.

The cottages, homes, and shops that pepper the island mimic the colors of a tropical jungle: shocks of fuchsia bougainvillea explode between coral and lemon cottages, peach hibiscus frame the crosswalks, and orange birds of paradise flower between lime-green traveler palms, red Poinciana, and soft-green pine trees leading to the beach. Sanibel's crescent shape and its position, perpendicular to the edge of Florida's peninsula, make it an ideal landing place for shells getting washed along the seabed, and shells on the beach mirror and mute the colors of the island: pink Florida fighting conch, cerulean lion's paw, and lavender olive shells blot out the cream sand.

Every year in February, the Sanibel Captiva Shell Club kicks off its annual shell fair ("Shellabration") with the Sanibel Stoop. The Sanibel Stoop is named after the stooped-over posture of shell collectors as they scour the beach for cockles, sand dollars, and coquina. During the Sanibel Stoop event at the fair, shellers gather along the beach en masse to mimic that pose. The fair includes other things—shell lectures, shell salesmen, shell books, to name a few—but make no mistake: people come here to hunt for shells. The hunt along the beach, the thrill at finding a perfect Scotch Bonnet, the ache in your lower back at the end of the day—this is Sanibel's allure.

Shells aside, Sanibel appeals to tourists seeking old Florida, or, at the very least, the picture they keep in their head of Old Florida. The island does not disappoint. It has no stoplights, no chain stores (except for one Dairy Queen, grandfathered in when the island enacted tight growth management practices). Sanibel still looks much as the *Guide* describes it, with bevies of birds, rainbows of wildflowers, and warm, welcoming water. While there is no shortage of colorful, quaint beach bungalows, time-shares, and inns, they come second to the natural splendor. Sanibel seems content to fade behind the brilliant colors of yellow frangipani, roseate spoonbills, and purple donax. This is not an island where you come with a purpose; this is an island where you come to absorb the scents and pace of Florida.

On the mainland, the route traces the crowded banks of the Caloosahatchee. East of Interstate 75 the buildings grow fewer. In parts, cypress swamps still meet the road, but farms and cattle are more prominent than low-lying swampland. As we pass Buckingham Road the road abandons all pretense of following the twisting river and shoots through the right angles of reclaimed swamp. This part of Florida is a study in right angles: the road, the crops lining the road, and the drainage canals dug to helpfully dry out the swampland and make the rich muck more useful as arable soil. Even the Caloosahatchee has succumbed to this idea of order. While the river still curves and bows in places, in parts its lines, too, straighten alongside the neat rows of orange trees, tomatoes, and peppers.

Was this the greatest idea? It depends on whom you ask. The farmers and the homes here think so; Everglades-huggers disagree. The system of drainage canals and pounds of fertilizer and pesticides used on these farms negatively impact the Everglades ecosystem. It appears some of the farmers have sold to developers (who, in turn, sell to unsuspecting folks from out of state), and signs of subdivisions marching south emerge along this road: a supermarket here, a diner there.

LaBelle exists at a bend in the Caloosahatchee. It is by no accounts a large city, but it is the main population center between I-75 and Lake Okeechobee along the route. It has not quite five thousand residents and is the Hendry County seat. According to the *Guide*, LaBelle's "big event" happened on Independence Day, when cowboys rode into town for a rodeo and "range hands compete in riding Florida broncos and 'bull-dogging' steers. Roping and whipcracking contests follow spirited horse races, on which wagering is heavy. A barbecue supper concludes the day, and in the evening square dances are enjoyed in jooks and homes to the music of guitars and fiddles, accented by the thumps of heavy boots."

The rodeo, since prewar Florida, has continued, but it has grown. Modern-day LaBelle also has an annual Swamp Cabbage Festival. The festival includes "Grasscar" (a lawnmower race), armadillo races, and, of course, the crowning of the Swamp Cabbage Queen. Swamp cabbage, for the uninitiated, comes from the white tender heart of younger cabbage palm trees. When prepared, they look like the logs of string cheese sold in grocery stores, although they taste nothing alike. I can't get enough of the squishy, sour-ish hearts, but I freely admit they aren't for everyone. Barry wrinkles his nose at them every time I try to get him to try one. The following exchange may give you some sense of the divisions on the topic: "Ate some in Holopaw," Florida literature professor Thomas Hallock wrote on an early draft of this manuscript. "What does it taste like? For me, like urine-pickled cauliflower."

Jono Miller, a cabbage palm expert, disagrees. He explains that swamp cabbage is the brand-new part of the tree. Like a brand-new baby, it doesn't have its own personality yet, so it tastes like whatever you soak it in.

"My suggestion?" he says in reply, "Avoid the urine-pickled swamp cabbage—the ease of preparation is offset by the result." Even cabbage palm experts, it seems, have a sense of humor.

While circling the Okeechobee I hope to feed my odd fascination with Florida's legless reptiles. Barry tells stories of crossing the lake on boat deliveries and stopping at the Roland Martin Marine Center for the night. Beginning at twilight, water moccasins would gather on the floating docks, patches of color darker than the dock that looked suspiciously like rope but most definitely were not. A more prevalent but decidedly less deadly evil, the mosquitoes here are so thick that when you sit down to dinner at the marina bar, the server hands you a can of insect repellant.

We stop the van and walk out to the levee, my eyes more focused on the ground than the water. Cottonmouth water moccasins are pit vipers with tiny heads and tails but fat, snuggly bodies. Curiosity compels me to see one up close. I don't want to cuddle it, exactly, but I do want to know if they're as fearsome as my childhood nightmares. I grew up a block away from a creek, and my parents warned me it was chock-full of the dastardly serpents. I never saw one, but odds are if I had seen one, it would have been a common nonvenomous water snake. Brown water snakes are far more populous in Florida, but not as good a deterrent for keeping a curious seven-year-old out of trouble. At the top of the levee I see a canal with four empty rowboats rafted up to grassy lowland; the lake itself remains mostly out of sight. In the distance I see an empty nesting platform, ready for osprey. I look carefully at the ground and the levee wall. I step carefully.

I see no snakes. We walk back to the van and continue circling the pond. Our next stop? Sugar Country.

If you've ever heard the phrase "Big Sugar," a term generally used derisively, the person likely meant US Sugar or Domino Sugar. Sugar is big business in Florida and a major player in the Everglades' downfall. Without Big Sugar, some say, there would be no need for the Everglades Restoration program. While I disagree somewhat—greed and avarice are powerful, potent motivators, and businessmen don't need sugarcane to buy, drain, raze, and sell land to the highest bidder—US Sugar's impact on Florida profoundly saddens me. The company irrevocably altered one of the sweetest, swampiest places on earth.

Clewiston sits at the southwest edge of the lake's rim. In *Guide* times, it was a company town, owned by US Sugar. The workers—the black workers—who cut the cane and processed the sugar lived south of Clewiston, in Harlem. In the 1930s the US Sugar Corporation owned Clewiston's water, power, and phone companies, as well as the town hotel, outright. Today, US Sugar dominates Clewiston still; there is no pretending US Sugar doesn't have a hand in everything. To the south, the Fanjul Brothers run a similar saccharine empire with Domino Sugar and Florida Crystals. While Florida Crystals, especially, markets itself as "carbon free" and prides itself on dredging "nutrient-rich" soil out of nearby (man-made) canals and reusing it on the fields, make no mistake: sugar is killing the Everglades.

If you want to preserve the remaining Everglades, stop eating sugar. Let me explain. The muck around Lake Okeechobee and the Everglades grows perfect sugarcane. Big Sugar came here, saw, planted, and—with an inordinate amount of help from government subsidies that they still receive today (almost $900 million in 2012 alone, and those are never on the federal chopping block when you read about the fiscal cliff or a sequester)—grew. They took what water they wanted, and if, during dry spells, they didn't get enough, they convinced the government to let them divert the massive amounts of water they needed. When they got too much, they flushed it out along the Caloosahatchee and the St. Lucie Rivers. They dammed it up behind a wall in case they needed it.

The result? Sweet, sweet sugar—fantastic news for US Sugar and the Fanjul Brothers but not so much for lands south of the sugarcane, which includes the Glades. Because of Big Sugar, the government—through the auspices of the South Florida Water Management District—can, at the governor's whim, turn Lake Okeechobee on and off like a big faucet. This, as you may well imagine, does not bode well for unique ecosystems accustomed to getting the same amount of water they have received every year since the last ice age. Without the seasonal, irregular flow, life in the Glades faltered.

In addition, sugarcane is not impervious to bugs and disease, so farmers use pesticides to keep that sugar coming. As with most plants, fertilizer makes sugarcane grow faster, but once they send those green stalks on a growth spurt, those chemicals don't disappear—they leach out into the Everglades. Since the first stalk of sugarcane sprouted from the muck, US Sugar and the Fanjul Brothers have steadily yet dramatically increased the levels of nitrogen and phosphorous, chemical cocktails that kill bugs, grow big sugarcane, and decimate the Everglades.

The *Guide* bragged about "intensive efforts to reclaim the swamp," that started with Florida getting legal ownership of the Everglades through a federal land patent. Two years later Florida politicians established the Everglades drainage district, which allowed for what the *Guide* writers called "drainage operations."

"The major problem was to control the overflow from Lake Okeechobee which inundated the territory to the south," the *Guide* says. "To that end, the southern half of the lake was rimmed with dikes, and a series of canals was constructed, radiating from the lake to both the Atlantic and the Gulf."

Optimistically, one may assume this happened because people failed to realize the environmental ramifications; in time, activists like Marjory Stoneman Douglas, a writer whose father happened to have founded the *Miami Herald*, helped people understand the significance of the Everglades, although she herself rarely ventured into the Glades, describing them as buggy, wet, and inhospitable.

Her personal distaste for the swampier aspects of the Everglades, coupled with her tireless passion—when she died at 108 she still campaigned fiercely for the preservation of the Everglades—to restore harmony in them resonates. We may not all like its razor-sharp sedge, its venomous snakes, or its larger-than-life collection of saurian green predators, but we should like even less knowing that we, as a species, drove an interconnected series of ecosystems to extinction. With Ms. Douglas's help—and others—people saw all too clearly that was where the Glades were headed. Work began on a "restoration program" to try to keep the Everglades from drying out and dying.

Except, of course, Big Sugar remains. Death of one-of-a-kind ecosystems or no, they have to worry about profit, and they will do anything to ensure state and federal laws continue to work in their favor. While US Sugar has the support of most of Clewiston—without Big Sugar, the best chance a local kid has for a future involves the NFL—most everyone else in Florida clucks their tongue and shakes their head when you talk about sugar and the Everglades.

After years of strife between Big Sugar and concerned citizens in Florida, Governor Charlie Crist came upon a seemingly perfect solution: why not just buy the company? For under $2 billion, the state could purchase 187,000 acres of Big Sugar land, close the refinery, and restore the flow of the Everglades, no easy task after years of soil erosion and degradation courtesy.

It sounded like a great, workable solution, and so of course it failed in quick stages. The governor announced the plan in June 2008. By

November the plan changed: for $1.34 billion the state could have 181,000 acres but not any of the processing facilities, including the refinery. To make a long story somewhat shorter, the numbers kept shrinking, and today US Sugar remains alive and well in Clewiston, much to the relief of its 1,700 employees, who depend on America's sugar industry to feed their families.

Clewiston's slogan? "America's Sweetest City."

....

While the sweet-toothed towns like Clewiston pave the road to Lake Okeechobee, the ring around the Lake itself (SR 80/US 27/SR 700/US 98/SR 700) has a mystique all its own. The wall keeping the water just out of sight, the possibility of crossing paths with a venomous pit viper, the migrant farmworker communities juxtaposed with the odd colonial home lined with massive palms and green, sweeping lawns. The southern edge is littered with liquor stores, markets, and other hastily lettered Spanish signs. No apparent middle class exists. Those colonial homes are few and far enough between that you start to believe the ruling class barely exists, either, but sugar's grainy white hand remains silently at work. It's not just sugar that rules the day here—anything that grows enslaves the poorest class in these towns.

Consider Belle Glade. The name itself crowns this town "belle of the swamp." Ironically, Belle Glade has perhaps Florida's most tragic history. "Welcome to Belle Glade. Her soil is her fortune," one signs boasts, and that may be so—but not for the people living here. Of the town's 17,500 people, 33 percent live below the poverty level. The town is 56 percent black people and 34 percent Hispanic. Along the roadside we see more Spanish signs than English, and the predominant roadside industry seems a mix of taquerias and drive-through liquor stores. There are more than six thousand homes in Belle Glade, more than half of which are single-family homes. As we drive through town, I find myself glancing toward the lake—or, more accurately, the dike keeping the lake from washing over these buildings.

Not that it couldn't if it wanted to. It's not like it hasn't happened before.

Here's the problem with putting houses down in this part of Florida: the land is low and wet, and no matter what humans try to do to make it higher and drier, it doesn't work on a long-term basis. The Hurricane of 1928 offers the best example of this. In his book *Black Cloud*, south Florida journalist Eliot Kleinberg explains how this happened:

> At the beginning of the twentieth century, water simply flowed unimpeded from the lake's south shore in a sheet, into the Everglades . . . For the early settlers and farmers, that simply would not do. So between 1923 and 1925, the state built a 47-mile-long dike of earth. It was about five feet high. Twice in the next three years, it would be shown as useless as a dam made of tissue paper.
>
> In the early 1920s, commissioners of the Everglades Drainage District, founded in 1913, decided to build a more permanent dike around Lake Okeechobee. The plan was for work to start on the dike in 1927. It would be 110 to 130 feet wide at the base and 20 feet wide at the crest and stand 27 feet above sea level. They concluded that such a levee would resist hurricane-driven surge from the lake. But the legislature didn't get around to approving the money for it.

When the 1926 hurricane hit Florida, a low dirt dike burst at Moore Haven, a town of 1,200. Estimates say the water rose seventeen feet, destroying the under-construction Glades County Courthouse. Officials buried the unidentifiable bodies in a mass county grave. By September 1928, the dike situation had not improved. Area farms still flourished in the rich black muck. Heavy late-summer rains and storms dumped more water in the lake. When a hurricane made landfall on September 16, water dammed in Okeechobee had nowhere to go.

"It woke up Old Okeechobee and the monster began to roll in his bed," wrote Zora Neale Hurston in *Their Eyes Were Watching God*, a novel set against the backdrop of the 1928 storm.

The dikes did not hold. What followed was a precursor to Hurricane Katrina: death of many poor black families on a massive scale. Forty miles inland the hurricane reclaimed Florida, destroying the levee, obliterating entire towns, flooding farms, and killing thousands. The water had taken back the land and reshaped the topography of Florida's lowest third.

Before human intervention, the natural system worked. Water flowed from the middle of the state at a shallow, slow pace down the meandering Kissimmee River. During the summer there was more of it; in the winter, less. Some water pooled in Lake Okeechobee; some went around, and still more flowed through. In late summer, heavier rains flooded the land south of the lake as well as the Kissimmee River's floodplain. At the edge of the Everglades, the excess water drained into Florida Bay.

However efficiently it worked for the birds, trees, and fish, this system did not work for those who wanted to farm or sell the land under the water. Under that ever-moving pesky water was black gold: soil so rich from eons of wet, decaying plant and animal life that anything would grow in it. Under that water was land that could hold houses, shopping malls, and condominiums. The land failed to make anyone money while flooded with water, so why not change it—just a bit—to make it more efficient for humans?

....

Tragedies rarely result from one single misstep; more often than not, a series of poor choices lead to catastrophe. The 1928 tragedy south of Okeechobee came about because of at least three bad decisions. Building a dike around Lake Okeechobee to contain the water proved less than prudent; altering the landscape so that the land surrounding and beneath the lake could be used for farm, cattle, and sugarcane compounded the problem; housing poor black farmworkers to live on that newly drained land completed the trifecta of bad decisions.

On September 16, 1928, these three decisions collided spectacularly. Nicole Sterghos Brochu, for the *Sun-Sentinel*, tells the story like this:

> As the category four monster raged westward, it saved its most crippling blow for the small farming communities that lined Lake Okeechobee's southern shore. Between Clewiston and Canal Point, 6,000 people lived and worked, and nearly half would perish before the light of day.

Hurricane winds can bend a bicycle around a tree. They can lift a roof off a home. They can pick up cars. In 1928, the wind powered a mighty wave of water through a wall supposed to contain it, crashing through the five-foot dike made of Everglades muck.

Today we know that Category 4 hurricane winds pushed the water around in the shallow lake, beating it to a boil. The water in the lake rose ten feet above the lake level, bursting through almost 22 miles of levee on the southeast side of the mighty lake. The wall of water rampaged through the town, turning houses upside down, washing them away, and drowning those in its path. There was no escape; the water fiercely and wholly reclaimed the land and swallowed the towns in its path.

Even today, no one knows how many people died. The first number, 225, quickly grew to 400. In *Black Cloud*, Kleinberg recounts the stories about the storm's aftermath.

"Ugly death was simply everywhere," Charles Young, a Glades resident who helped collect the dead, would later recall. The work was one part rescue, most parts body recovery. Young found the bodies of a family, including a dead man clutching his stilled child. Another rescuer, Festus Stallings, found the bloated body of a toddler wearing a bracelet. Stallings recognized the bracelet. The month before, the tiny girl wearing it had shown it to him. It was a gift for her second birthday.

Some bodies were given a coffin burial, but not many. The Florida Health Department officially claimed just over 1,800 dead, but historians put the toll higher. Most of the dead were black farmworkers. In 1920s Florida, an unidentified black person didn't get a coffin, especially not with the weight of dead bodies crushing relief efforts. No records exist of the farm owners dying in the storm, perhaps because they lived elsewhere.

Relief workers stacked bodies in piles and burned them, burying the remains in mass graves. At some sites, they took the time to count the corpses. At others, workers were too overwhelmed to keep track. Most black survivors and many white ones never found out what happened to their friends and relatives. The young girl with the bracelet? She was thrown onto a funeral pyre, her body burned and buried with the others. Festus Stalling never forgot her. Memories of that child—and the many other dead—stayed with him until he died, his son Frank said.

"He said the hardest thing he ever had to do," Frank said years later, "was throw that little girl's body on that fire." Today, the majority of homes and stores by the lake's southern stretch lie less than a scant half mile from those levees.

Farther north, Pahokee looks poorer still, perhaps because of more of those colonial-styled estates interspersed with even more decrepit housing projects and shuttered businesses. Sugarcane is everywhere. As we drive I wonder about the unmarked graves from the 1928 storm. A cane fire burns in the distance, de rigueur in cane farming. Burning the fields leaves only the stalk, making it easier for the few remaining workers—machines do most of the work today—to harvest the cane.

Port Mayaca is the lone spot along the road where we can see the lake instead of a neatly mowed levee. It is also where we begin to leave the cane fields behind. Between here and the top of the lake, lunkers, not sugarcane, are the order of the day. Lunkers, or largemouth bass, make for big business. Fishing camps dot the northeast quadrant of the lake between Port Mayaca and Okeechobee. If agriculture has attempted to triumph over the lake and Glades on its south side, fishing has learned to harmonize with both on the north end. It is a wholly more pleasant sight for me; I've never caught a hawg, or even tried, but after the desperation of Pahokee and Belle Glade, the unassuming fish camps soothe me with their contrast. There are still farms here (largely palm farms, but the presence of something at work with the environment instead of against it eases the ache I felt in Belle Glade.

Taylor Creek marks the top of the lake, and also the least impoverished city along the pond, although it, like the others, contains a fair share of derelict buildings. It caters more to tourists, although judging by the wealth of fishing camps and bait shops, visitors here have a different idea of paradise than those flocking to Disney just two hours away. At the western edge of Taylor Creek we stop and walk out to the levee. We park, this time taking an antsy Calypso, and walk up the levee.

Here the lake seems less wild; there are more buildings and boaters and a man collecting trash from the ramp leading up to the levee. A tractor rests on the inside of the levee on a patch of grass, and a blue heron stares at us. East of our vantage point, a chain link fence separates the heron from a neatly mowed backyard. West of us a barge sits unattended, a colorful sign advertising "ICE SNACKS" in hand-painted lavender letters. White marshmallow clouds over the lake lower themselves and start to darken.

It's time to go.

In Moore Haven, we see a landfill on the lake side of the road, easily the highest point along the route and marked by crows and vultures soaring overhead. Prison inmates help with road construction, holding "STOP" and "SLOW" signs as we chug along the lake's perimeter. When one of them switches "SLOW" to "STOP" and we stop at the front of the line, he pantomimes asking for a cigarette. We shake our heads no, and I find myself wondering what one does in this area of Florida to get thrown in jail. The Moore Haven jail offers no more than medium security. It houses fewer than one thousand inmates, all male.

Once we come full circle around the pond, I am still at a loss to describe the lake. Despite severe alteration to the landscape, it feels like a forgotten and untouched part of the state. It also leaves me with an alternating sense of wonder and melancholy. Part of me looks for a way to empathize with the needs filled by businesses and farms whose owners shaped these tragic decisions, but I cannot find it. Part of me is in awe of the lake and the surrounding communities; earning a living here cannot be easy, even for the wealthier: they battle mosquitoes, snakes, gators, and the threat of storms with alarming regularity. This part of Florida is still frontier.

On its west side, Okeechobee grows wilder as it seems to spread out. Here we find fewer signs of development, save the odd gas station, house, or government building. Fields of cattle interspersed with cabbage palm line most of the roadway. On its east, neatly ordered rows of farmland escort the route east until the Loxahatchee area, where subdivisions, strip malls, and golf courses rise up to meet the road until it ends in West Palm Beach at A1A. From Loxahatchee east, the density of the Palm Beach suburbs are a blur after the wide-open rolling green of the southernmost interior. It is almost a culture shock to see farms pushed up against the rows of development, and I laugh as I recall the Guide's description of an 1880 homestead application for what was, by the 1930s, the business section of West Palm Beach. Irving R. Henry wrote on his application that he lived 3 miles from his nearest neighbor. The homes line up along the road in much the same way, just moments ago, sugarcane and tomatoes and peas did.

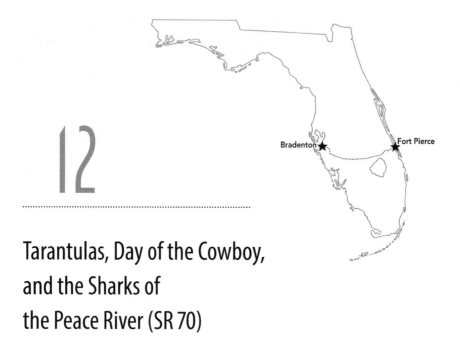

12

Tarantulas, Day of the Cowboy,
and the Sharks of
the Peace River (SR 70)

The farther south these driving tours take me, the more I marvel at the change in the state. I cannot specify one thing that marks the metamorphosis, such as the houses or vegetation or people; the changes are diaphanous, a delicate haze that covers parts of the state but somehow brings it into focus. The air hangs thicker; the trees grow a clearer shade of green. As the roads approach the mighty swamp that nestles against the state's limestone mattress, the spiky stalks of palm fronds and the teeth of the sawgrass bite through that gauzy veil of Florida's tourist-friendly image and leave no doubt that you stand at the edge of wilderness.

State Road 70 demarcates that wilderness. The tour starts in Fort Pierce, and as the road pulls away from the edge of North America and into the center of the state, the hinterland rears up and announces itself with ferocity.

Even when most of peninsular Florida, if we believe the *Guide*, seemed a swampy wilderness, something altered perceptibly along this route. The writers described farms to the north, but soon tours with that ordered description give way to one of winding through a swamp bearing the Seminole name for "alligator water." This, the *Guide* said then and our travels now announce, shares little with the land to the north.

First up on the order of letting you know you're not in Kansas anymore, much less northern Florida? Tarantulas.

Tarantulas have found a home in Fort Pierce's St. Lucie County. Mexican redrump tarantulas, to be precise, although for most of us, "tarantula" is all we need to hear to reach for the shotgun and the vodka. The fuzzy invader first made its presence known in the summer of 1996, when a citrus grove worker near Fort Pierce found a half-grown tarantula, a find that must have given him cause to ponder his career choice. A week later, other workers found a female tarantula and a few of her children, which could not have helped employee morale. The Department of Agriculture decided to head down and check out the Fort Pierce tarantula population. They found about one hundred tarantulas. As best as the experts can figure, the spiders descended from pets imported from Central America, because what's fluffier than a puppy? That's right: a huge furry spider with a thousand eyes. OK, eight. But still . . . more than we have, which no matter how you slice it, is creepy. The south Florida environment has enough in common with the spider's native land—the Yucatán—that the velvety nightmare-maker can survive quite nicely outside the exotic pet keeper's terrarium. So far, the state believes the tarantulas confine their ever-expanding population to this lone citrus grove, but in south Florida, hope springs eternal and, once again, life finds a way.

As the road leaves I-95 behind, for a great expanse the only businesses are a Ford dealership and mini-marts. Cattle, however, thrive. Cattlemen here sell more than 150,000 head of cattle annually through the Okeechobee Livestock Market. Thought rodeo clowns were just for the West? Nope. The Okeechobee Cattlemen's Association holds two rodeos every year, one in March and one over the Labor Day weekend, and of course they have rodeo clowns.

In neighboring Highlands County, the Lykes Brothers raise one of Florida's largest herds of cows. They own 367,000 acres of Florida real estate, making them one of the state's largest landowners. They use much of that property for cattle ranching, citrus, forests, and sugarcane. Descendants of Dr. Howell Tyson Lykes, who practiced medicine before going into Florida agriculture in the 1800s, still own Lykes Brothers. Today, the Highlands County ranch covers a good bit of the county. Before the Lykes Brothers—and others like them—bought and drained this land and went about the business of straightening the pesky curves of the Kissimmee River and trying to change its floodplain, this land was all part of the Everglades system. It still is, although ranching has forever altered what the upper part of the system feeds the Glades. Today, if you look south over the heads of cattle, you can see the Everglades in the distance, on the far side of Lake Okeechobee.

Unlike some other routes, a lack of development—other than the cattle ranches and citrus groves—marks our trail. Signs note several state-designated "natural areas," areas studied by the Florida Natural Areas Inventory (FNAI), which catalogues the plants and animals in these places. These evoke thoughts of the frontier, even where cattle graze next door. Oak and pine and palm dot the pasture, which grow thicker as the ranch ends and these specks of first nature overtake the landscape.

In Okeechobee, at the apex of the lake of the same name, the road has its first (and some of its only) stoplights. Rural Okeechobee maintains a narrow focus: fishing and cattle. Since 1965 the town has hosted the Speckled Perch Festival; unlike other Florida festivals, they do not crown a queen. In addition to the biannual rodeos, in July Okeechobee also holds the "Day of the Cowboy," which culminates with a cattle drive through the town. A modest set of buildings are strung together in a traditional main street. Although you can find the odd fast-food restaurant and may take your pick of gas stations, the town gives the impression of favoring local businesses over franchises.

The Peace River runs through Arcadia, a stopping-off point between its home in the Green Swamp and its destination, Charlotte Harbor. During the Miocene epoch (5 million years to 26 million years ago), the now-inland river lay at the bottom of the ocean. That means today's fossil hunters can sift through the shallow riverbed beneath the blackwater river and find sharks' teeth, dolphin bones, and other prehistoric remnants.

I went to the Peace River in search of these fossils and put in with my kayak no more than two hundred feet off the tour route. Traffic speeds by on a four-lane highway as we off-load our kayaks, ready to paddle back in time. Before we can, though, the dynamic of the river changes as we happen upon families running their all-terrain vehicles through the shallow riverbed, wondering if, in their enjoyment of the moment, they fail to notice us. We paddle around another bend, and the incessant monotonous drone of the ATVs fades. We paddled a peaceful, straight stretch of blackwater.

After a series of bends takes us less than a mile from the main road, we find a bed of black rocks, visible underneath the running water. I crouch; I sift. In twenty minutes time I unearth a handful of sharks' teeth and what more experienced fossil hunters will later identify as inner-ear bones from a dolphin. Satisfied with my haul, I let the slow current push me downriver to the road.

We soothe our waterlogged souls with deep-fried corn at Wheelers, a breakfast and lunch diner down the road. The pies change every day, as does the vegetable. Deep-fried corn may not feel like a vegetable, but according to the folks who run this small, no-nonsense eatery, it most certainly qualifies.

In May 1939, Arcadia held its first cattle sale. The Arcadia Stockyard continues the cattle sale every Monday and Wednesday at noon, although several owners have claimed the stockyard since the *Guide*'s first printing. The Seaboard Air Line once ran parallel to the road, and railcars used to move the cattle across the country; today, trailers full of cattle take the living steaks to their final destination.

Our tour ends at the junction with US 41, where the relative order at the route's western terminus echoes the past of a fruit-orchard- and packinghouse-dominated landscape. Today parking lots and strip malls hem in the water, keeping the wilds of Florida safely to the south. The sense of civilization remains just that: a sense. Scant miles outside of town, beyond the remaining farms and nurseries of which the *Guide* speaks, Myakka River State Park offers a different sort of order: natural. Here humans remain interlopers in the wild. The undeveloped areas within the park offer a glimpse of what the entirety of the area once looked like (and much of it still does): pines, oak, and palm hammocks protecting the banks of the gnarled, ancient river. The river itself winds between grassy, wet shoreline, the water the sole connection with the prairie.

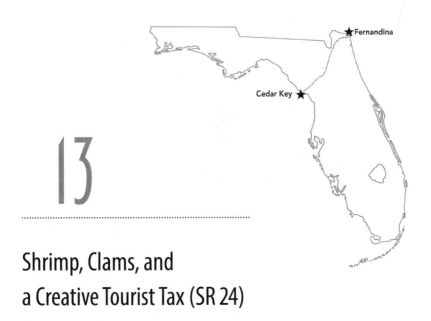

13

Shrimp, Clams, and
a Creative Tourist Tax (SR 24)

Aquatic pastoral.

The *Guide* paints the countryside along State Road 24 in vibrant hues: the "dark green mass" of slash pines, the "brilliant scarlet" of wild hibiscus, and the white blossoms and heavy fruit. In describing either salty waterfront—be it the Atlantic or the Gulf—the *Guide*, to pardon the pun, misses the boat.

Here's what the *Guide* says about Fernandina, Florida's northernmost beach: "an industrial city in which the shrimp and menhaden fisheries and the manufacture of pulp paper are the leading industries." And for Cedar Key, the route's western terminus (not counting the offshore Seahorse Island) for physical description, the *Guide* describes a "fishing village on a white sand island" before leaving readers with a none-too-riveting history of the railroad, Timucuan burial mounds, and a brief parting description of the area's economy and its "muddy tidal shores." Descriptions of both areas use words like "commercial," "industrial," and "factory," painting—perhaps unintentionally—a mental picture of waterfronts cast in gray undertones, caught perpetually in the throes of the Industrial Revolution with its iconic smokestacks.

....

Viewed differently, the gritty pull of a working waterfront is irresistible. The deep Atlantic beaches, while lovely, fascinate me less than Fernandina's series of boat docks where fishermen and shrimpers with salt in their beards, callouses on their hands, and the sea in their soul off-load the day's catch. Fernandina has a long-standing reputation as a vibrant waterfront that gets tourists but, perhaps, doesn't really need them. The *Guide* tells us as much, true then as now: "Although the city does not depend on tourists for its livelihood, its exceptional beach attracts visitors from all the southeastern states." In Fernandina, we drive the historic downtown and see shops that look appealing in their brick buildings but resemble many other small towns desperately seeking their individuality, but when Centre Street dead-ends at the Amelia River, we stop the van.

If some people idealize working the land or owning a herd of sheep, I have my own idea of the pastoral, and it involves brine. The beauty I see when I look at a working waterfront could not have less in common with those boilerplate downtowns if it tried, because there's no way to off-load tons of dead fish on the regular and still look like a chamber of commerce postcard. In college, I worked at the Madeira Beach marina. Ever since then, the smell of fish comingled with salt air and diesel exhaust acts as an aphrodisiac on my soul, and this is almost the exact smell that fills my nostrils as I step out of the RoadTrek, onto the grungy fishing docks, and into a dockside shanty offering the day's catch.

I stand, staring at nothing, slack-jawed and smiling like a fool, for a long moment before I pull open the door to the fish market.

For readers who have only purchased fish from the local supermarket, prepare yourself. You should not expect to see a tidy young man in a heavy apron over an embroidered polo shirt with only a passing knowledge of the fish you see spread out before you. As with most grocery stores, you will find a goodly amount of dead fish watching you from behind glass cases and a refrigerator full of less-than-premium beer. But you must also envision the bulk of the fish with clear eyes on heads still attached to their bodies, and you should also include a much-erased chalkboard with the day's catch listed and priced in less-than-perfect handwriting. In one corner you may find an old metal rack with a small assortment of Crystal, Tabasco, and Everglades seasonings as well as a few local additions; in another you may spy a sparse collection of dust-coated boxes of parboiled rice, paperboard cylinders of breadcrumbs, and bags of hush-puppy mixes. In the center of this dark wood haven, a gruff man behind the counter with a big, oyster-colored mustache, meaty hands, and few unnecessary smiles waits for your order. I ask where he gets the shrimp, and he looks at me—for just a moment—as if he has no patience for idiots before explaining he gets them off the boats docking fifty feet away. I buy a pound of shrimp, a six-pack of Corona Light, and beat a hasty, embarrassed retreat.

We detour off the tour to find our sandy respite for the evening at Little Talbot Island State Park, following the rope of road called the Buccaneer Trail, so named for tidbits of pirate history littered along the roadside. According to the *Guide*, Fernandina was something of a pirate "resort." Slave runners in 1807 and 1808 had to not only navigate past government ships but also outwit "hijackers" like the brothers Lafitte (Jean and Pierre).

The next morning we head back to the route and push west, leaving the deep blue of the Atlantic to follow the road west and south toward Cedar Key. The *Guide* writers described willow trees, elderberry, and fiery shocks of hibiscus lining State Road 24, but today, courtesy of I-95, Burger King, Krystal Burger, and an embarrassment of gas stations all cultivate the immediate western edge of Yulee. Privately owned tracts of pine yield to infant subdivisions. The stands of pines yet to surrender to development frame the for-sale signs at the edge of the hammock.

We reach Callahan quickly—the Eisenhower interstate system leaves the backroads to us slow travelers and not the folks intent on making good time—and recognize Callahan when we see it: it's Anytown, USA at its finest. Drugstore chains, regional supermarkets, and fast-food eateries abound. Callahan also marks the start of A1A or, in our case, the end. Here it turns into 301, a road immediately recognizable to any driver who ever cut across the state from the northeast corner to her southwest segments.

Lawtey follows next, known to many drivers as one of the only two speed traps recognized by AAA in the United States. Florida, it is important to note, has never instituted a state income tax. Over the years her cities found other ways to generate revenue; Lawtey opted for a tourist tax of sorts, because locals know the Lawtey segment of 301 as a strict no-speeding zone (as does anyone who can read the ominous black-and-yellow billboard warning you as you enter town). As a teenager and a twenty-something, I had a lead foot. Police officers pulled me over with such regularity that I added "tickets and traffic school" into my budget. Just as often as they ticketed me, though, they would let me go with a warning or a lesser ticket (I once received a ticket for "failure to obey a traffic sign"—referring to the speed limit sign) if I smiled and spoke honestly ("No, I don't know how fast I was going, officer; I just got out from behind an octogenarian Canadian, and honestly, it just felt good to *go*" saved me a couple hundred dollars once). I am dancing with middle age these days, and a hefty sense of my own mortality coupled with a writer's budget keep me driving the speed limit (mostly), but even as a kid, I would never have sped through Lawtey. These guys have a reputation to uphold, not to mention that, if officers let speeders go with a "free pass," their police force may not have gas for their cruisers next year.

The city's population—under seven hundred people in 2000—doesn't require much, and US 301 delivers almost half of what they do need. In 2001, 48 percent of the town's budget came from speeding tickets.

Next up on 301, Starke, the Bradford County seat, known to 1930s America for exporting strawberries and turpentine to the nation (although, one assumes, rarely together). If people outside the immediate area know of Starke, they know of it because it houses the Florida State Prison. Serial killer Ted Bundy slept here, as have a host of other killers.

Florida doesn't have the Broadway shows of Manhattan, or the movie houses of Hollywood, but when it comes to bizarre crime, we win hands-down. Florida novelist and columnist Carl Hiaasen makes this point brilliantly. "The Florida in my novels," he says, "is not as seedy as the real Florida. It's hard to stay ahead of the curve. Every time I write a scene that I think is the sickest thing I have ever dreamed up, it is surpassed by something that happens in real life."

For twelve years I earned my keep as a reporter for a small weekly paper, and Mr. Hiaasen ain't just whistlin' Dixie. We are a strange, wonderful state; in the summer of 2013, our small town had a rash of duck thefts and then duck deaths. The state had to get involved with the necropsies, and our paper received a lawsuit threat when we published a police report containing the names of two duck thieves. Excuse me, *alleged* duck thieves. We've also held a voter referendum about the location of chicken coops, and, on the eve of the city's 103rd birthday, we had a 250-pound pig running through my neighborhood. I should mention that we are in no way a farm community but a city on the southern tip of Florida's most densely populated county.

Duck theft, at least in my hamlet, doesn't carry jail time, but as far as—let's call it "nonstandard"—as far as nonstandard crime goes, that's just scratching the surface. Google "Florida Man" and you'll see what I mean. "Florida Man Arrested for Calling 911 after His Cat Denied Entry to Strip Club" and "Florida Man Steals Ambulance with Patient Still Inside" typify the results. Those more hardened than people misusing 911 or stealing wild ducks end up near Starke, at the state prison in Raiford, which currently houses almost nine hundred convicted criminals as well as the state's now-unused electric chair, built by inmates in 1923 and used through the end of the twentieth century.

Before the modernization of electric execution, each county could execute capital crimes as they saw fit, usually by hanging. Instead of an electric chair, Floridians on death row now die by lethal injection. The state pays an anonymous executioner $150 to administer the injection. Prison officials regularly test the electric chair to make sure it still works, just in case.

Down the road from Starke, Waldo awaits . . . with radar guns. Taking a page from Lawtey's budgeting process, Waldo, too, earns a hefty chunk of change from drivers in too much of a hurry to mind the speed limit. The town has just over eight hundred people and covers less than 2 square miles, much of which borders 301. AAA designates Waldo as the nation's second speed trap, and with good reason. In 2010, the City of Waldo collected just under $150,000 in property taxes but over $450,000 in court fines. Speeding tickets covered all but $100,000 of the city's entire public safety budget.

The towns along this route, save for Gainesville, are whistle-stops. Waldo and Lawtey typify the sort of town you find along US 301: small towns settled around the Seaboard Airline Railway that relied on the railway to export citrus and import visitors. Trains still run along the track, although they rarely stop. Freezes decimated the citrus crops that once grew in the center of the state. These towns, former winter playgrounds offering a respite of warm weather and tinge of culture, appear as sophisticated shells along the roadway.

While these towns have limited appeal for tourists seeking a beach vacation, hunters and naturalists will find plenty to do. Don't expect a variety of posh resorts or chain hotels, especially compared to the ubiquity of hotels lining much of the coast. Camping and the odd mom-and-pop motor inn, endearing in its basic amenities (Color TV! HBO! Phone! Indoor Plumbing!), epitomize area lodging. A short drive will take you to the Santa Fe Swamp Conservation Area, Lake Butler Wildlife Management Tract, Paynes Prairie Preserve, and the Austin Cary Memorial Forest as well as Belmore and Etoniah Creek State Forests.

The chief difference between these tiny dots of population along the roadway and the larger cities are not the speed traps, blue-collar families, or the lack of salt water. No, what you will notice first is the trees. Between Fernandina and Starke, statuesque foliage consumes the landscape, parting only occasionally for the odd business or restaurant. West of 301, this tour diverts to State Road 24 and heads through Gainesville. There, the trees don't bother to part for the homes, businesses, or even the University of Florida. Through town, the route contains more stands of pine and oak than strip malls. Rolling hills (think gentle Florida hills) rise up to meet your car.

Gainesville is a university town—aggressively so—with a football team. Students, former students, and professors populate this college town. This, of course, is Florida's "public Ivy," a school with origins dating back to before the Civil War. The town itself drips with the physical manifestation of academia, from the university's fifteen-story carillon built in memory of students killed in both world wars to its oak-lined streets and hills completely at odds with the university's website description of a "subtropical" climate. The trees, the shade, the hills, and the brick feel more New England.

Downtown, the Hippodrome State Theatre transports patrons about as far as they can get from the Florida "sun and surf" lifestyle. Built in 1909, the building was formerly the post office and federal courthouse and features classical revival architecture, rich plasterwork, stately columns, limestone construction, and terrazzo floors.

The collegiate tone of Gainesville fades abruptly and gives way to Levy County, the last county on this tour. After more miles of trees and the refreshingly nonfranchised eateries along the roadway, the road narrows to two lanes as it drifts out to the coast.

A small green sign marks the town of Rosewood, although the *Guide* fails to mention the town. By the time the Federal Writers' Project made its way to the coast of Levy County, only ashes and overgrown lots remained.

In early January 1923, a white woman accused Jesse Hunter, a black man, of assaulting her. Despite an eyewitness account that the married woman's white lover, not Jesse Hunter, hit her, a posse of white men from Gainesville summoned their dogs and the Ku Klux Klan and came to Rosewood. What transpired next was a hate crime of epic proportions: white men torched homes while onlookers did nothing but watch, although later county officials would not be able to find a single eyewitness. A posse of white men murdered every black person they could find, forcing at least one man to dig his own grave before they fatally shot him. When the smoke cleared, black bodies littered the town, left where the white men had felled them.

Some black families hid in the swamp; others at the home of a local shopkeeper; those who could, fled the area. The *St. Petersburg Evening Independent* reports no more than two white men died in the assault. Mr. Hunter was never found, dead or alive.

Thus ended the town of Rosewood. Today, historical markers let you know you have arrived; nothing more exists.

In nearby Cedar Key, I push open the door of the history museum and inquire about any Rosewood records they might have. Nothing, they tell me, that I probably haven't already seen on the Internet. An older white man, almost certainly a volunteer, smiles thinly as he tells me the news accounts exaggerated. "You know," he says, "a lot of those folks just left."

Yes, it's peculiar how the threat of racially motivated mob violence compels folks to desert their homes. I show him a thin smile of my own, thank him, and go looking for clams, because that, and not the museum's not wholly impartial look at Rosewood, is Cedar Key's treasure.

The *Guide* describes Cedar Key as a "fishing village on a white sand island in the Gulf of Mexico, three miles from the mainland." A more apt description of the town would evoke images of an outpost. Do not come here seeking sun-soaked beaches; you will find nowhere to stretch out your towel, butter yourself with sunscreen, and read a book on the sand. Cruise lines bus in tourists on day excursions, straight to the shops on Dock Street, a boardwalk of tourist-centric T-shirt shops and restaurants. The cruise ship passengers unknowingly motor past Cedar Key's treasure: clam farms.

In the late 1800s, Cedar Key served as a central shipping point for food and wood; goods from Mississippi would come to the town's deepwater port. From there workers would pack them into railcars and send them throughout the state. In addition, the town produced crazy amounts of oysters and pencils—Cedar Key and Rosewood both had cedars in abundance, hence the names. When millionaire Henry Plant couldn't buy the railway lines at Cedar Key, he moved his base of operations to Tampa and essentially shut down Cedar Key; the 1896 hurricane finished the job.

Today Cedar Key clam farms raise 175 million clams every year, and such farms allow five hundred men and women to make their living off the water. The town's one market doesn't sell clam chowder, which I find odd, but they have a reputable craft beer selection. We have our pick of clam farms where clammers will sell us one hundred clams for next to nothing. For us, that's a two-day supply, but we may not be representative in our shellfish gluttony.

Other than eating clams and staring into the blue of the Gulf of Mexico, Cedar Key also offers tourists kayaking through the mangroves, bird-watching, and airboat rides. The Suwannee River empties just north of the town, a fitting end to our sojourn from one watery paradise to another: a shallow estuary pulses with life and soothes all at once.

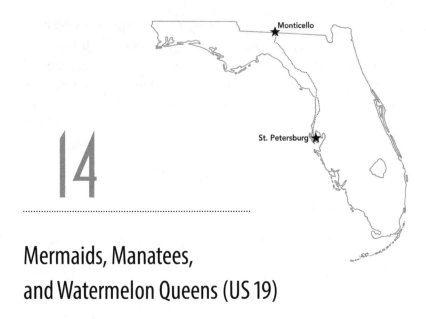

14

Mermaids, Manatees, and Watermelon Queens (US 19)

When I was a kid, cars had bumper stickers on them that read, "Pray for me—I drive on US 19!" That aptly describes modern-day US 19 at its southern terminus, although at the time *Guide* writers toured this road, today's most horrific portions of US 19 did not yet exist. That road entered the state, then and now, as a delight, a series of rolling hills and red clay and leafy green trees, running through what the *Guide* described as "many old towns in which little of importance has happened since the 1860s."

Although the *Guide* remarks on the area's steadfast qualities with apparent disregard, today travelers, rare as they may be—the first town at the top of the road, Monticello, has only three bed-and-breakfasts and three hotels—can find one of Florida's few Deep South pockets here. This town, at the intersection of US 90, emits a distinctly southern vibe, with antebellum homes, an 1890s opera house, and a crumbly, senescent cemetery. The pre–Civil War construction, so rarely seen in Florida, exists solely because of poverty—when residents couldn't afford to build new homes during the Great Depression, they instead renovated the older ones, many of which still peek through the stately live oaks lining the streets. Homes have roomy porches, maid's quarters, and gingerbread trim.

I linger in Roseland Cemetery, trying to make out the inscriptions on the moldering tombs. The cemetery dates to 1827, and I find out later that I could have taken a ghost tour through the cemetery. I enjoyed wandering alone among the headstones, and if I want a party instead of solitude, I will return in June, when Monticello crowns a Watermelon Queen. In the late 1800s, Monticello and surrounding Jefferson County provided the country with the bulk of its watermelon seeds. The annual festival honors this juicy slice of the town's history and includes bed races, plenty of food, and watermelon carving.

Farther down the road at Capps, the road joins with US 27 and US 19 and runs south through Lamont.

Here's the thing about the *Guide*'s description of Lamont: these writers relied heavily on local lore rather than other sources for telling a town's history. Clearly, this left room for a wide margin of error. The *Guide* tells us that in 1890 the villagers changed its original name, Lick Skillet, to Lamont because "Cornelius Lamont, vice-president of the United States, had been a recent visitor." While that sounds great, there is one slight problem: the United States has never had a vice president by that name. In 1890, President Harrison's second-in-command was Levi Morton. While in office the first time, President Grover Cleveland employed a private secretary named Daniel S. Lamont who served as the secretary of war during Cleveland's second term—but never as vice president. In their book *Florida Place Names*, Joan Perry Morris and Allen Morris explain that Lick Skillet changed its name to Lamont to honor not a mythical vice president but the real Lamont.

The road passes through a town called Eridu, so named, the *Guide* reports, for the mythological river Eridanus, which Virgil—among others—counted as one of the rivers of Hades. Appropriately, Eridu is less than a thirty-minute drive from quite possibly Florida's most toxic river. As you head south into Perry, a town described as "industrial" even when *Guide* writers toured it, roll down your windows, take a deep breath, and smell the sweet smell of contamination that is the Fenholloway River.

The river looks untouched and serene, and it is—largely because the locals know better than to go anywhere near it. To give you a better idea of exactly how contaminated the state allowed the river to become, Florida uses a five-level system to classify the surface-water quality of every waterway. Class 1 waterways provide drinking water. Anything below a Class 3 is unsuitable for swimming. In the 1940s, the state designated the Fenholloway a Class 5 river, the only one in Florida. "Class 5" is another way of saying "open sewer," and the state allowed for disposal of whatever anyone wanted—treated wastewater, cellulose, biomedical waste, you name it—into the river. This designation lured Procter and Gamble to the area, where it commenced turning the area's trees into cellulose and dumping upward of 45 million gallons of waste per day into the river. Buckeye bought the plant in 1993 and pats itself on the back for helping "save" the river by bypassing it entirely, piping mostly treated wastewater directly to the Gulf of Mexico. It did this grudgingly, blaming the trees for the contamination.

Yep, that's right: the paper mills blamed the trees for the contamination and the smell. According to fenholloway.com, the website where Buckeye explains how it's doing good things for the river, the treated waste it discharged into the river stopped grasses from growing because of lignin from the trees. While technically true, it also shifts the onus of the river's smell and elevated levels of nitrogen and phosphorous from the people cutting down the trees to the trees themselves. Nevertheless, the plant—good corporate citizens that they are, especially when so ordered by various governmental agencies—made some changes to help offset the devastation it wrought upon the river. The smell, however, remains. Some call it swamp gas, but locals and environmentalists know better. It is the smell of death. Today it is a Class 3, with limitations. Hampton Springs, a few miles from the Fenholloway, was once thought to cure rheumatism "and kindred ills," and, according to the *Guide*, people would pay to visit a health resort surrounding the springs. Today, as perhaps a great unintentional metaphor for the river water shared by the spring, the hotel has fallen to ruin; all that remains of the health resort crumbles at 30.08148882 N and -83.66284597 W—just off Hampton Spring Road, sandwiched along Spring Creek between US 98 where it splits from US 19 and the

Fenholloway River. With hope, belief, and a not insignificant amount of government intervention, the Fenholloway stands a chance. Until then, kayak the river, but I'd suggest not taking a dip.

While area residents may complain that they know better than to drink their own well water because of Buckeye-related contamination, it doesn't stop them from going to work every morning. Buckeye remains the largest employer in the area, providing almost a third of the Perry households with work. Remember, this is not a burgeoning metropolis. This is Taylor County, and while it has many fine things, employment opportunity is not one of them. Locals may not like Buckeye, but they like starvation less. It's a pragmatic type of love.

....

Off the river, this area has one thing on offer you won't find in too many other places: Florida's finest jellies and jams. I restock my supply of mayhaw jelly, Tupelo honey, and whatever vegetables the unfailingly cheerful roadside salesmen have on offer. Mayhaw berries grow in wet, low-lying areas with sediment-rich, acidic soil. They look like cranberries but taste nothing like them. They taste like . . . well, they taste like mayhaws: somehow sweet and tart and gentle and sharp. You must taste the mayhaw to appreciate it. The trees grow in swampy north Florida, in the panhandle and along the east side of the state as far south as Marion and Volusia (think Ocala and Daytona Beach) Counties, but I find the tastiest jelly along this stretch of US 19.

And what a lovely stretch of road it is, yawning greatly before us as we trundle toward the Tampa Bay area: trees in multitudes of green, the odd store or gas station, and not much else. I wouldn't want to break down here, but I love the drive along the wooded highway. If one gauged the wealth of the residents by the number of shopping malls, they would call this poor man's country. If one looked instead at the wealth of birds, pines, and foliage, one might find the people here are rich indeed.

Our tour crosses the Suwannee River at Fanning Springs, close to the river's communion with the Gulf of Mexico at Cedar Key. One does not come to this area of the state for beaches, though; one comes for the springs. Every hole and dip in Florida's limestone floor glitters with teal and sapphire sparks of water, and Fanning Springs burns its radiance as brightly as any.

Florida springs gurgle and prattle along their way, their blues and greens coalescing to the moonless midnight as they traipse through pine flatwoods, swamps, and hardwood hammocks. At the spring-heads, though, the halcyon water shimmers with teal sunshine, an aqueous rainbow revealing infinite depths. Fanning Springs State Park fronts the route, offering primitive camping for hikers, bikers, and paddlers. Car travelers can opt for a modern cabin (no pets permitted) or, as we did, head to nearby Manatee Springs State Park for RV camping or tent camping. Either spring offers a glimpse into Florida's depths, and both feed the Suwannee. I do not trust my ability to out-swim a gator quite enough to relax in Florida's blackwater rivers, but I snorkel, swim, and dive the springs with abandon. Manatees and Fanning Springs alike allow and encourage these things, their crystalline waters the perfect invitation.

Manatee Springs State Park is William Bartram territory. He came here two springtimes before the American Revolution.

For those not familiar with Early Florida literature, Bartram offers a breath of fresh air compared to the flat-out lies told to the royalty who financed most Florida expeditions. "Early Florida Literature" is a creative euphemism for "reports to my boss that justify my large government travel budget." The Ernest Hemingways of the day did not apply for these posts; these men were bureaucrats with an often-fatal sense of adventure. I envision them, perhaps incorrectly, as pre-cubicle desk jockeys with dreams of seeing the world. Traveling the world on the queen's dime for the small price of having to send home expense reports likely sounded awfully sweet compared to a lifetime spent grooming the king's horses or filing reports. Yes, the threat of death loomed large, but Europe was crowded and no picnic itself. An explorer could live in relative peace in La Florida, far from the Inquisition, Ottoman invasions, and plagues one might face in Europe.

Consider the narrative of Jacques Le Moyne, a mid-sixteenth-century explorer, cartographer, and artist who traveled Florida with a group of fellow Frenchmen. The pictures contained in this government report include water dragons (I'd guess alligators) with snakelike heads and manlike arms. The account also includes a sketch of the Indians stabbing an explorer through the penis and sawing off his other extremities with Stryker-like precision.

Fun stuff, good times, but not exactly accurate. And that's just an overview of how Europeans described the natives. Couple that with how a few Europeans can beat down limitless indigenous Americans (read Pizzaro's account of what he did in Peru) and you now know the party line for basically every exploratory account of the New World: plenty of vicious creatures, warring heathen masses, ultimate victory in the name of state-run religion.

Enter William Bartram. The guy liked plants, which don't read well as vicious, man-eating beasts. It also helped that he explored Florida well after the Spaniards and the British wove themselves along the eastern coastline of America; it's harder to lie when less than an ocean separates you and your boss. They could pop in any old time and see that those dragons were, indeed, tarpon.

I like Bartram. He wrote about what he saw up and down Florida, Georgia, and the Carolinas in what I consider more realistic terms. He loved his birds and plants, so documenting them rather than slaying dragons and natives consumed much of his time.

As I gaze into a spring so blue and encircled with knobby-kneed cypress that I never want to leave the waterside, I notice a plaque honoring William Bartram as the European finder of this spring in the late 1700s. The plaque bears a transcription of his notes about the springs but says nothing of how he happened across the cerulean oasis. I amuse myself supposing he arrived via the Suwannee River, although I later learn he followed the same route *Guide* writers and, later, I will, the route from Fernandina to Manatee Springs. In his day, it was a native path turned trading trail, which later became a railroad line and then a series of roads.

The method of travel and travelers have changed, but the destination has not: a spring shattered by sunlight into a deluge of blue and green. Cypress trees ring it on three sides; on the fourth, it flows out to the Suwannee River, where its shimmering translucent blues turn quickly to inky black. A wooded boardwalk leads over cypress knees out to the floating dock; the spring and the creek that leads 100 million gallons of water per day to the Suwannee and, shortly, the Gulf, are narrow and shallow. The Suwannee is vast and dark. The clear water will hide under the black blanket of the Suwannee for twenty-five twisting and turning curves, pushed ever-forward by the water thrashing from the spring behind it, until it emerges again, unsullied by the deep secrets of the Suwannee as it shows its clear, cool face to the emerald waters of the Gulf of Mexico.

I learned to scuba dive because I wanted to get closer to the rainbow of life on the reefs. My first for-real dive, though, took place in a murky, frigid sinkhole south of these springs: Hudson Hole. I had no intention then to dive freshwater, and that morning at the sinkhole cemented that decision. It was January. It was 50 degrees. It was not fun. Our dive instructors, clad in snuggly warm dry suits, laughed at us as they dumped hot water down the backs of our wet suits. Their breath made steam clouds as they smirked and suggested we pee as soon as we jumped in the water. We entered the sinkhole and snorkeled a circle around the lake, then dropped to a platform twenty feet beneath the dismal, dusky surface. We ran through drills—clearing our mask and recovering and purging our regulators—but not once did I think about drowning. No, I was too busy worrying about hypothermia and alligators. At least, I thought to myself at one point, if a gator bites me, I'll be too numb from the cold to feel it.

Hudson Hole did nothing to entice me out of the salt water and into the fresh. However, Florida's first-magnitude springs—springs that push more than 100 million gallons per day out from the state's spongy limestone center—share few similarities with that dank, creepy place best used to train rescue divers. Manatee Springs is a glorious, serene, warm, and—this is crucial—first-magnitude spring. Fanning Springs pumps out "only" 65 million gallons of inner-earth water daily, which ranks it a second-magnitude spring. Those are just words, though, and don't truly convey the force of the water pouring out of the earth. It gushes over limestone and out into the sun, tumbling over itself in its rush for the surface. You can't, in all practicality, dive to the source—the pulse of the water will push you back to the outer edge of the planet. You can, however, often find tiny fissures where infinitesimal jets of water stream upward, a small but unique delight in a wild aquarium.

Back on dry land, we head south.

At Otter Creek, the route passes State Road 24, the one way in and out of Cedar Key. Bronson, just east of this junction, had 694 residents when *Guide* writers passed through. Today, the town has grown to just over 1,100, a small portion of the Levy County population, although Bronson is the county seat. Its honor as such stems, according to the *Guide*, from the railroad running through the town. David Levy Yulee, Florida's first senator and the first Jewish senator in the nation, built the Florida Railroad Company, which ran through Bronson and effectively shifted the population east from Levyville, a now-extinct town 7 miles west of Bronson.

As the road approaches Yankeetown (south of the more populous Chiefland), it turns toward the coast and traces its contours closely for the remaining 137 miles. In 1961, Elvis came to Yankeetown to make *Follow That Dream*, a movie about a family that settled in Florida when their car ran out of gas on a deserted stretch of road. The family starts what becomes a thriving fishing business, outsmarts the mob, and befuddles bureaucrats, emerging triumphant at the film's end. The short story on which it was based, "Pioneer Go Home!," sets the stage in New Jersey; filmmakers thought the story made more sense in Florida. In tribute to the film—and Elvis—the town renamed State Road 40 "Follow That Dream Parkway." The sign still hangs between the traffic lights as the tour crosses the "Parkway."

From here south, the route grows steadily more populated, although the *Guide* glosses over much of the route between Williston and Weeki Wachee. The *Guide* does tell us that the route unites with another tour, US 41, along this section, which explains the description as a road that "climbs and dips over a series of round hills."

We opt for the new section of US 19, the one that hugs the coast and passes through Crystal River. Here, scallops and manatees beckon. Tours offer scallop trips for the uninitiated, but during scallop season (July through September, although the actual dates vary) anyone who wishes may snorkel for scallops. Scallops live in the green grass, have thirty-two glittering blue eyes, and slam their shells shut (*escalop* means "shell" in French) to swoosh out of harm's way. Bay scallops, once bountiful in the Gulf coastal waters, have declined in number. Speculation puts the blame on water quality, as scallops (like clams and oysters) filter their food from the water. Shellfish populations cannot thrive in contaminated water.

Instead of scallops, we're hunting manatees. Well, not hunting, exactly, but looking for them awfully hard. In Citrus County, boat captains can take passengers out to swim with and pet the marine mammals if they're doing it for educational purposes. Our boat captain does give us manatee facts and talks about preserving the species, but we're not fooling anyone: we all boarded this boat with plans to pet a giant gray water beast. It's a gorgeous summer day, and I'm delighted to be out on the water, but I didn't think this through. You see, all the photos advertising the tour showed manatee frolicking with humans in an opaline springhead. These gentle, awkward creatures do lumber toward the spring when the water temperature outside the spring dips below 70 degrees, but that is not the case on a hot summer day.

Now is a good time to mention the three types of rivers flowing through Florida: alluvial, blackwater, and spring-fed. Alluvial rivers, often carved out by years of floods, carry loads of sediment along with them. Their levels and flow are usually tied to rainfall. Blackwater rivers rise out of swamps and generally have a dark tea color derived from tannic acid, made from the decaying plant matter in the water. Clear springs gush out into spring-fed rivers. One such river, the Crystal River, starts at a springhead, but do not assume that means the length of the river shares that transparency. The river grows deeper in color the farther we motor from the springs. We do this, the boat captain explains, because the tiny-headed sea cows only hang out in springs in the winter.

I refrain from smacking my palm against my forehead. Of *course* these creatures won't linger in the spring today. Of course they will hang out in the "I-can't-see-my-hand-or-that-alligator-in-front-of-my-face" portion of the river. I enjoy paddling Florida's rivers, but few exist in which I will blindly jump, manatee or no. I remember my father's warning that every body of freshwater in Florida has gators in it and, trying to sound casual, ask the captain if he sees many gators.

The boat captain assures me I need not worry about gators or snakes. This strategy would have worked better had I considered the possibility of snakes *before* he mentioned them. I do not know if I believe him, but I accept my swim noodle (we may not use our arms to swim lest we hit a manatee or, I imagine, anger a gator), slip my mask and snorkel over my face, and slide into the water. The manatees wait a few yards away, the guide tells us, but the murk makes it hard to see anything. Something wraps around my leg. I scream.

River grass. Not a snake. I feel like an idiot but take solace in knowing that when I put my head back under the water, it's too stained with tannic acid for the others to see me blush.

I see a great hulking shape before me. A manatee. My heart accelerates. I reach my hand out to pet it tentatively, and the beast doesn't seem to care. They have more bumps than I would have thought and are about as motivated as one would expect. She just floats in front of us—manatees are excellent floaters, what with all their fat—and even lets us pet her calf. I can only tell she's there by feel; I cannot see her other than to make out a massive darker blob against the ochre water. I have no visual clues as to what I'm touching. My only reassurance is that gators have almost no body fat, ergo, this must be a manatee.

After we've worn out our welcome, our boat captain takes us for a swim in Three Sisters, a nearby cluster of springs, vents, and boils. He ties his small launch to a river tree. Here, clear water reveals tiny springs, their exit from the earth announced with a rushing gurgle I can almost hear with my eyes. I step off the boat into water far colder than 72 degrees, the inexact standard for Florida rivers and springs. We walk toward the larger spring, through a group of wood posts set in water, designed to keep watercraft out of the springhead. The dizzying force of the water pushes against us as we move toward the springs, but as the narrow channel opens into a springhead, it gets easier. I can see the edge of the abyss; I peer over it, the clear blue sky reflected in chalky-white limestone. Deeper down the color turns from an easy blue-green to a persistent and ancient blue. Cypress and oak ring the spring but do not cover it, letting the sun and sky dance prisms of light across and through the spring water. We find no manatees here, but that's just fine by me. The springs, uncluttered with kayaks and canoes and too many people, offer a rarer and fuller experience.

If you don't feel brave enough to take your chances in a Florida river, you can watch these giant water cows through glass that lets you view them at their beady eye level—Homosassa Springs State Park, just down the road, also boasts an elevated boardwalk that lets you stroll past cougars, Florida panthers, deer, and the ever-present alligator, but the underwater observatory offers a less intrusive way to see manatees. It's worth it to see their fat Shmoo-like bodies in all their blubbery glory, if only just to marvel that Florida folk wisdom holds that sailors used to mistake these creatures for mermaids.

To see real mermaids, though, head down the road to Weeki Wachee Springs State Park, where another underwater show takes place seven days a week, several times a day. These mermaids, of course, are quite real. No, they don't really have tails instead of legs, and they don't get their oxygen with gills. Nevertheless, they do perform underwater shows, breathing through air hoses and performing in tails.

Mermaid shows started with Newt Perry. Perry trained World War II Navy SEALS—then called Frogmen—in underwater maneuvers; in 1946, he trained women to drink grape soda underwater. They learned to eat bananas, have picnics, and swim in unison—all while battling a 5-mile-per-hour current wrought by a spring that pushed 177 million gallons a day from the earth. Perry took a spring just off a two-lane dirt road and created a theme park that, long before Disney thought to do so, allowed people to pay money for the privilege of believing in a fantasy.

At Weeki Wachee, that fantasy is mermaids who perform beneath the big top of Weeki Wachee Spring, with audiences watching them from an underwater theater. Today the shows continue, as do reunion mermaid shows that feature retired mermaids, some of whom swam with Elvis. Underwater, these "legendary sirens" as the park calls them, have grace equal to—if not greater than—their younger counterparts. Young mermaids perform the bulk of the shows. These elder mermaids help out with mermaid camps for those who want to swim in a mermaid's tail for a day. The park also has kid camps for aspiring mermaids and mermen, but the reunion shows offer Floridaphiles a peek at the past.

The reunion shows started in 1997, when park management called former mermaids out of retirement to celebrate the Springs' fiftieth anniversary with a *Tails of Yesteryear* show. Lines wound along park paths and out into the parking lot to see twenty-six former mermaids—some in their seventies—twirl and pirouette under the sea. One show turned into three that day, and the former mermaids' show found its place alongside the current mermaid performances. Once monthly, former mermaids don their tails and slip into the 72-degree water. They look nothing like their younger counterparts. These mermaids bear the scars of forty years of life on land. They birthed babies, had careers, and adjusted to life with legs. Few have model-thin figures. It doesn't matter; once they slip into the spring, they are agile, graceful creatures again, eliciting applause from the crowd. The spring washes away weight and wrinkles, and they play out a script from forty years ago—dancing in the water, suspended in time.

"It's like water in your veins. We're still a part of the river, a part of the spring," Mermaid Vicki Smith, in her early seventies, says. A tiny, compact woman who lives on the river, she still giggles with glee when she talks about meeting Elvis as a mermaid.

The audience claps at the regular mermaid shows. At *Tails of Yesteryear*, people weep. Something—perhaps the joy on the Legendary Sirens' faces—speaks to the crowd.

Not everyone loves Weeki Wachee. Florida scholar Thom Hallock relishes Florida springs but calls this park "the dullest park I've ever visited," and he's a guy who finds early accounts of French explorers coming to Florida positively riveting. I see his point. You have to truly love the kitsch of Florida roadside attractions to get this place. Before you eschew it, though, try to imagine it in its heyday. Picture yourself in the 1960s, driving a Chevy big enough to hold a softball team, down US 19. Suddenly, bathing-clad ladies—mermaids!—beckon you into the park. You're from Michigan, where there's three feet of snow on the ground, and even when there isn't, this sort of thing simply does not happen. You have no clue what to expect, but as you take your seat in the underwater theater and the blue curtain rises, lithe, nubile women twirl and pirouette before you. Weeki Wachee was unparalleled; these women had no competition. The wild bird show, the parrot show (because no Florida roadside attraction was complete without a cockatoo on roller skates), and the chance to meet a real live mermaid enchanted generations of visitors.

Roller coasters, castles, and water parks have all faded the glory of roadside attractions like Weeki Wachee, and folks used to Pixar animation and Disney special effects may look down their nose at those of us who marvel at ladies drinking soda pop underwater. Weeki Wachee, taken over by the state in 2008, pays homage not only to generations of mermaids but also to the dying breed of Florida's roadside attraction. The park may be paler than the bright world of modern tourist attractions, but it has a patina all its own. Of course, even this happened well after *Guide* writers chronicled Florida. If you had uttered the words "roadside attraction" in 1930s Florida, people might have thought you meant the cattle. Florida's earliest tourist attractions consisted of gator wrestling, "health resorts" such as the one at Hampton Springs, a glass-bottom boat, and a couple of large-scale gardens.

Of course, those seeking natural attractions had plenty of chances along the road. The springs feed the Weeki Wachee River, and today, just as in the 1930s, no invented roadside attraction can compete. The river runs clear with a swift current—at 5 miles per hour, it takes just over two hours to reach the Gulf of Mexico. The park service operates a kayak and canoe livery, and they will pick you up at Rogers Park 6 miles down the road.

Today, as I often do, I paddle upriver from Rogers Park, then lazily drift back. The sojourn past the houses nearest Rogers Park takes minimal effort and gives me plenty to ponder. One side of the river redolent with palms and marsh life, on the other, cartoonish sea life murals adorn sea walls, residents pay homage to Jimmy Buffett with Middle American Tiki-bar decor, and every variation of rope and tire swings dangle from spidery oak trees standing guard over the Weeki Wachee. Farther upriver the homes thin out and the water gets clearer.

The odd rope tied to a branch lets people climb trees, dangle over the river, and plunge, feetfirst, into the crystal-clear water.

As the river gets closer to the springhead, homes disappear into copse after copse of trees. The river twines a thin cordon of blue around a marsh forest. At a stand of trees with a wood platform, I tie my kayak painter to a slender tree trunk and stretch my legs while I eat a sandwich. The water is clear, and I see no gators, so I let Calypso stretch her legs, too. When we set off again, we're headed back, carried by the current. Calypso curls up on a towel drying on the kayak's bow. We float by a school of mullet, struggling their way upstream. Like a shot Calypso heaves herself in the water, but we're moving too fast for her to catch the mullet. She swims instead to where I sit and puts a paw on the side of the boat. I pull her in the cockpit, use the towel to squeeze river water from her black fur, and have a moment of thanks for clear water and no gators.

South on US 19 a giant dinosaur waits. I first found it as a kid, when my dad had a construction job at nearby Timber Pines. He worked for Scarborough Construction, the company that installed most of the water and sewer lines in central west Florida. The parent company, Weyerhauser, sent me through college on a scholarship, and I try not to focus too much on the fact that the company that actively participated in resurfacing much of Florida's landscape paid for the education that made me to fall in love with what they destroyed.

Before that education, though, I was going into sixth grade, and Scarborough paid for the guys on the construction crew to stay the week in the Weeki Wachee Holiday Inn, so my mom and I spent a few days hanging out on the then-deserted stretch of US 19. We visited the brand-new Kmart, went to the pool, and visited the mermaids. She also took me into a taxidermist's shop—I guess you'd call it a shop—and I stood transfixed by all the animals rooted forever in death.

My favorite thing (after the mermaids, of course) was the great green plaster dinosaur. The hulking giant used to signal a Sinclair gas station, but those, too, died out. Today an auto service station, Harold's, changes water pumps and rotates tires beneath the belly of the beast. It's not a traditional tourist attraction, but that doesn't mean people don't stop and take pictures. I have a painting of Dino in my study, and if the brute ever topples, to storm or sprawl, US 19's meta-morphosis from sleepy two-lane road to clogged arterial highway will be sadly complete.

Well hidden from the highway and south of the dinosaurs you can find the stilt houses. If you don't live near New Port Richey, you likely don't know they exist; I only knew about them because I wanted to get over my fear of flying. In an attempt to not get physically ill at the idea of boarding a plane, I took flying lessons. Among the best things I saw from the right, then the left, seat of a small plane, was a crop of nine homes. I knew, of course, of Stiltsville in Biscayne Bay, but I didn't realize that stilt homes stood so close to my own home, just south of Green Key.

Just past Green Key's shimmering sands, this cluster of stilt houses rises from Pasco County's clear waters. These fish camps, perched high above the Gulf of Mexico on wooden legs, stand in silent tribute to Florida's fishing past. The *Guide* makes no mention of these homes, although they were there. Instead, *Guide* writers talk of stone cot-tages built on high riverbanks—the Pithlachascotee River continues into the Gulf between the fish shacks—and shaded by oak trees. They write only in passing of the Gulf, failing to note that here the water is calm and shallow, and clear enough that, the one time I paddled out to nearby Durney Key, I could see redfish and crabs darting beneath my paddleboard.

Tucked amid the watery stilt city, Durney Key attracts paddleboard-ers, kitesurfers, kayakers, and boaters. Paddleboarding into the Gulf, the world beneath your feet comes alive. Cownose rays—tiny, timid stingrays no bigger than a dinner plate—flutter over sea grass. Mul-let twist and toss themselves into the air. Redfish zig, then zag, just beneath the surface of this oversized aquarium.

....

In stark contrast to the spacious green country hills surrounding Mon-ticello at the northern reach of 19, the most crowded place in the state waits at the end of the tour. Pinellas County, the most densely popu-lated but second-smallest of Florida's sixty-seven counties (Union County has 40 square miles fewer than Pinellas County's 280) greets you with sponge docks and Greek food. After divers picked over the Key West sponge fields, they headed north to Tarpon Springs. Eventually, synthetic sponges replaced natural sponges, but today locals still refer to Tarpon's downtown as "the sponge docks." The city boasts Greek food, Greek-oriented gift shops (think lots of olive oil-based products), and an annual Epiphany celebration. The Greek community celebrates the Epiphany, or Cross Day, with a blessing of the fleet. As part of the Epiphany, a Christian holiday celebrating the baptism of their Christ in the Jordan River, a processional (complete with doves) to the water ends with a priest from the local Greek Orthodox church throwing a cross in the water. Young men dive for the cross; the one who retrieves it receives a blessing from the priest and, legend holds, divine beneficence for the coming year.

Today, US 19 runs the eastern length of the county, but the old route followed Alternate 19 and what we now call the Pinellas Trail, which parallel and twist over each other on the western edge before ending in Seminole. The Pinellas Trail, a former railway line now converted to paved trail, travels the length of the county with spurs into local communities. The trail has rest stops, water fountains, and a host of bike shops and restaurants along its 33-mile trek through the county. Art styled to recall the railroad's glory hails each town as you pass through it along the trail. Between Wall Springs Park—a historic spring once marketed as a health spa—and St. Petersburg, the route devolves into a glut of supermarkets, gas stations, and car dealerships. In St. Petersburg, a detour off the road over to Fourth Street takes you to Sunken Gardens, where you can descend into the pit of a sinkhole covered in flowers and greenery. At one time, the flowered sinkhole boasted a plastic Jesus—no one there can tell me why when I ask—but it's long gone.

The writers take us only far enough south to neighboring Shell Key, a five-minute boat ride from the mainland. This bird sanctuary, home to nesting terns, skimmers, and oystercatchers, also offers shell-seekers sand dollars, sea urchins, and dolphin sightings. Even here, the *Guide* simply tells readers, "The shores of the key are favorite hunting grounds of shell collectors." They make no mention of Fort De Soto, a county park and a former fort at the mouth of Tampa Bay. The fort and park are on five islands interconnected by a chain of bridges and lagoons; the 1,100-plus acres of the park are prime beachfront real estate, fronting Tampa Bay and the Gulf of Mexico. The park offers a 13-mile bike trail, fishing piers, camping, beaches, paddling, a boat ramp, hiking paths, and a beachfront dog park. This park, expanses of sand and pines and pockets of nature, offers an oasis from the homogenized shopping experiences dotting the tour. It is here that you realize you have reached, as one local hotel bills itself, island's end.

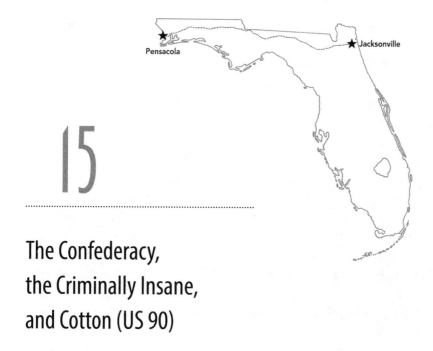

Pensacola

Jacksonville

15

The Confederacy,
the Criminally Insane,
and Cotton (US 90)

Fun fact: Florida still has a handful of tobacco farms. Turns out the panhandle's red clay grows better tobacco and cotton than grapefruit and sugarcane. Of all the roads we traveled, US 90 seems the least touched over the past eight decades. The *Guide* called the road "Florida's longest and most heavily traveled east and west highway." I doubt that's still true, but the rest rings true: "It traverses pine lands, where lumbering and the production of naval stores are important industries, penetrates the State's principal cotton and tobacco areas, and passes through many plantation towns of ante-bellum days, and a few large cities. The people, architecture, and economic conditions of this region, first in the State to be settled and the first to have a railroad, remain largely untouched by the seasonal tourist influence, standing in sharp contrast to the Florida pictured in resort literature" (*A Guide to the Southernmost State*).

"Naval stores" refers to anything made with pine sap, including turpentine. Workers would scar the trunk of slash pines to get the sap, a practice that died out sometime during the 1950s. As for the rest of the description, I could stop right there and leave you with a not wholly inaccurate picture of US 90 as it runs today, but then you would miss so many things.

For one, you'd miss the scarcity of palms. North Florida is all about pine trees and flowering trees and hills, wholly unlike the rest of the state's sandy beaches, pine scrub, and swamp.

Jacksonville still has maritime industry, and its downtown charms me more than I expect. Trees pop up in odd places, interspersed with museums and theater and cultural experiences not as common in many of the city's outlying areas. As we drive west out of the city, though, the charm is replaced by industry. Rail yards follow the road, and I remember that Jacksonville remains a shipping center, as it was in the 1930s.

Here the architecture looks older and the people appear poorer, with buildings begging for fresh paint. While the *Guide* writers said both black and white folk used to frequent this area of town, midcentury white flight to the suburbs seems to have changed the balance. The faces we pass are all black; these are people who still feel the weight of living so close to the Deep South. In this predominantly African-American district, Jacksonville had, until 2013, a high school named after a KKK grand wizard and confederate general, Nathan Bedford Forrest.

Moving westward, the industrial lots gradually grow more and more interspersed with tall stands of pine trees, both slash and longleaf. By the time we cross 301 into Baldwin, we are ensconced in pine forest. Baldwin, the *Guide* reminds me, used to ship pine logs to Jacksonville. I'm guessing the majority of the pines we see between here and Macclenny are younger pines planted to replace those felled since the 1930s.

Macclenny, the Baker County seat, has its share of feed stores, reminding us that agriculture, not tourism, is big business here. Although it could be, I think as we coast through the small town, if it didn't have to compete with beaches. The land here is filled with trees, not housing developments; the buildings, old and stately. The largest ones I see are an Ace Hardware easily the size of a Home Depot superstore and the county courthouse, a red-brick affair unlike the peninsula's more casual, modernized courthouses of the late twentieth century. It looks like a sleepy, welcoming town, the sort of place that epitomizes southern charm.

The *Guide* describes a different Macclenny altogether, one with inbred clans of folk who did not trust outsiders but cut loose when no one was watching. I love this sentence perhaps more than the aforementioned glut of "rogue cattle" warnings: "Their social affairs are strenuous, not to say violent." The text continues to describe men sneaking away from the dance hall to "refresh themselves" with alcohol and tells us, unsurprisingly, "there is often as much fighting as dancing." On occasion, a knife flashed or a gun appeared. People stepped outside to settle things. The police did not get a phone call.

Never judge a town by its courthouse.

Oaks and pines part occasionally to reveal houses with large yards. Like most of north Florida, it feels less like Florida and more like Georgia. We're in the Okeefenokee Swamp, and the area is rife with cypress. We stop next at Olustee Battlefield State Park.

Florida has less Civil War history as compared to its southern neighbors to the north, although some historians suggest that had Key West not remained in Union hands, the South would have won the war. In Florida's northern reaches, where most residents lived during the Civil War, Tallahassee never fell to the Union. Soldiers fought relatively few battles on Florida soil. I always wondered if that was because no one saw enough value in Florida, save Key West's port, the saltworks, and cattle, to brave its swampy frontier. Remember, this was well before doctors worked out that quinine cured yellow fever, and in the 1800s the Sunshine State was actually more of the Swamp State, filled with bogs and hogs and mosquitoes. Dysentery and gunshots were awful enough without throwing alligators and yellow fever in the mix.

Florida's biggest Civil War battle took place in Olustee. For some southerners, this battle is a source of pride. Confederate soldiers beat the Union troops back to Jacksonville, where they stayed for quite a time. For northerners, the source of pride came from the African-American Fifty-Fourth Massachusetts Volunteer Infantry Regiment, the first all-black unit in the North.

In 1912, veterans gathered at the site to dedicate a monument. There are, however, not one but two monuments there today, which typifies the state's conflicted history. One monument refers to it as the "Battle of Olustee," and the other, a smaller one built by the Daughters of the Confederacy, calls it a memorial for the "Battle of Ocean Pond."

....

Both east and west of Olustee there are work camps, not the last we see along this stretch of road. Despite a disproportionate number of prisons, the drive here is a handsome haven of pine and oak clasped together, alone in the copper and jade landscape. A sense of peace prevails along the road, with no stoplights and no urgency within the confines of Osceola National Forest. That overwhelming feeling of peace follows us through a chain of small north Florida towns, and the lack of people, shops, and signs of development along this road washes the following towns of Watertown and Lake City in tones of quaint and charm.

West of here, through Live Oak and on to Tallahassee, remains delightfully the same with one notable exception: the flatwoods start to gradually give way to hills as the state's elevation rises. I know that beneath the roadway, the soil is shifting to a red clay.

We pass through Live Oak, easily the most populated town thus far, and head over the Suwannee River. The water level is disturbingly low. A glance at the local paper reveals something strange, at least to this downstate Floridian: northern Floridians consider hurricanes *good* things. The rains keep down the risk of fire, recharge the floodplains, and keep the water levels elevated. With no major hurricanes near north Florida recently, the rivers and forests are suffering. It's odd to realize that the force of nature that devastates the rest of the state on a regular basis is welcomed here.

Of course, a look around can explain that easily enough. There's no fear of storm surge here, no levees to swell and burst. These people will get the rains after the storm weakens over land, not as the storms first make landfall. They seem not to fear hurricanes like the coastal towns do; they have chosen, it would seem, more wisely than their southern neighbors. No beaches, that's true, but no ridiculous insurance premiums and no family heirlooms lost to sand, salt, water, and wind.

Between here and Monticello, the road leans out between small towns, vast expanses of pine and oak broken up by Lee, Madison, and Greenville. Many of these small towns appear to be struggling, and Dollar General stores dot the landscape. I wonder how Dollar General headquarters determines where to build a store. These stores unfailingly herald a town with economic issues, representing flagging economies and the ultimate devastation of every great, yet unappreciated, small town in Florida. Every time we see one, we remark, "Oh, look. A Dollar General. We must be in a struggling small town."

It would be funny if it didn't bear out over and over again. These yellow-and-black signs are everywhere we travel, save the affluent areas and some of the middle-class ones. I see fewer surf shops on these tours than I do these franchises, and along US 90 I see far, far fewer mom-and-pop general stores (one, to be exact).

Between Monticello and Tallahassee, the route is lined with crape myrtles, pink and white explosions of color along the roadway. The *Guide* mentions Mahan's Nursery in conjunction with Monticello but neglects to mention that Mr. Fred Mahan donated those crape myrtles to the state in the 1932. The nursery grew pecans and ornamental shrubs. Mahan gave the plants to Jefferson County for highway, church, and cemetery beautification projects. The county's unemployment relief commission paid forty-five men an average of thirty-nine dollars a month to plant these trees as well as the palms, ligustrum, and forty thousand other plants and trees lining the route into Tallahassee. In 1953, this stretch of road officially became the Fred Mahan Drive.

The road dips slightly south to cut through Tallahassee, the state capital so chosen for its equidistance between Pensacola and Jacksonville. West of the capital, it passes through Quincy, then Gretna. Gretna is one of the prettiest rundown towns I've seen, even if the best-kept homes do have bars on the windows.

The route brushes up against Georgia in Chattahoochee, where I want to see one thing only: Florida State Hospital. It was the state's first mental asylum, not to be confused with the neighboring Capitol Building, and opened in 1876 as the Florida State Hospital for the Insane. A drive through the immaculate grounds reveals historic white buildings, among them the administration building with a place on the National Register of Historic Places; it dates to the Second Seminole War, when it housed officers. During *Guide* times, when segregation remained a way of life, both black and white patients stayed here. It's a small triumph; the *Guide* also speaks of a beauty parlor built to offset the "chronic rage" among the female patients. As late as the 1970s, the hospital faced a lawsuit for holding a patient against his will.

Today, inside these buildings, somewhere, the state's most severely mentally ill wait—some for recovery, some to recover enough that doctors will find them competent to get executed. Others, those declared "not guilty by reason of insanity," may wait forever—the state places no time limit on their confinement. The white buildings and rolling landscape combine comely with creepy. I step out of the van to take a photo and find myself wondering who is held behind the white stately building on the other side of my camera lens.

As we exit the ground onto US 90, I have to laugh. Directly across the street is a Dollar General store.

West of Marianna near Cottondale we see, appropriately, our first cotton crops along this route. Combined with the donkeys and mules starting to dot the roadside acreage, I feel us slipping into the Deep South.

At Chipley we turn off the route and head south to Falling Waters State Park, checking into our campsite as a heathery red dusk falls over the pines. The ranger tells us the waters aren't falling, and, in the most neighborly way you could imagine, warns us to look out for snakes. In the failing light we walk through the woods down a boardwalk to where the waterfall would be in wetter times. It's a sheer wall of no water this evening, but in the fading light the cool abyss below, the cliff in front of us, and the pines above make a lovely end to the day all the same. Walking out of the woods, I hear something above. I look up and follow the slow, decisive, wings of a horned owl, and then a second.

At the edge of the woods I look back through the longleaf pines and see the outline of an owl, perhaps watching us or waiting for a moonlit feast.

When we do get to the campsite, I hop out as Barry backs our van into place, mindful of but not alarmed by the ranger's warning of snakes. When a green tree frog jumps on me, I reflexively yelp, then laugh at myself. The frog, for her part, seems unamused.

After an evening of screeching owls and bellowing tree frogs, nearby Bonifay just makes me sad. The buildings on US 90 tell me the town likely had a thriving center at one point, but now it just looks used up, run-down, and deserted. The parking lot for the Jehovah's Witness Kingdom Hall has nary a space left.

A note about the county extension services here: they're bigger—much bigger—than those along the coast. While on the road, I imagined the big buildings had some sort of agricultural use, perhaps for teaching farmers plow techniques or tractor repair. In reality, I discover, the Extension in Bonifay offers a multitude of housing counseling services for people in trouble with their mortgages or in need of help finding low-income or public housing.

While the state hospital east of this area may have espoused a more progressive practice toward race relations, the *Guide* tells another tale of race about the area west of Bonifay, near Ponce de Leon Springs.

The *Guide* describes a group of people called "Dominickers," mixed-race people who lived in the backcountry. The writers tell the story this way: At the dawn of the Civil War, a white man lived in nearby Ponce de Leon with his wife and some slaves. He died, and his wife married one of the slaves and had five children. Her husband—her second, former-slave, black husband—took her deceased husband's name: Thomas. Some of the kids married white people, and some married black people. Their descendants remained in the backwoods, shunned by the school system. The *Guide* describes the culture as having men "of good physique" with women worn out too young. "All have large families, and the fairest daughter may have a brother distinctly Negroid in appearance. The name originated, it is said, when a white in suing for a divorce described his wife as 'black and white, like an old Dominicker chicken.' Dominicker children are not permitted to attend white schools, nor do they associate with Negroes. About 20 children attend a one-room school. As no rural bus is provided, the pupils often walk several miles to attend classes."

That's what made it into the official guide. Here's what the *Guide* writers wrote that didn't make the final edits:

These people are sensitive, treacherous and vindictive. They never start a disturbance but if any one bothers them—the whole family will do childish things to get revenge, to steal a hog or mutilate a crop is as good as a want. They are pathetically ignorant and an entire family will work hard for little compensation.

The women are low in stature, fat and shapeless, they wear loose-fitting clothes and no shoes. One woman 74 years of age has never owned a pair of shoes. When a person is the smaller type his is almost dwarf-like in size. There seems to be no in-between size. The people move from one hut to another, often living alone for awhile and then moving back into the family group. Men, women and children work in the fields. Some houses are scrupulously clean while others are filthy. They just live from day to day—certainly not an ambitious group. Each generation marries into the lower class of white people, their original group will soon be extinct. Common law marriage is practiced, as a matter of fact—most of them "take-up" with each other.

Local people claim that the Dominickers are 95 percent Negro. This statement is absurd. They are about three fourths white and one eighth Negro and one eighth Indian.

I could find no record, historic or anecdotal, of what happened to these people.

....

Not far from Ponce de Leon, DeFuniak Springs has a pleasing historic district. Of course, go a few blocks outside the district and it's a different story. The walking/shopping district borders the Springs neighborhood on one side and US 90 on the other, and the Walton County Courthouse has a Confederate monument. Welcome to the South.

Unlike the coast, everything—everything—curves and twists and bumps here. Despite the antebellum vibe, it feels northern, too—almost New England in nature. The red clay of the soil dominates the landscape, be it cotton or forest, evoking a marked Georgia feel as we push west.

At Crestview we see a copse of new homes. For whom, I wonder, are they building? There is nothing but clay and pine and cotton here. The area doesn't seem to have businesses or any indication whatsoever of a population. Nonetheless, census takers did document more than twenty thousand Crestview residents in 2010.

The Perdido River ends the Florida portion of US 90. The *Guide* tells us a ferry once crossed this river, connecting Pensacola stagecoaches with Mobile.

"It was acquired in 1849 by Henry Allen Nuñez. Rumors circulated that Nuñez had large sums of gold buried here, and he was seized in 1861 by raiders who demanded to know its whereabouts. When he refused, a rope was put around his neck; he was hauled up and only cut down when his terrified wife betrayed his secret."

Fun fact about Florida: Some historians suggest Henry Nuñez was Henri Nuñez, a pirate with Jean Lafitte. As with most Florida piracy tales in the *Guide*, I could not verify this one (pirates, it seems, kept lousy records). However, Pensacola has no shame in claiming its pirate heritage, from pirate festivals to the sports teams at Pensacola State College. And, in a way, pirates still live there, with the treasure they covet not cotton or tobacco, but tourist gold.

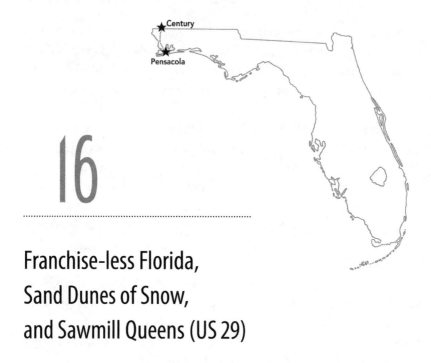

16

Franchise-less Florida, Sand Dunes of Snow, and Sawmill Queens (US 29)

Look at this road on a map, and it seems unremarkable in the way it hugs the Escambia River and follows the flow of the hills. The thing about it, though—and even in the 1930s, this was the route's claim to fame—it follows the route Andrew Jackson and several thousand soldiers used to leave Florida after a massive killing spree. Of course, the *Guide* doesn't *exactly* describe it as a killing spree. It doesn't tell us why Jackson and his men took this route at all, saying only the tour "follows the route of an old trail over which General Andrew Jackson marched from Pensacola to Fort Montgomery in 1818."

Here's what the *Guide* writers don't reveal to us: During the First Seminole War, in 1818, General Jackson, acting on behalf of the US government, took several thousand troops into Spanish-controlled Florida and killed an unrecorded number of Seminoles. In his spare time in the panhandle, General Jackson managed to slay a not-insignificant number of Spaniards, too. This led the Spanish to conclude that perhaps they didn't need Florida after all. Shortly after Jackson's government-sanctioned killing spree, Spain traded Florida to the United States in exchange for Texas and promises that the United States would assume about $5 million in debt from damages caused by Americans rebelling against Spain.

If Jackson were leading an army out of Florida via US 29 today, he'd have to deal with the congested mess of traffic at the southern end of this 45-mile route. That is, if he could tear himself away from the sandy grandeur of Gulf Islands National Seashore. At its southern end, US 29 connects with State Road 30, which leads you out to sand dunes so white they look like snowdrifts. These dunes go on for miles, and just beyond them the Gulf beckons with sapphire water that splits into bands of jade and emerald. That sort of experience does tend to create unrealistic expectations of whatever comes next.

Even during Friday rush hour, the congestion lasts only as long as the 10 miles it takes us to reach Old Chemstrand Road, just north of US 90. Pensacola boasts many fine attributes: It's steeped in southern history yet remains a bike ride from some of the finest sand in Florida; it boasts quirky yet skilled public art; and it also showcases a wide range of architectural styles. You may, however, fail to notice these things along the most traveled roads, as these stretches tend to lend their character to franchises and chain stores. The ubiquity of this sort of commerce falls away as we head north to the Alabama state line. The *Guide* describes Cottage Hill's "gently rolling terrain." That description still fits: gentle. North of US 90 the towns and the road have a Florida-country feel, and just south of Molino I catch a glimpse of something white and fuzzy: cotton. I honestly had no idea we grew cotton in Florida. In 2011, Florida cotton farmers planted 122,000 acres of cotton, making it the second-smallest cotton grower in the southeastern United States. (Virginia grew the least cotton, with 97,000 acres.) Passing by field after field of these plants, though, it didn't seem as though we were the second-smallest producer. Remember, too, that the inland panhandle differs from the flat peninsula; everywhere we looked we saw another small hill adorned with these diminutive white gossamer trees growing in between tall green forests.

Many towns across the country crown queens, and many of those crowns relate to the local industry, be it past or present. Florida queens come in all flavors: strawberry, tomato, swamp cabbage, watermelon, and—my personal favorite—a gecko queen, who rules alongside a mullet king.

Just south of the Alabama state line, in Century, the town crowns a sawmill queen in homage to its sawmill history. Built in 1900 (hence its name) by what the town website calls "Yankees," the Alger-Sullivan Lumber Company produced more southern pine board than other local mills, thanks in no small part to the mill manager, who replanted trees as the company cut them down and extended the life of the mill by an estimated fifty years. Another mill, the Bondurant mill, closed in 1987, although the family still runs an Ace Hardware. On a building emblazoned with the name Bondurant a sign proclaims "Century: The Heart of the South."

"The winding highway dips and rises, occasionally cutting through red clay hills; herds of cattle and goats graze in the clearings," the *Guide* promises just outside Century, and, in this corner of the state, time has stayed true to this description. Far from my mind as we bump over the hills is General Jackson, terrorizing Spaniards and Seminoles alike. Instead, I drink in the *Guide*'s description made real: hilly terrain as the road hugs the river.

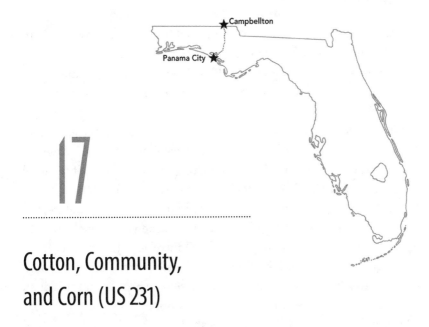

17

Cotton, Community, and Corn (US 231)

A Guide to the Southernmost State has only black-and-white photos, but its words splash Technicolor onto the parched pages. US 231, the *Guide* tells us, "traverses fertile rolling country" where "crops of cotton, peanuts, corn, and bright-leaf tobacco" grow. "Dense forests of shortleaf pine, hickory, sweet gum, and cypress grow in the rich red loam of this territory; the streams flowing through limestone beds are unusually clear and blue, except during spring freshets."

Campbellton, a town nestled against the Alabama state line, calls itself the "Gateway to Florida," and we soon find ourselves adrift in a white and gray sea of cotton and donkeys. Upon entering the state along this route, I start to truly appreciate how Florida lands as the brunt of so many backwoods jokes. Even in the 1930s, when the bulk of the tours centered around the panhandle, *Guide* writers described locals as "backwoodsmen," crackers who existed in one-room shacks with poorly made mattresses and no apparent protection from the elements. Pack animals and fields of cotton do little to drive this image from my mind, and I *know* I know better. These rolling red hills streaked with valleys of blue sky reflected in limestone pools pale in comparison to the *Guide*'s harsh description of the locals. Even today, tourism boards don't market this Florida, her cotton and mules perhaps implying too much of a hick farmer vibe for those seeking sun and sand.

We first sense the heartbeat of this route at, of all places, a Tom Thumb at the junction of US 90 in Cottondale. Admittedly, I don't associate the gas station lunch counter with getting the pulse of the local community, but this Tom Thumb is the northwest Florida equivalent of the town piazza. In perhaps one of the poorest areas of the state, the men and women waiting for biscuits and chicken at the deli counter of the gas station all laugh and smile. Only after a few moments do I realize they are not merely friends, but neighbors. The jovial mood simultaneously acknowledges and dismisses the notion that it is at all odd to buy fried chicken and collards at a store that also sells fuel, Fix-a-Flat, and condoms. Outside the gas station, discarded soda cans and plastic bags line the curbs, but inside everything is clean and convivial. It's not that customers don't notice the run-down buildings, but they share a sense of community *despite* those things. I get my biscuit and fried chicken—which are delightfully tasty, especially for a gas station at 9:00 a.m.—and we head south.

I hope this short stretch of road, from Alabama to Panama City, allows me to satiate today's single-minded, gastronomic purpose: field peas. Prior to our trip, food historian Andrew Huse assured me that field peas rule this area of north Florida when in season—which they are. In the midst of the still-present "rolling agricultural section" the *Guide* mentioned, I find a promising roadside vegetable stand. We stop along the four-lane, divided highway—an anomaly around these quiet, two-lane cotton- and pine-lined roads I've quickly grown accustomed to in the inland panhandle—and I get out, eager for peas.

A sun-weathered, stooped-over man with yellow teeth, white hair, and red clay under his ragged fingernails greets me. He and his wife work a makeshift tent at the edge of the parking lot, and they sell not only field peas but also ears of sweet corn and butter beans. He peels an ear of corn like a banana and punctures a golden kernel.

"We call it candy corn," he says. I am unsure how much of everything I want; I stopped only for field peas, but that corn looks glorious. The woman tries to help me, but he snarls at her, and she acts like she does not notice his rude, dismissive tone. I ask the woman how much; she turns and asks him.

When he names his price—$19.50 for five ears of corn and two quarts of beans—I am tempted to walk away. This would cost me four dollars at any grocery store. I see his wife almost roll her eyes behind him and, illogically, that makes the price OK.

....

"Remote from towns of any size, the people of this section retain many strange beliefs and superstitions handed down from generation to generation," *Guide* writers said of the area's hamlets. "Many 'cure-alls' and 'conjures' are still in use. To drag a rake through the house or to stand a broom on its grass end brings bad luck; to hear a screech owl at midnight is a certain sign of death—unless the hearer immediately turns his right shoe upside down; a stiff dose of asafetida is a popular remedy for malaria."

I remind myself that this is probably as close as these folks will ever get to making a living off tourists, many of whom likely still think of them as backwoodsmen who can't properly shelter themselves or believe in upending a shoe to prevent death.

Back in the van I downplay the money I just spent and bite into the raw corn. The sweet kernels explode in my mouth; juice runs down my chin, and a giggle burbles out of my mouth before I can stop it.

Suddenly, $19.50 doesn't seem so bad.

The road rolls on, a series of swollen helices, and only as we get closer to Panama City do we see signs of life. The most notable are billboards asking drivers if they have "oil spill stress" and giving them a number to call for relief. It's been a year since the oil didn't destroy Panama City, but clearly the town, in one way or another, is still feeling effects.

The tour ends when US 231 meets US 98 in Panama City, although here US 98 runs through the north end of the city, not the beach. A marl of traffic, billboards, and franchises—the backstage few tourists ever see—separate the city from the beach, and it dissolves into Bryson's Anywhere, USA. I glance at the road behind us, not in any hurry to see more of the same congestion, wishing instead we had time to linger in the fields and talk to the farmers. I want to take the color the *Guide* reserved only for the countryside and have it burst into the lives of the so-called "backwoodsmen," ask them their best recipe for field peas or if they hold any superstitions. I want to come back, not to mock their customs, but to celebrate their lives. I want to disprove the *Guide*'s condescending tone and see for myself the swamp maples the same writer reverently described as bursting into "large clusters of scarlet flowers."

Lake City ★

★ Flagler Beach

18

Death Row,
the World's Best Grocery Store,
and Finding Gold (SR 100)

Humid heartland.

As we cross Florida's northeast countryside on State Road 100, that is the image painted in my mind. This road takes us southeast from Watertown to just shy of the Atlantic at Bunnell. Between them, the two towns have roughly 5,300 residents; this is not metropolitan Florida. The pine-dominated road follows State Road 100 for the entire stretch, although State Road 100 starts farther west, at the state line. It runs through Jasper, past the Stephen Foster Folk Culture Center State Park, and ends farther east, at Flagler Beach.

Once upon a time, well before the farms south of Okeechobee made use of the fertile Everglades muck, farmers worked the land along this road. The *Guide* chronicled homes separated by pecan groves and vegetable gardens.

While this area turned a fine trade in naval stores, with a stately democracy of slash pines for tapping, the writers noted "lumbermen follow at the heels of naval-stores operators, leasing the land for timber. Gradually the forests become open pastures, or are grubbed, fertilized, and cultivated by small truck farmers."

For the first leg of the tour, the community appears unaffected by the eight decades between the *Guide* writers passing through and our adventure. We don't see many houses between Watertown and Starke; instead, we see rows and rows of planted things along this two-lane stretch of highway and, of course, the odd tractor or other unidentifiable-to-me farm equipment. We also find an abundance of fundamentalist Christian churches, more than one cemetery, and no indication of where the sometimes-dirt, sometimes-paved roads lead when they leave the highway.

Lake Butler is the exception. The town, a former turpentine and resin producer, also had two plants that built farm equipment. Today it has plenty of trees, but the main street—appropriately if not imaginatively titled Main Street—runs past a newspaper, used-car lot, fried-chicken restaurant, and a miscellany of businesses. The town's small center has few chains, save a CVS drugstore and a Mercantile Bank, but it also has few recreational shopping opportunities. The utilitarian downtown serves its residents and doesn't appear designed to attract outsiders.

The buildings here come in two flavors: functional structures that create a stylistic void, and brick, historic-looking edifices. The Union County Courthouse, built in 1936, fits the latter classification; most of the shops fit the former. The jail included with the original construction gave way to a newer, less dignified structure at the midcentury mark, but it still stands. Along this road, too, you will find the Supervisor of Elections, the Health Department, the State Attorney's Office and, less than a block away, the public library. As the county seat for the smallest county, at least in terms of geography, in the state—Union County encompasses 240 square miles—this Main Street may well serve as the hub of the county.

Lake Butler is not a tourist town. It's not even a particularly attractive town. In this I find its appeal. Florida sold citrus, then it sold land, and now it sells paradise vacations. Lake Butler doesn't sell anything; it just chugs along, same as it ever did.

Down the road, past pine trees and more rows of vegetables and trees, Starke houses a prison and Florida's death row. The town of Starke has impressive architecture along the Call Street Historic District, much of which is lost against the backdrop of poverty. According to the 2011 census, Starke residents earned an average of fifteen thousand dollars a year; almost 30 percent of the city's residents lives below the poverty level.

The route continues south out of Starke, and as we approach our campsite for the evening we start to look for a grocery store. The Yelp app on my phone tells me we can find something called Hitchcock's nearby. Hitchcock's is a market—it does not call itself a supermarket—in the Alachua area. They've been around for more than sixty years.

In most of Florida, Publix supermarkets dominate the grocery landscape. I used to joke that if you grew up in Florida, the law required you to serve a term of employment at Publix. Their refusal to sign a Fair Food human rights agreement with Immokalee tomato growers cemented my disgust with a once-wonderful grocer. All the same, I know what to expect from Publix. I'm used to Publix; it's akin to rooting for the Tampa Bay Bucs. You don't expect them to be good; you just expect them to be consistent. On that count, Publix delivers.

When we walk through the door at Hitchcock's, though, the familiar, forgotten smell of sawdust hits my nose, and I can't help but smile. Hitchcock's is easily as large as a Publix, but it lacks the facade of Florida's green giant. The bag boys still wear aprons and the fresh, young eagerness of farm boys, or at least boys who know farm boys. Is the selection of foods I can easily prepare in a camper as broad as at a supermarket? Nope. But the food—especially the vegetables—cost less, and the people are delighted to assist. I fell in love with the store when an aproned stock boy offered to help me find canned tomatoes and insisted on making sure he found the best-priced brand. I hold out hope for a store like that to make its way down the state and bring a touch of sawdust back to our urban beaches.

Armed with canned tomatoes, bacon, a yellow bag of Wise butter-flavor popcorn, and a six-pack, we head for the campsite. Today has been a shorter drive, and we still have plenty of daylight left; tomorrow is also kind of a free day—we don't have reservations, although we have a route planned—so it feels almost like a weekend.

Mike Roess Gold Head Branch State Park opened the same year the WPA published *A Guide to the Southernmost* State. Mike Roess donated the land, and the Civilian Conservation Corps built the park. The *Guide* perfectly describes a subtropical wooded Eden, which is how you will find the park today when you visit:

> At the head of a ravine from which emerges Gold Head Branch, a crystal-clear stream rising from a group of springs and flowing over a bed of white sand. A footpath descends the steep slopes to the bottom of the ravine, 65 feet below the highway. The gorge is a natural garden, overspread with wild flowers, shrubs, palms, and other subtropical growth. There is a motor road along the edge of the ravine to the site of a mill dam.

Crisscrossing the state, we talked to a lot of park rangers. Without fail they proved friendly, knowledgeable, and helpful. They all agreed that September was a slower time for the state park system. It makes sense. The kids down here are freshly back in school, and up north it isn't cold enough yet to head for Florida. At Gold Head Branch, we were among few others at the park except for the ranger, who told us that one of the tiny white cabins had someone in it and that the campsite had one other camper, but we didn't see another human for the length of our stay.

My friends call me a misanthrope, and I can't disagree. Calypso is my best friend, and I thank God every day Barry can put up with my moods. A crowd of people makes me itch; I start scanning the room for the emergency exit. The emptiness of the park soothed me. The only sounds we heard were birds and squirrels and other animals, including the soft rustle of deer that had Calypso's tiny body tense with instinct and her nose twitching with the rapidity of a power tool. I realize, though, that being the only people in more than one thousand acres of land might make a horror movie soundtrack start playing in some heads. If so, this serene, beautiful park may not be for you in September, because it was blissfully deserted.

Gold Head Branch State Park lets you see north central Florida in a (mostly) untouched light. We parked our camper between longleaf pines on a carpet of pine duff. The ranger told us the elevation was almost two hundred feet, but in my mind it feels more like a mountaintop with crisp air and the sound of light breezes. On our walk, Calypso levitates about two feet off the ground with all the smells. Within moments we see deer circling an empty camping loop; they see us and race down the ravine. Birds flit from one turkey oak tree to the next, sending leaves fluttering to the floor. I rinse away the smell of the road under a hot-water stream in a deserted bathhouse; the park is still empty, and I don't bother dressing to walk back to the camper. I simply wrap myself in a towel and traipse across the leaves and rocks. The sun sets over the woods, and the light dims, the forest backlit in orange blazes. Once darkness settles over the park, it's nothing but a void with white pinholes high above us.

The next morning we hike down into the ravine. The water level at the ravine is low. A good hurricane would fill it, but that hasn't happened yet this year. We circle the ravine on a single-file path, Calypso stopping every five or ten feet to smell or roll in something.

I hear people talk about the quiet of the woods, but I disagree. The woods and rivers and forests, especially Gold Head Branch, thrum with a cacophony of sounds. I heard leaves twitter down, anoles scatter over the ground, and the snap of twigs and branches as the earth moved and settled. The ravine never fell silent.

Back on US 100, the route crosses Etoniah State Forest on the way to Palatka. Tall pines line either side of the road, blocking the horizon and casting a cool green feel over the road. Few fences and gates interrupt the stretch of forest; longleaf pines, not homes or shops, are our roadside companions. It feels enchanted and surreal, as though there is no world outside this green tunnel. The forest offers refuge to wild turkey, rattlesnakes, and the unusual assortment of Florida's usual critters. It is also home to the cheeky scrub jay and an endangered plant called Etonia rosemary.

As the road emerges from the forest and the sky casts its blue warmth down upon us, the trees become shorter and less dense. Cows along the south Florida roadside are commonplace, but here we find few cows and fewer horses. Instead we see goats, as we did along US

17 near this same latitude. Keystone Heights, just south of the turnoff for Gold Head Branch, houses the Florida Dairy Goat Association. In 2010 the *Orlando Sentinel* reported an increase in goat farming—from thirty-six thousand animals in 2005 to sixty thousand in 2010. I am not kidding when I tell you we drove past most of these goats.

Just over the St. Johns River in Palatka, the route crosses US 17 and sidles south along the edge of Dunn's Creek Conservation Area. Two different state agencies run this area: the St. Johns River Water Management District has responsibility for parts of the conservation area not owned by the state parks department. Both agencies have a similar goal: keep the area as untouched as possible. Before becoming a conservation area the state park land was used for turpentine production, cattle ranching, and logging. Today it's used for camping, hiking, and horseback riding.

The *Guide* last noted the area southeast of San Mateo, describing it as a dairy and potato region with farms bordering both sides of the road. What I've just seen, I realized, is Florida's heartland. It doesn't look the same as it did in the 1930s; I haven't seen exactly what the federal writers saw. Palpable waves of late-September humidity radiate over the farms remaining, blurring the air, and if I squint between the sultry corkscrews of heat, I can see the ghosts of the *Guide* towns. They follow me out of the heartland to the east as the road beelines for Bunnell, a surprisingly forested near-coastal end of the road where US 1 smacks against the Kodachrome of Flagler Beach, with its ruby, rusty sand and small-town vibe.

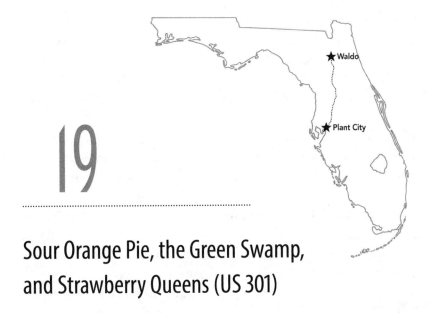

19

Sour Orange Pie, the Green Swamp, and Strawberry Queens (US 301)

Writers of post-boom Florida tend to avoid the beaten tracks of the tourist, and by doing so have uncovered parts of Florida little changed from pioneer days. Marjorie Kinnan Rawlings has practically staked out a domain of her own, the interior scrub country and its elemental people. . . . Her faithful reproduction of "cracker" speech and backwoods customs, destined soon to disappear with the invasion of modern highways, becomes a presentation of the conflict between man and nature.

A Guide to the Southernmost State

This comes from the *Guide*'s chapter on Florida literature, but editors could have easily included it in the final chapter, the one that carries drivers down modern-day 301. This route—one some might call utilitarian or nightmarish—bisects the state, heading almost due south from Waldo, crawling only slightly west after the midway point.

At first glance the road appears a humdrum conglomeration of franchises, forgotten storefronts, and traffic. At least, that's what I once believed. Most Floridians drive 301 only as a means to an end— if you live in central southwest Florida and want to get to the east coast of America, US 301 allows you to get there faster than any of the interstates, even accounting for two of the most speed-restricted towns I've ever known. However, if you look at it as a true tourist—one touring—and not someone impatient to just get through the speed trap in Waldo, it's a different ride altogether.

Waldo had 1,015 residents when census takers walked through town in 2010. That's 312 more residents than the town had in 1939, which may be some kind of nongrowth record for a Florida town. Oh, and when I say walked the town, the emphasis here is on walked—the entirety of the town encompasses slightly more than one and a half miles.

Down a skinny road, skirted on both sides by lakes, is Hawthorne, and if you skitter far enough off a side road toward Cross Creek, you wind up at the Yearling Restaurant. Named after the Marjorie Kinnan Rawlings book, the restaurant serves sour orange pie.

Sour oranges, also called Seville oranges, originated in Southeast Asia and came to the States by way of Spain. While not as common in Florida as, say, navel oranges or Valencias, you can find the odd tree in a yard and or a copse of trees growing wild in some state parks. Sour oranges look like big, bumpy lemons, and if you pick one and show it to an orange-ignorant person, that person will argue passionately that you are mistaken and this is a lemon.

That person would be wrong. While Sevilles don't taste as sweet as, say, a honeybell or a navel orange, they don't exactly taste like lemons. That doesn't mean most people want to peel away the thick, knobby rind, section themselves off a piece, and take a bite. Sevilles taste bitter and work best in mojo sauces. I take mine in pie form: juiced, mixed with five eggs and sweetened condensed milk, and poured in a graham cracker crust and thrown in the freezer for two hours. Drizzle it with chocolate, or not, and that's dinner. And breakfast. And dessert. After I quite literally stumbled into a small grove of sour orange trees by Fisheating Creek in south Florida, I used some to create a sour orange Margarita. It's tequila, sour oranges muddled with brown sugar, and triple sec. If that still sounds too bitter, try throwing in a scoop of orange sherbet for the perfect cocktail/ice cream float. Cheers!

At the Yearling, the waitress seats us in a booth and sets down our menus. Rawlings and the lifestyle she has come to epitomize surround me. Each room re-creates a scene from *The Yearling*, and, by extension, sets you in the midst of Cross Creek, where Rawlings wrote both *The Yearling* and *Cross Creek*, a quasi-autobiographical book of life in the big scrub. A meal here is also a throwback to Marjorie's time, and while you'll find chicken, grouper, and other mainstream dishes on the menu, you can also try what the restaurant calls "traditional" Florida dishes: quail, cooter, frogs' legs, venison, and gator.

Just down the road toward Island Grove is Miss Marjorie's homestead.

I feel a kinship to Rawlings, even though I suspect her tales of frontier life in *Cross Creek* are not wholly true. I empathize with her flawed writings about her life in Cross Creek. I empathize with the way she saw the state—with its imperfect nature and people—and loved it anyway. She didn't try to make her neighbors better or different; she just wrote what she saw. She had limited room in her life for anything else—although things and people wormed their way in—unless it was cooking. I get that, too.

When studying Florida, there are three Marjories of significance: Marjory Stoneman Douglas, Marjorie Harris Carr, and my Marjorie. Douglas tried to save the Everglades; Carr tried to save the Ocklawaha River. The Marjorie of 301? She tried to show the world who inland Florida was. I suspect that, of the three, she had the most success. Drunk, destitute, and remarkably in love with Florida, she died quite young, but not before she showed the world her state. So she was a bit of a storyteller, so she was slightly bigoted, and so she was wildly alcoholic. Her gift to us was allowing us to see Florida through her eyes.

Past Miss Marjorie's place, a variety of orange shops in Citra sell orange candy, tupelo honey, and, of course, orange juice. Most of the orange juice sold in supermarkets hails from Brazil or Mexico and gets pasteurized for our safety. Here you can find unpasteurized, hyperlocal orange juice—usually from a tree out back. The taste is a saffroned gold, sweet and heavy and crisp and light at the same time.

All the towns south of Cross Creek and Citra blend together for me, dulled by the brightness of Miss Marjorie. The Withlacoochee, though, is a great, scary river, glistening black and hissing a song of the River Styx as it crosses a boggy paradise. I gladly put in my kayak and push myself around a series of turns, expecting to see a snake or a gator or a swamp ape at every apex.

The river and the surrounding forest swallow me in a wilderness not far from the hustle of downtown Tampa or the crowds of Ocala, and while it's a short drive to the office buildings west of the Tampa Channelside district, the feel of the Withlacoochee gives the impression of a forest of northwest Florida, not one an hour or two from people trading stocks and forging real estate acquisitions.

Before you get to Tampa, you pass through bottled-water country. In Zephyrhills, Nestlé bottles its spring water. While bottled water itself has precious few regulations placed on it, the nomenclature falls under stricter guidelines. To call water "spring water" it must burble forth of its own accord; companies may not label water pumped out of the ground as such. For this exact reason, Zephyrhills matters greatly to Nestlé. In the early part of the millennium, the company contracted with the Southwest Florida Water Management District for the rights to take spring water—as long as it pumped water from another source back into the aquifer. Put another way: if Nestlé wants 70 million gallons of spring water every day, it could take it—as long as it found a way to pump just as much *back* into the aquifer. Legally, it's still spring water. Ethically? Well, Floridians don't usually think of bottled water companies when they think of ethics.

On top of the aquifer in this area, the Green Swamp feeds the spongy limestone tunnel of water as well as surrounding rivers. The Green Swamp Wilderness Preserve, controlled and managed by the state, reaches into Lake, Polk, Pasco, and Sumter Counties. Four significant rivers flow out of this 110,000-acre swamp: the Withlacoochee, Ocklawaha, Hillsborough, and Peace Rivers.

The Green Swamp, like the Everglades, doesn't consist of just one type of ecosystem. Cypress ponds, stands of oak, marsh, sandhills, and flatwoods all comprise the swamp. Each system has its own population of plants and animals, and the *Guide*'s descriptions of each—as a "deep narrow stream," an "inland waterway," a citified river with tropical foliage and cypress and palm-lined banks, and a "broad valley," in that order—still hold true.

As with the Withlacoochee, the Hillsborough River abuts 301, crossing it at one point and grazing it at another. Unlike the Withlacoochee, this river offers both urban and wild escape. It leaves the Green Swamp and flows through Crystal Springs in Zephyrhills. There, courtesy of those springs that corporate water loves so much, it receives an infusion of freshwater before formally becoming the Hillsborough and traveling through the state park of the same name in Thonotosassa. As it closes in on salt water, the river runs through downtown Tampa.

Florida has one alligator for every fourteen people. Many of them either live along the Hillsborough or visit an awful lot. I put my kayak in the water at Thonotosassa's John B. Sargeant Park, and before I make my way down the creek to join the river, I see the telltale nubby snout set between two unblinking eyes. On a whim, I decide to see if I can paddle the tricky Seventeen Runs. It's a run littered with deadfall, submerged trees, and, of course, gators. As I try to wind my way around a branch and get stuck in the vee of an underwater tree, I notice a congregation of baby alligators watching me with eyes too old and mean for their oddly adorable, bright-green bodies.

It is precisely at this moment that Calypso decides she's tired of waiting for me to get the kayak unstuck. She sees the small gators and decides, I suppose, to chase them. As she leaps out of our boat, I see visions of not-so-cute mama gator lurking just beyond her babies. Gators, as I've mentioned, are all about furthering the species. So much so that the babies are never far from mama. I grab Calypso by the tail as her paws touch the black water not three inches from the baby gators and yank her back in the boat, where I stuff her in the bow between my calves, confused but well out of sight. With an increased sense of urgency, I unstick my kayak, point it back from whence I came, and forsake Seventeen Runs for open water.

As I round a bend a few minutes later, my eyes meet a gator watching me from the shoreline. As I get closer, he slithers into the water, and I realize he is what locals would call a "real" gator—easily twelve feet long. He disappears beneath the water as I pass.

This puts me even further in awe of this wild, beautiful river as I paddle more urgently, my heart pounding and Calypso now subdued, curled up and asleep in the cockpit at my feet.

Less wild and not nearly as fearsome is the Plant City Strawberry Festival. Plant City still has—as it did in the 1930s—strong ties to berries. The berry industry depends on slightly cool winters for red, juicy fruit. In 1939, Plant City provided the United States with 75 percent of its strawberries grown in the middle of winter. Today, the Florida Strawberry Growers Association asserts that strawberries grown in Hillsborough County (home to Plant City) account for "virtually all" the winter strawberries and 15 percent of all strawberries in the United States. Hillsborough County produces 18 million flats of strawberries every year. Pick-your-own farms abound, as do hydroponic, organic, and traditionally grown berries. Many Floridians—especially those spoiled by berries picked the same morning they arrive at the farmer's market—will only eat strawberries about two months out of the year, because the rest of the year they come from somewhere else, and after a long road trip, no one—not even the once plump and juicy strawberry—is at its best.

The *Guide* called strawberry farming a "thirteen-month-a-year-job" and the late-February Strawberry Festival its climax. Today it's held in either late February or early March and includes music, livestock, and strawberries in every incarnation from strawberry pie to strawberry mashed potatoes.

The event, of course, also includes the crowning of the Strawberry Queen and her royal court. Starting in 1930 Plant City has crowned a Strawberry Queen every year except for 1942–47. The queen wears a flowing red cape adorned with strawberry patches. She rules her court from a red chair shaped like a colossal strawberry.

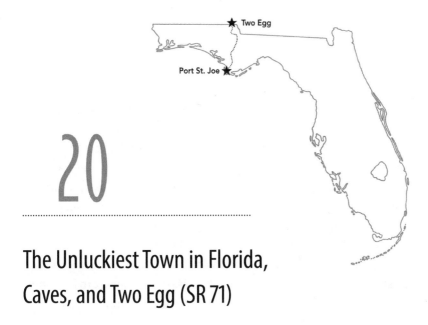

20

The Unluckiest Town in Florida, Caves, and Two Egg (SR 71)

All along the panhandle's coastal route, tiny towns sprout between the pine forests, each one with an ephemeral seaside image of an illusory Florida, as if an artist stepped in and created the vintage beach town that exists in the unwashed corals and teals of your imagination. State Road 71 leads into Port St. Joe, which, coupled with Mexico Beach a few moments west, offers prime examples of this. They're sleepy coastal towns with simple footpaths leading over the dunes and out to the Gulf of Mexico. Port St. Joe has a few remaining older beach cottages, and everywhere you look, weathered wood is either exposed to the sun and salt or stained with understated tropical beach colors.

The *Guide* mentioned a different town with a similar name: St. Joseph, a ghost town today almost completely consumed by Port St. Joe. When the state held its constitutional convention there in 1838, St. Joseph boasted six thousand residents, making it the largest town in Florida. Two years later, nothing remained of the town but a cemetery.

St. Joseph's industry hinged on a thriving seagoing trade, so in all likelihood no one thought anything of it when a ship docked there in July 1841, fresh from the Greater Antilles. At least one of the passengers—in all probability, more than one—suffered from yellow fever, a deadly disease carried by mosquitoes and marked by a yellow jaundice in those afflicted. It's also quite contagious: three-quarters of St. Joseph's residents died from yellow fever, while others fled the town, which is why, of the six thousand residents, fewer than five hundred remained when a hurricane struck on September 14. The storm destroyed many of the buildings and pushed the remaining folks out of town. Soon thereafter, forest fires ripped through the (now almost certainly all-but-completely) deserted St. Joseph, burning every building left standing. This should have completed the town's trifecta of bad luck—after all, things happen in threes, right?

Not so much for this unlucky seaside hamlet. In one final attempt to resurrect the 1840s equivalent of modern-day Jacksonville, some residents returned to St. Joseph after the virus, hurricane, and fires ravaged the town. They started to rebuild the city, but on September 8, 1844, yet another hurricane made landfall. After two days of wind, rain, and storm surge, the Gulf won, flooding the town. After that, one can only assume that even the most intrepid settlers tapped out, heading for safer pastures.

In a move echoed later by south Florida officials in 1928 and New Orleans in the aftermath of Katrina, many yellow fever victims received a mass burial in unmarked trenches. The St. Joseph cemetery off State Road 384A marks the graves of other yellow fever victims.

It is also the only vestige of St. Joseph.

To the north, Wewahitchka—Seminole for "water eyes"—holds onto a healthier history: bees and honey. Before we drive through stands of swamp and tupelo trees, we stop for shrimp.

At a small roadside shrimp store, the Shrimper's Lady, we buy head-on Apalachee Bay shrimp. There really is a shrimper's lady working behind the counter, and in addition to shrimp she maintains a hearty collection of Danielle Steel, Debbie Macomber, and many other authors who have graced the Harlequin editorial desks. The shrimp she sells for $4.50 a pound; the books she exchanges with customers. We talk about Debbie Macomber and cooking shrimp. She has never heard of boiling shrimp in beer; I have never heard of most of the authors on her bookshelf. She promises to try boiling the shrimp in beer; I trade a book to try when my next bout of travel insomnia strikes.

During the Depression, this small town shipped one thousand barrels of tupelo honey a year. The *Guide* explains the value of the tupelo as medicinal: "Tupelo honey does not granulate or become rancid, and is used largely for pharmaceutical purposes. Apiarists from adjoining states bring their swarms to this section each spring by motor trucks and on rafts floated down the streams. Tupelo, a hard wood, is used as flooring and in making bowling-alley equipment."

The tupelo tree, which some call a "black gum," grows in and near swamps, and here, in north Florida, beekeepers build walking docks out to tupelo trees, over swampy no-man's land, to ensure monofloral honey, or honey from one type of blossom. Honey created from tupelo blossoms does not crystallize, but I do not care about that; I seek its rich taste. At one time the primary purpose of this honey may have been medicinal; today, however, it is regarded as a regional artisan delight, and for good reason. Tupelo honey tastes like sweet, dripped gold, not nearly as dark as clover honey and not as tangy as the less expensive honey sold in plastic bears with squeeze bottle heads.

Swamps abound in south Florida, but tupelo trees do not, so only here in northwest Florida will you find jars of the prized honey at every roadside stand and grocer. In the panhandle, tupelos grow along the Chipola River, which starts in Marianna and feeds the Apalachicola River. In high-water times, the Chipola River offers whitewater, an anomaly on top of Florida's flat rivers. Today, though, the water only dreams of rapids. The local paper quotes a forest ranger saying they need "rain with a name," meaning a hurricane. The winds and storm surge of a hurricane may have devastated nearby St. Joseph, but just a few miles away, in hilly north Florida, those heavy rains suppress forest fires, keep the aquifer filled, and the state's few rapids running.

Torreya State Park abuts a ravine far above the Apalachicola River. As we gaze down at the Apalachicola from the high ridges of the park, the trickle of water below settles between the bluffs in sharp contrast to the steep banks. Behind us is the Gregory House, a plantation house from across the river. The Civilian Conservation Corps (CCC) dismantled the house and moved it across the river piece by piece, with thoughts of using it as a hotel. There, CCC workers restored it, although the 1849 home never functioned as a hotel. Its backyard overlooks a 150-foot sheer drop. No more than two vertical feet have ever separated my feet from a Florida river; this feels nothing like Florida. The ravine grabs at my heart and squeezes, because I was not prepared. If I were in Tennessee? Sure, the place is lousy with sharp precipices. After eight or nine hundred, you just sort if glance at it and say, "Meh." It seems somehow more dangerous in Florida, as if the scarp is a threshold between two Sunshine States: the sandy, flat Florida and the parts of the state that belong more to the Deep South. I creep forward, mindful of the obvious lack of guardrail between me and the far-below banks of the Apalachicola.

The high walls lining the river are not the only spectacular thing here, however. Not far from the Gregory House we find a stand of torreya trees, so named for an 1800s botanist, John Torrey. The torreya grows almost exclusively inside the park. Fewer than two hundred of these tiny, adorable Christmas trees remain, although the tree has distant relatives in Japan and California. This cheerful wisp of greenery lives one wildfire away from extinction.

Consider the torreya tree's alternate name: gopherwood. In case you aren't up on your Old Testament, that's the tree Noah used to build the ark. Of course, the epic flood happened nowhere near the Apalachicola, at least not judging by today's trickle of a water level, held in check against its will by the Woodruff Dam. The Apalachicola River actually begins its southward journey north of Atlanta, in the Appalachian Mountains. Despite its origin and terminus, in Georgia people know it as either the Flint or the Chattahoochee. The Chattahoochee River marks the state boundary between Alabama and Georgia; the Flint runs to the east of it. Both rivers meet just north of Chattahoochee, Florida, at Lake Seminole, and this is the official beginning of the Apalachicola River. It is also where the dam holds back the water, providing electricity but also creating Lake Seminole to the north.

The dam holds back the water united by the confluence of the Flint, Chattahoochee, and Apalachicola Rivers. While the biblical flood may not have happened here, in the event of a hundred-year storm event (a storm with water so high that its probability, on average, is only once a century), the lock would go underwater and, with enough rain, the area could have a flood of mythic proportions. The biblical allusion is perhaps lost on area hydrologists.

South of the dam, the Apalachicola meanders in twists and turns that shape the waterway into a Christmas bow, ending its journey with a great watery exhalation into Apalachicola Bay.

Marianna, at the north end of State Road 71, is west of the river. Two nearby attractions divide my attention: Florida Caverns State Park and Two Egg.

At the edge of Florida, at Florida Caverns State Park, I take a dark tour through the dry air caves of north Florida. Everything I see in the underground chambers looks like melting candles; I can't tell a stalagmite from a stalactite, but it doesn't matter: the idea of caves in a state where most folks hit water if they dig too deep thrills me. In the back of my mind, the caves could, you know, cave in at any moment. My favorite story about these caves—after the idea that they exist at all—involves Indians escaping Andrew Jackson. Jackson did his best to disguise the keeping of slaves and killing of Indians as "defining the boundaries of the Louisiana Purchase," but ask a bear: a hunt is a hunt is a hunt. This hunt took Jackson to a spot north of Marianna. The Indians, who had inferior firepower but superior knowledge of the land, hid in a cave while the troops walked overhead, searching for them.

Not a long story, perhaps, but a fun way to understand how Florida's first natives defeated the northern aggressors with true American ingenuity.

I can hardly contain myself as we go through the caves. Room after room, I wait to hear the tour guide tell us about the crafty Indians fooling the silly northerner (if we may consider a Carolinian "northern," which I totally do), but she fails to mention it. Finally, at the tour's end, I ask her, and she tells me to follow a separate, unguided nature trail.

At the end of a thirty-minute trek along an uneven trail, we spy a hole in the side of a piece of land. This looks more like a short, squat tunnel that spans less than fifty feet than a cave. I can see light from the end at its start.

This fooled a future president? I crawl through the tunnel for "histori-cal purposes," but secretly I revel in walking where Indians hid from a man determined to erase their existence.

If the Indians hid in a cave that wasn't, well, that just fits in nicely with Two Egg, a town that isn't.

The TwoEggFla.com website explains the town's name:

> Two young boys came into [a local] business so often on errands from their mother to trade two eggs for sugar that regulars jokingly began calling the establishment a "two egg store." The name caught on and was picked up by traveling salesmen and others who spread it to nearby towns.
>
> The story may seem light-hearted on the surface, but at a deeper level it reflects an effort to put a good face on very hard times. Many local families then were barely surviving and at times of the year, when fresh fruits and vegetables were not available, sugar provided one of the only available sources of carbohydrates. Although it is difficult to conceive in today's era of "low carb" diets, but carbohy-drates are a vital necessity of life. They provide the body with energy and help key organs to function.
>
> A little sugar added to the diet each day provided just enough en-ergy to help struggling families make it through to the next day. In other words, two eggs worth of sugar could make the difference between life and death among people already living on the edge of collapse.

To this day, Two Egg exists as a speck of a town in Jackson County. It has no city government whatsoever; it's not a city but a census-desig-nated place. Even as the economy improved, the town name stuck. Two Egg is, for legal purposes, an unincorporated part of Jackson County. You should not expect to find any more eggs there than in any other part of rural Florida, and you can no longer pay for sugar with eggs.

Most shops accept cash.

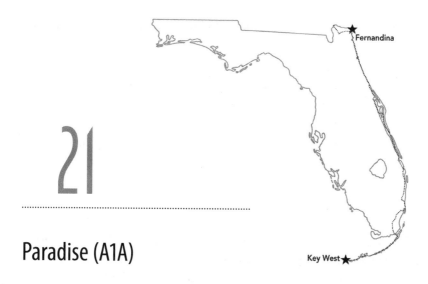

Fernandina

Key West

21

Paradise (A1A)

In the sixteenth century, the French captain Jean Ribault led a star-crossed expedition through northeast Florida. According to the *Guide*, two 1565 expeditions—one from Spain and one from France—made landfall on Florida's east coast, two days apart. France sent six hundred explorers (in reality, colonists) to help the three hundred Frenchmen who had tried to settle Fort Caroline the year before. Just around the corner—literally, as the two expeditions landed less than 50 miles apart—Pedro Menéndez de Avilés led six hundred Spaniards who hoped to Christianize (by force or reason) the indigenous people. The Spaniards and French knew of one another, with the French on the St. Johns at Fort Caroline and the Spaniards farther south at St. Augustine. Each expected to have problems with the other, and, of course, neither was disappointed. Accounts differ, but according to the *Guide*, both forces took the offensive. An oncoming hurricane shipwrecked Ribault and cloaked Menéndez's attack. Had Ribault paid more attention to the weather, French-named forts and parks might pockmark Florida's east coast today. However, we do have one remaining vestige of the French settlement along the St. Johns: the ferry that carries cars and passengers is named the *Jean Ribault*.

The *Jean Ribault* connects Fort George Island with Mayport via a pleasant yet quick, unremarkable sail; more interesting than the journey on the *Jean Ribault* is the patchwork of fishing nets, shrimp trawlers, and working boats lining the river's edge here. This, like Fernandina, is a working waterfront, and my blood zings at the way Floridians still live off the land . . . and sea.

Although this ferry ride isn't at the top of A1A, it epitomizes the surprises waiting along the stretch of road that whispers along the edge of Florida's east coast.

Not everyone in the car was anticipating A1A the way I was, and even I didn't know how hard I would fall for this sandy spit of road. When we started our great Florida adventure, I had Barry's unrelenting support, but he had no qualms about telling me he dreaded A1A. At this point in the trip, too, we were tired. We smelled a bit like road. Florida had overwhelmed us, exhausted us with her diaspora of cultures, economies, and ecologies.

Most people—and this included us at the top of this road—have driven roughly 10 miles on A1A and subsequently painted the whole of the road with the tiny brushstrokes they see in those 10 miles, often part of a drunken spring break, early-morning surfing safari, or sightseeing tour of South Beach. None of these things is the whole of A1A; none of these experiences prepare you for the sandy seaside villages interspersed with silver saw palmettos.

In parts, A1A runs right on top of the sand dunes and fronts the cobalt-blue Atlantic. In other parts, it runs through a horrid glut of T-shirt shops and low-rent tourist traps, but every inch of this road speaks to a different part of Florida's soul. It is, if you will, a compendium of the entire state, although it didn't exist when the WPA writers toured the state. Instead, the writers toured US 1. I did not do that, thanks to Pop, my great-grandfather.

Pop died before I turned five, so I don't remember much about him, but I believe I inherited my penchant for road trips from him. He lived in New York, but every year he would head south on US 1 to Florida. He started before Eisenhower created the interstate system, but long after the interstate lay a 2,000-mile trail of black asphalt from Maine to Miami, Pop still drove US 1. He loved it and saw it through the eyes of the *Guide* writers:

> US 1, and its extension State 4A south of Miami, the longest and most heavily traveled route in the State, enters north Florida over the St. Marys River, runs along the coast, and goes to sea to reach Key West, Florida's southernmost coral island, only 90 miles from Cuba. For most of its length it runs close to a chain of salt lagoons, separated from the ocean by low-lying islands and narrow reefs. These lagoons, connected by canals, form a section of the Intra-coastal Waterway, a popular yacht and motorboat route to and from southern Florida waters.

As we perched at the top of the state, it quickly became clear: The road described above? Pop's road? It had shifted. And disappeared.

Guide writers, though, had left us an alternative: They detailed side trips east to an unconnected chain of barrier islands, separated from the mainland—and each other—by a salty spray of shallow tidal lagoons. A1A would later connect those low-lying islands across those lagoons, forming the Intracoastal Waterway. Those islands? We know them as towns like "Fernandina Beach" and "Daytona Beach" and yes, even "South Beach." Bridges and no small amount of dredging make traveling A1A stem to stern a practical reality, with a few relationship-testing exceptions. *Guide* writers had no such road to tempt them toward the sand and salt, but they did pepper their travels with a seemingly infinite number of diversions across mangrove islands and barely paved roads, out to the seaside. Today, the by-products of development litter US 1; it has morphed from a low-lying road showcasing tidal pools and the splendor in the sand to a haven for homogenization, symbolized most greatly by the repeated presence of franchised surf shops.

Some things remain unchanged. US 1 still brings you into Florida by crossing the St. Marys River, and that is where we start our journey: at the top.

Picture the first of twenty-two tours of an unknown state, and re-member, the *Guide* came before the whole country dreamed of owning a piece of the Florida dream. For this new beginning, consider US 1 as it enters the state: two two-lane bridges spanning the tea-colored St. Marys River.

Today, this is not the Florida you expect; it is not the Florida the hotel brochures promise. You can't see a sandy beach anywhere, and even the river appears dirty, as many exclaim upon gazing with horror into the blackwater river, but tannins (a fancy name for the substance produced when leaves and twigs rot), not toxins, stain the river a watery dahlia.

The *Guide* described this river as "a deep narrow stream," and, although it did not address the color of the water, it did extol the benefit of the tannic acid, saying, "because of its acid content, the water remains fresh for many months when placed in casks."

The St. Johns River flows south to north, one of the few North American rivers to do so. The river starts at an inland Florida bog, its headwaters south of those leading to the Everglades from the Kissimmee. The waterways pass one other. The Kissimmee River, which flows south into the famous River of Grass and, ultimately, Florida Bay, starts just south of present-day Discovery Cove outside Orlando, while the St. Johns River starts south of Yeehaw Junction and flows north through Indian River, Brevard, Putnam, Clay, St. Johns, and Duval Counties.

The St. Johns River Water Management District, the state agency charged with managing the St. Johns River and its associated waterways, including the St. Marys, claims the St. Marys has excellent water quality: "Though black, the river contains little suspended sediment. Because of its extensive bottomland swamps and marshes, relative lack of urban development and few pollution discharge points, the St. Marys is considered to have excellent water quality," the website proclaims. The agency gets one thing wrong: where the river divides Florida from the rest of the Union, it is not black. It is red, like Georgia clay or the afterglow of a long winter sunset.

Remember, though, that the 1930s traveler knew none of this. Even now, the wilderness permeating parts of Florida can be downright daunting; eight decades ago, Florida didn't exactly offer *easier* living. The *Guide*'s side trips to the beach likely promised a traveler relief from the mosquito colonies living in the swampy woods swirling around the road, on which travelers should, according to that deadpan warning (at least I hope it was intended as such) "watch for cattle."

Cattle aside, the *Guide* describes US 1 in a manner that now better befits A1A: "With each mile, as the route proceeds southward, the vegetation becomes more tropical. Birds and marine life not found in other parts of the United States inhabit marshes and rivers. Almost every side road leads to a sandy bathing beach or to a resort with fishing and sailing facilities. And with each mile southward the temperature rises; the winter visitor, topcoated on entering the State, is often in shirt sleeves on reaching Miami.

"Almost every Florida town along US 1 is a winter resort; boom towns of the 1920's stand between settlements that flourished in the 1700's; night clubs are within tee-shot of crumbling ruins built when Florida was a part of the Spanish Empire. Smoky pine woods, dense cypress hammocks, marshes, and glittering sand dunes relieve the flatness of the coastal region."

While the beach portion of A1A starts in Fernandina Beach, the road itself begins in Yulee, named for David Levy Yulee, an islander from Charlotte Amalie. He used slaves to work his sugar plantation in Homosassa, built a railroad from Fernandina to Cedar Key, championed statehood for Florida, joined the Confederate Congress when the state left the Union, spent some time in jail after the South lost the war, then rebuilt his destroyed railroads. He was the first Jewish United States senator. His life's trajectory, I think, says much about how Florida works.

A1A kisses the coast first at Fernandina's thriving, working waterfront. Prior to this I'd only seen A1A as I passed through Daytona and Cocoa Beach, and Barry shuddered as he recalled more than one clogged afternoon in south Florida. But forget spring break and Miami Beach, at least for now: A1A's northern end gives you a quiet and wonderful surprise, beginning at Fernandina.

One stop worth making is PuttPutt Florida, which has been around since 1959. Its charm comes from the hyperstyled designed mini-golf holes it lacks. If you are over thirty-five and played miniature golf as a child, you'll feel right at home. If you're a child of the 1980s or later, you will find the charm in the retro feel of the place. What makes this one of Florida's two coolest putt-putt places—the other is Goofy Golf along US 98—is its proximity to the sand. It's smack-dab on the beach, just behind the gorgeous piles of mounded sand.

Florida has no mountains; most people notice this almost immediately. It's hard to miss. One of the chief complaints Floridians hear is that their state is too flat. I find this funny, because anyone who looks can find plenty more wrong, starting with the 2000 elections and ending with the myriad of news bits with a Florida dateline that end up in every "weird news" column in America. The fact that I can ride my Panama Jack beach cruiser bike almost anywhere in the state is not a negative in my mind.

Besides, it's not wholly true. We're not flat, we just lack mountains. We have hills, mostly in the panhandle, and right down the state's middle is a ridge rising out of the limestone that used to connect sand islands during the Pleistocene era. And, of course, we have sand dunes. Sand dunes support vegetation like sea oats and railroad vines, which hold the sand together and let more things grow in them. Eventually, they'll support trees. Along the water's edge, these sand mountains prevent beach erosion; in Fernandina, we see high dunes inland as well as along the beach, where they sink into creamy, fawn sand that meets the ultramarine sea.

Just south, Amelia Island evokes images of the South Carolina low-country, although we Floridians don't tend to use that word related to anything along our water. Grass peeps through the water, creating brown and green mazes through the Tiger Point marina and fronting boatyards. The route then flows into beach forest. A canopy of green closes over the road, trees punctuated only occasionally by a glimpse of the Atlantic. If you peek hard enough, you can find American Beach. A simple sign marks the area. If you're speeding, you will miss it.

American Beach was the state's first beach for African Americans. Abraham Lincoln Lewis, president of Florida's first insurance company and, not coincidentally, Florida's first black millionaire, founded American Beach for his workers. He bought two hundred acres of beach in 1935 with the intention of creating a respite where black people could recreate or, if they so desired, own property, calling it "recreation and relaxation without humiliation."

Bethune Beach by Daytona Beach was another Atlantic beach where African Americans could "enjoy" their separate-but-equal status, but American Beach is the only one remaining relatively undisturbed after Florida eased unwillingly into integration. American Beach lacks the glitz of the Ritz Carlton to its north and the luxury of Amelia Island Plantation to its south, but the American Beach families held on to their land. Some houses stand empty, some crumble in disrepair, but others still shine. Whatever their physical state, the spirit of the beach remains strong.

Florida's Department of Environmental Protection runs the state park system, and at the northeast end of the state, parks cover much of the prized real estate. Fort Clinch, Amelia Island, Big Talbot, Little Talbot, Pumpkin Hill Creek Preserve, Yellow Bluff Fort, and Fort George Island State Parks dot the northeastern edge of the state, fostering palms, sand dunes, hiking trails, and wildlife.

We follow A1A (also called the Buccaneer Trail at this end) as it passes through dunes and driftwood, opening occasionally to reveal alabaster beaches and beryl water. The name evokes images of pirates adorned with fancy black boots and flamboyant puffy shirts, swash-buckling across the dunes, sword-fighting perched atop cabbage palm driftwood, all the while swatting at mosquitoes, then retiring with a stein of down-island rum. I tamp down that image as we cross Myrtle Creek, and Little Talbot Island reveals grass-over-water vistas framed with moss-draped oak trees surrounding our campsite. In our nightly ritual, Barry commences connecting the camper to power and water as I clip a leash on Calypso and explore the park. We're about 150 feet from the water, and I walk over to let her have a back roll in the sand.

As she does, I notice a fisherman crouched by the water's edge, fiddling with something. I move closer and see he's holding what looks like a young rattler in the water. Under the water, to be precise.

"I caught it with my rod and reel," he says, then explains how snakes can swim "if they want to." He intends to drown it.

"But don't tell no one, 'cause it's illegal," he finishes.

"I know," I say, watching and debating how much to say. His attempts to hold the chiseled, tiny head in the sand under the water don't appear successful. Barry comes over and asks the guy why he wants to kill the snake.

"Well, you wouldn't want it waiting for you when you walked outside your camper, would you?" he asks Barry, who regularly sleeps on boats in Lake Okeechobee and must navigate water moccasins on the dock. Also, as a Boy Scout, he suffered a rattlesnake bite. I can see him trying—and failing—not to condescend.

"No, but he wouldn't want to be there, either," Barry finally says and walks away, shaking his head. The man moves the snake to land and tries to stuff its head into dry sand. How, I wonder, does he not get bitten?

Finally, the guy's buddy comes over and points out the vast expanse of trees and underbrush ten feet from the beach. After a brief debate, the fisherman sends the snake sailing through the air into the marsh where, I like to think, it lands safely, then slithers away, likely gasping for breath and trying to figure out what the hell just happened.

....

A1A does not cross the St. Johns at its junction with the Atlantic Ocean. Instead, cars may opt to leave the coastline and twist across 28 miles of Jacksonville traffic. Alternately, drivers can take a five-dollar ferry on the aforementioned *Jean Ribault* and disembark in the small seafood-dominated town of Mayport.

Jacksonville Beach contrasts sharply with, well, everything north of Mayport. Its built-out, no-view-of-the-beach, chain-store stretch reminds me of A1A between the St. Lucie Inlet and the Florida Keys—a suburb on the sand.

This capitalistic stretch doesn't last long; at Ponte Vedra the landscape changes back abruptly and the route grows forested again. Large homes perch on ecru dunes on the Atlantic side, almost entirely shrouded from the road by soft walls of rustling palms and oaks. On the west, a salty tangle of palm, oak, and pine thickets shield homes from the rest of the world. Finally, the beach forest triumphs, and we see nothing but sand dunes, saw palmetto, and the occasional cabbage palm peeping out. It is a long, narrow stretch of gorgeous nothing, and A1A's two lanes offer the only way in or out of this salty jungle. Briefly I catch glimpses of the Atlantic, its waves curling and beckoning like foamy fingers.

South of Vilano Beach, A1A does not cross the water, turning inland instead, toward St. Augustine. A1A turns south again at Davenport Park, running smack into the merry-go-round that dates to 1927, although it has only lived in Davenport for two decades. We pay a dollar each to ride the unassuming carousel, climbing aboard painted horses and taking pictures of each other in full tourist mode.

After spending the night at Anastasia State Park, we head into St. Augustine. America's oldest city predates 1607 Jamestown by almost a century, which may explain why the region is called "Florida's First Coast." Here we find the first everything, at least according to brochures and signs. We also find the Fountain of Youth. "Finding" it perhaps is not the proper word, as the chamber of commerce has it clearly marked on bright waxy maps of all the local sights. The Fountain of Youth, allegedly "discovered" by Ponce de León, is one part tourist attraction, one part museum, and no part reality. Remember, if he even stepped off the boat, Ponce de León had no illusions that he had stumbled upon the Fountain of Youth; that came from political enemies who mocked him posthumously. From here, St. Augustine locals crafted Florida's First Urban Legend.

Throughout Florida's history, tourist-dependent groups in every corner of the state have claimed that Ponce de León found a potential spring of eternal life in their town. Imagine how that would have gone for him. Every other day his group probably found a spring—in Florida, we have roughly two gazillion and three—which meant he would have sent letters to the Crown a few times a week: "Found a spring that will cheat death; send more gold." I paraphrase, but certainly the monarchy would have caught on to this game.

I sit by Señor Ponce de León's spring—I like to think of it as his First Spring, in keeping with St. Augustine's marketing—white Dixie cup in hand, waiting for a sip. An "attractions host" fills my cup with water from the spring in front of us.

But if this is the Fountain of Youth, it stinks. Literally. The smell of rotten eggs assaults me, and I'm not the only one; everyone around me wrinkles their nose, too. Our host assures us that what we smell is "only" hydrogen sulfide gas. Before we can dump our water back in the spring, he adds that it will not hurt us, and if we pinch our noses, it won't bother us anymore. Apparently you can't taste the gas.

I pinch my nose closed and take a swig.

Did the water work? Did it grant me eternal life? I can't say for sure, but I can tell you I have yet to die.

St. Augustine, of course, offers more than sulfur water: the Colonial Spanish Quarter, Flagler College's amazing gilded architecture, the city gates, and, well, all of the city. We devise our own walking tour, making it up as we go, turning whenever a fuchsia flash of bougainvillea catches our eye or when Calypso feels the need to tug the leash a certain way. She's not, shockingly, interested in the Colonial Spanish Quarter (truthfully, it looks somewhat commercialized, so I can't say I blame her), but we do pause for a long while in front of Flagler College and stroll through the gardens in front of city hall. We move on through the town, stopping to remark that so much of the neighborhood by the waterfront looks like the New Orleans Garden District, which makes sense as they share latitude. There are flowers everywhere, and the houses, while close together, are separated by curtains of foliage. Odd, brilliant bits of color spring forth from gates, surprising the unexpecting pedestrian.

We finish our walking tour at the water, where we stroll by homes crowned with widow's walks. I picture a boat captain's wife, pacing the roof, wringing her hands and waiting for her husband to return home from sea. The city gates are here, too, proudly looking every bit their age (just a shade over three hundred years), as is one of the only remaining parts of the wall that once encircled the city. On the other side of the road, Castillo de San Marcos still stands, a masonry fort unlike the coquina shell I expect from Florida's historic monuments. The national park makes a valiant effort to show visitors how St. Augustine has earned its place in the history books. Across from it, I spy a cemetery. I walk past it, stopping and looking over the wall, wondering who was lucky enough to get buried here, beneath the oaks. Then I spy the historical marker and see that, far from lucky, the inhabitants were victims of yellow fever.

St. Augustine is lovely, but I want to go back to the ocean. We cross the Bridge of Lions, stop by the lighthouse, where I bail on the view after the second flight of steps and continue south.

South of Marineland, a vintage aquarium featuring dolphin shows along A1A, the road widens and we find ourselves separated from the Atlantic by blocks, not feet. The air never loses its tang, and the buildings never get tall, and before I can blink at the development, we're back in a forest of palm and pine and sand. At Flagler Beach's north end, a whole lot of glorious nothing surrounds us. Flagler Beach, at the terminus of US 100, is the beach town time forgot. Everything here has the patina of a Kodak Instamatic photo, and that's more than OK. Even the sand has a saturated cinnamon tint, and the aged orange roofline of the beach pier intensifies the feeling of slipping back in time.

A1A runs atop a sand dune along this stretch, with the beach fifteen or so feet below us. We make a slow circle of the town—it really doesn't take much to circle the town—noting that one building houses all the city services and everything seems blissfully underdeveloped. I discover later that height restrictions in the town center, Veterans Park, don't allow anything taller than two feet in case someone ever wants to develop a hotel just behind the park—the town had a public outcry when a shuffleboard box breached the two-foot mark. The town removed the boxes.

The slow, sleepy town has only one chain store I can see, and I groan: Dollar General. Even that, though, is less flashy than its counterparts, without its yellow roof and prefabricated building. Everything else appears locally owned and doing well enough, and as we park the car and stroll down to the beach, I start to plan a return trip in my mind. After a day or so, I can't imagine there's much to do other than bob in the surf and bury my hands in the sand, and after almost 5,000 miles crisscrossing Florida, that sounds divine. I can see myself at the aptly named Beach Front Motel, one of the few buildings fronting A1A, walking to get shrimp at the Funky Pelican, and falling asleep to the sound of the waves crashing against the pier.

I turn to look back for Barry and realize the sand dunes and sea oats almost completely obscure the view of the road. It's like a subterranean seashore, a seaside hobbit hole secluded from the onslaught of development.

Everyone who loves Florida wants to believe places like Flagler Beach exist, sandy and time-honored Kodachrome memories, but in reality, these places lose ground every day to development. The best thing that ever happened to modern Florida? The real estate crash in 2007. Countless coastal communities stared down the barrel of imminent condo canyons and steroidal McMansions replacing the classic Florida ranch; when the bust came, developers went belly-up and Florida regained some ground—literally. While countless homes and beaches escaped Ponzi schemes and dollar-sign dreams, other beach communities lost vintage buildings to a new, northern Florida dream—one with plenty of amenities prior residents didn't need, such as homes with three story-aquariums, lazy rivers, and no more public beach access. The hardest hit, though, were communities with the dream half-realized. That meant when the bottom fell out, it fell hard—leaving buildings half-built, sometimes with no windows or even a roof. Every summer storm worked over these buildings, turning charming coastal communities into eyesores.

Flagler Beach escaped all this, and finding it is like finding Florida, except it's a Florida you assume no longer exists. Flagler Beach represents more than just a town; it's a seaside vignette.

As we leave Flagler Beach, just past the 1960s-style aqua water tower, saw palmettos cover dune after dune, often on both sides of the road. Welcome to North Peninsula State Park. It's only 2 miles along the coast, but the wild thickets, fawn-shaded sand, and sapphire water remove anything else as we float through paradise.

The road in south Flagler County and north Volusia County streams along the coast, blacktop balanced on sand, as if daring the salt water to topple it. These are cliffs, Florida-style.

Daytona Beach offers a sharp contrast to Flagler Beach, although it, too, retains a sense of a 1960s photograph, complete with a roller coaster and a Ferris wheel on the sand. The intersections are pink and blue brick, and the hotels all have funky signs and names like Aku Tiki and Ohana Luau. Hawaiian Falls Golf has a tiki hut office and volcanoes I suspect erupt with every hole-in-one.

A Bealls department store signals the onset of civilization, and Ormond-by-the-Sea is the opposite of North Peninsula. It's odd, though, how it doesn't bother me; parts of the beach, I reason, must go to the tourists, or else how could we ever know to value the Flagler Beaches and sand dunes? People have to be able to see what they're protecting, and, likewise, they should also be able to see what happens when they fail to do so.

The throngs of hotels, shops, and people thin as we near our stop for the night: Canaveral National Seashore. Jetty Park, a campground run by the Port Authority in Cape Canaveral, is at the tip of the cruise-ship ports, and, if it were crowded, it looks as though it would be a cramped nightmare. Tonight, though, we can count our fellow campers on one hand. The beach does not expressly forbid dogs, and Calypso and I both go off-leash and run down the sandy expanse, she, wriggling her back along wet shells coated with sand, and me, digging my toes into that same sand.

In the morning we string our way down between a series of beaches intended for tourists, but not before a nasty turn inland along US 1. This inland connection—necessary courtesy of Canaveral Air Force Station and Kennedy Space Center—confirms our decision to travel A1A instead of US1. I would go into detail, but, honestly, just stay on A1A. It's exhausting to drive past strip mall after strip mall interspersed with a random oddity that tempts you, although never enough to stop. Our reward, though, is Cocoa Beach, a haven for surfers with its majestic Atlantic waves. Through town, A1A splits into what I can best describe as a divided highway, but it isn't really. It's two one-way roads separated by short buildings: a cigar bar here, a restaurant there. There is nothing divine and planned out about it; it simply is what it is. Cocoa Beach, I sigh after breakfast, is one of my favorite places. Bear in mind, this is the twenty-second time Barry has heard me say this. At one time or another, they're all my favorite places.

Roberto's, a Cuban cafe in the downtown, has had the same owners for decades. Pray it stays that way, and if you go, order the Surfer Special: an egg over black beans and yellow rice. Then go back north to Ron Jon, because this is the original Ron Jon, and if you want to understand surfer culture, you need to visit surfer Shambala. Yes, they have T-shirts. Go ahead and get one. But maybe also get a surfing lesson, or at least look at the statues out front. This is Graceland.

Nonsurfers know this stretch of land for two other reasons: we sent a man to the moon, and this was the setting for *I Dream of Jeannie*. A walk through Kennedy Space Center at Port Canaveral (also called Cape Kennedy) deals primarily with the former; a trek through Cocoa Beach, where almost everything has a space motif, deals with both, slanting only in Hollywood's favor with "I Dream of Jeannie Lane" in Lori Wilson Park.

South of Cocoa, the land is still populated, but by Sebastian Inlet State Park. The park covers a long expanse of A1A, and, on impulse, we stop, lucking into a waterfront campsite.

We make camp on the dock of the inlet. So far things are wonderful and frightening. Wonderful because a leisurely drive down A1A reminded me that not all of our coastlines are chain stores and trinket shops; frightening because so much of the state no longer looks so unspoiled.

The fright doesn't last. It can't. Manatees lazily lumber on by in the bay; great blue herons pick their leggy selves through the rocks. I take a walk and talk to a grizzled old man netting for fish. Wildflowers escort me down the bay.

At sunset, I grow introspective as I type my notes into my computer, my mind drifting to the people inland, the migrant farmers and the city-dwelling poor, who certainly came to Florida enticed by the seductive drifts of sand framed by beach sunflowers and emerald seas. Somehow, somewhere, something changed and they ended up inland, picking strawberries or packing guests into Space Mountain at Walt Disney World.

Of course, I remind myself, even inland Florida beats Iowa. It's still a wonder of swamp and freshwater and sweet oranges and berries. I close my MacBook and let the setting sun wash over me.

In the morning we head south, stopping at the McLarty Treasure Museum, built near the site of a 1715 Spanish shipwreck. We learn that the Spanish queen at the time, Elizabeth, wouldn't consummate her marriage until she received her dowry, which included emeralds, pearls, and a coral rosary—eight chests in all, worth 14 million pesos. According to the parts of the museum video, the treasure sunk in a series of shipwrecks. It seems a high price to pay to get the queen to give it up to her king, but I may have missed some of the story because the woman seated in front of us never learned how to quietly watch a movie.

Before she opened her mouth, I thought she looked stately. Once she started speaking and I realized she did not mean to stop but rather intended to narrate the narration, I alternated between trying to hear over her "Did you hear *that*?" exclamations and watching the social drama before me. The couple accompanying her and her husband, who did an excellent job of feigning deafness, apparently had traveled with her before and seated themselves slightly apart. This, of course, failed to deter her. She would simply lean across the empty chair separating them. A moment later she would look at her husband, who sat ramrod straight, pretending, perhaps, to have never seen her before. She would parrot parts of the documentary she found amusing. "The bloody queen!" she would chortle, never noticing that everyone nearby was actively ignoring her.

....

Back on the road, things remain blessedly quiet. That is, until a blue . . . thing . . . materializes on the road. For the next few miles, giant blue land crabs attempt to cross A1A, a small-scale B movie come to life. Why do the crabs cross the road? No, this is not a joke. Even though they're land-dwellers, mostly, they lay their eggs in the shallows. So basically, these crabs aren't just playing some sort of real-life Frogger on A1A, they're doing it in labor with somewhere between thirty thousand and seventy thousand babies. When I cannot avoid crunching over a crab—and I try, I really do, but these guys (well, gals) are everywhere—I'm not just killing one crab. I'm potentially killing 70,001 crabs.

The homes along the way prove paradise: cabbage palm and sand pine thickets buffeted by sand. Few condos dot the road, and mom-and-pop hotels are the dominant types of lodging. Vero Beach and surrounding cities don't seem as tourist-oriented as their northern sisters. South of State Road 60 we jog back to the mainland. The second time we made this journey, we stopped in Stuart when a nautical thrift shop caught my eye. We were in my car, not the camper; in retrospect, the camper might have made more sense.

Now, the term "thrift" implies, at least to me, bargain. This was not the case here. Having recently purchased a home, Barry and I had grand landscaping ideas about the yard. Like most self-respecting boat captains, he thought using dock pilings strung together by lengths of boat line would make nice edging. I agree, and when we see just what we needed draped over a weathered fence, we ask the shopkeeper for a price. He names it: several hundred dollars. I laugh and walk away. The guy doesn't know who he's dealing with; Barry is wonderfully unemotional about purchases and also, when he's not careful, can sound like a hard-ass. This serves us well when we negotiate.

After stretching my legs around the shop, I return to the two men tying several hundred feet on top of my Volkswagen Rabbit. They assure me "it will be *fine!*" and the owner's girlfriend, Jeanette, surreptitiously hands me a book we had asked about and deemed not worth the owner's high price.

"He wants to hold on to everything," she says, shaking her head. We chat for a few moments about books and state water issues and how exactly I intend to cross the state with what the owner now estimates to be seven hundred feet (spoiler alert: it's not) of heavy line crowning the German compact car.

The next day A1A tests our relationship. Toward the southern end, drivers wishing to follow A1A must zigzag back and forth to the mainland. This would be frustrating but fine if the signs were (*a*) clearly marked and (*b*) more than two feet in front of the turn. Both times we drove this route, we made the same mistakes. We know this because our wrong turns all looked familiar the second time. We're not clever, but we are consistent. It does not help that A1A, in addition to US 1, runs inland, and so when I took my turn at the helm (leaving Barry to navigate) on our second trip together down A1A, I found myself repeatedly asking, "Are you sure this is A1A and not US 1?," not wanting to doubt my beloved but all the while aggressively doubting my beloved. I was hungry. We had not yet found a place to stay, and I wanted desperately just to get out of the car. Barry, for his part, was just as tired of driving. He, I should mention, is so infrequently wrong it infuriates me, so it was almost with excitement that my doubt grew as I asked, about every five minutes, "Are you sure we're not on US 1?"

Finally, he pursed his lips and started reverse pinching his iPhone screen with his fingers.

"You know what?" he says slowly, "There, uh, was another A1A. You need to zoom to see it, but it's there."

I do not kill him. I turn the car around, retrace our steps, and detour through McArthur State Park. I also manage to blow a red light at a monitored intersection, and three weeks later I open a citation in the mail that shows my squat red Volkswagen Rabbit, bogged down by about a metric ton of braided line, chugging through the intersection. The lesson here? Always zoom in on your maps app when navigating the southern end of A1A, and don't be afraid to, very gently, doubt the love of your life when he navigates, even if he's never, ever wrong. A1A is a tricky mistress when it comes to navigation; Magellan himself would have had issues.

At Palm Beach, we head back out to the barrier islands, where A1A makes more sense. The Lake Worth Casino, fronting the Atlantic, invokes the traditional usage of the word. It's not a casino but a public hall, in this case an oceanfront park, cabana rentals, and ballroom (yes, you read that right). Its 1920s architecture contains several restaurants as well as a fudge factory.

This is the last vestige of anything open to the public in sight, because here's where the road gets rich. Not just garden-variety rich—Ivana Trump rich. Hedges, easily stretching twenty feet into the air, protect mansions from the road and chicken-neckers like myself. We twist and turn through a moneyed shopping district and enjoy the roadside landscaping—designed to offer homeowners privacy but also allowing drivers to feel alone on the road. We pass through a tunnel of twisted and beautifully gnarled sea grapes and emerge in Briny Breezes, where everything gets small: the hedges disappear and so do the mansions, but these homes are certainly worth, to me, their weight in gold. Briny Breezes is a more residential version of Flagler Beach. It's a blip on the map, but a vintage blip, a throwback, especially obvious given the walls of wealth on its north and southern ends, and I am not sure why this town too isn't developed within an inch of its boundaries. The small beauties of seaside towns like this, with slash pines meeting sea grapes over our head on the road, makes one see the ridiculousness of Palm Beach's manicured beauty with those large mansions plopped so close together. When we reach Highland Beach I am reminded of the parable about the foolish man who built his house on the sand. This stretch of A1A again boasts an inordinate number of ostentatious displays of wealth, but as the sun dips and we start to seek lodging, I am struck by the area's natural beauty. In parts, yes, it's hidden by homes and hedges, but all you need to do is look up to see the sky streaking pink and purple as the sun sets.

The next morning we set off for the final hour of the official A1A, starting our day at Hollywood Beach, which looks like a lovely town to get mugged in, although we can see the promise of a future. By the time you read this, in fact, Jimmy Buffett and his crew will likely be mostly done building a Margaritaville Resort in Hollywood Beach. That makes sense. The area may not look great now, but we are on the cusp of Miami–Dade, an animal unto itself along this roadway. We're already starting to see a lot of turquoise paint, jalousie windows, and deco buildings.

The odd marriage of grand architecture juxtaposed with extreme poverty is jarring. North Beach has once-beautiful, now-hollow buildings, and just as you think the devastation has no end, you're in South Beach. The southbound lane, like the northbound, oceanfront lane, was once exclusive but now houses a Gap and an Alvin's Island "tropical department store." The northbound lane offers the version you saw in the Robin Williams/Nathan Lane movie *The Bird Cage*. If you wondered at the time, no, the movie exaggerated nothing about South Beach. On either side, the buildings offer Florida's best examples of art deco. Everything is painted in extreme versions of the colors that wash over the smaller towns, only in more intense hues. Everything here is more intense, more vivid. South Beach is a different Florida reality.

To go any farther south, we must leave A1A and head to US 1, which will deliver us to the Florida Keys. You can follow US 1 into the Keys, or just before the Last Chance Saloon, you can turn left and take Card Sound Road, the celebrated back door to the Florida Keys.

I didn't see the Keys until college. Of course, I had heard of them. I knew that people wanted to go there. I just didn't know why.

As an undergraduate at St. Petersburg Junior College—now called St. Petersburg College—I enrolled in a class called "Identifying Florida Biota," a nondissection alternative to "Anatomy and Physiology." While I enjoyed the outdoors enough and liked my state just fine, this class revealed to me the Florida I wish everyone could see.

Dr. Jerry Smith took us on a field trip every Tuesday, for the entire day. We also had one trip to the Florida Keys. I wanted to go because I was a college sophomore and it seemed like the weekend would be a good time.

That weekend was more than a "good time"; it, along with Dr. Smith's course, changed my entire life. We drove through a tangled straight of mangroves, and when they spit us out we came to a small bridge over Snake Creek, and I saw a high-and-dry marina. Just past us was the greenest water I had ever seen; "green" doesn't even begin to describe it.

Something bubbled up within me that I couldn't name; I had a feeling, not unlike when the seven-year-old me first saw Florida's salty green water, of coming home without knowing I had been away.

A few years ago "road improvements" in the form of a fixed-span bridge altered my familiar homecoming vista, so now I take Card Sound Road; this less-traveled route winds through infinite mangroves and past a lot of spoken-for, anonymous stretches of land. There is a wonderful bar at the toll booth: Alabama Jacks. I've only ever stopped once for a celebratory "we're in the Keys!" drink. On our way in I am generally too eager to get there, too busy chasing that green watery paradise, to stop. Upon leaving, I am generally too melancholy for the sign on the blue canopy of the toll booth that gently, happily reminds me, "Don't Forget Your Keys!"

As if I could.

Crab traps stacked by the side of the road are the main sign that the tourists aren't the only things they catch down here. Fish and crabs and even Florida lobster are big business, and there is hardly a Key along A1A where you can't stop and taste something caught locally. You can get salmon and tuna in the Florida Keys, but why? Yellow-tailed snapper, mangrove snapper, grouper, flounder, and a seemingly infinite number of local swimmers offer themselves up to you on a more-than-daily basis.

Nowhere else in Florida are you farther away from the South. The Florida Keys could be their own country, and at one point, they almost were. The story that gets told is largely folklore; in the words of part-time Keys resident Jimmy Buffet, it's a "semi-true story." It goes something like this: In the 1980s, the DEA set up a roadblock on A1A to catch drug runners. Keys residents, who referred to themselves as Conchs, rebelled at the idea that they couldn't get on or off the islands. They seceded from the Union, hoisting the flag of the Conch Republic, and declared war on the United States. They then immediately surrendered and demanded reparations.

....

Perhaps like many people, my first snorkeling experience was in the Keys. At the start of the Florida Keys—the end that really doesn't quite feel like the Florida Keys just yet—is John Pennekamp Coral Reef State Park in Key Largo. This is the country's first underwater park, and while it has a few beaches, ample kayaking opportunities, camping, and walking trails, this park is made for people who want to look below the glassy surface of the Florida Keys.

Tour boats take snorkelers out to whatever reef the boat captains feel have the best snorkeling conditions—meaning calm and clear—and let them slip into and beneath the warm water.

If you have never snorkeled or scuba dived, think of it as getting dropped inside an exotic aquarium with boundless nooks and crannies to explore at your leisure. With a shark. Or two.

That weekend so long ago, my classmates and I slid under the surface at North Dry Rocks. I realized my swimming skills were counterproductive; my biggest frustration was diving just beneath the surface of a coral ledge, getting a sneaky glimpse of whatever was under there, and then finding myself helplessly buoyed to the surface, a prisoner to the remaining air in my lungs and curvy figure. Even from just beneath the surface, though, I saw a rainbow. Blue things, purple things, pink things. Graceful dancing plum-colored fan coral, intriguing matrices of brain coral, fire-engine-red fire coral. Tangelo-colored starfish, speckled snarky eels, green and purple and blue stoplight parrotfish . . . everywhere my eyes came to rest made them jump alive again. The silence of the reef replaced the voices in my head, becoming a meditative soundtrack I would carry with me back on land.

Even the barracuda, silver and torpedo sleek, didn't slow me down. I recalled reading a Jacques Cousteau anecdote about how barracuda appeared eager to "play" in a manner that, while it made the diver uncomfortable and somewhat jumpy, brought no harm. They would swim a few feet behind the diver's fins until the diver grew nervous enough that he would turn and try to shoo the toothy fish away. The barracuda would then swim straight at the diver's mask with what must have seemed definite intent, veering off only at the last minute. Within moments, the barracuda would be back at the diver's fin. This, Cousteau said, could continue for hours "with no apparent lassitude to the barracuda."

So, no, the barracuda didn't scare me. When one of the professors on the trip stuck her head out of the water, spit out her snorkel, pointed, and said, "shark," I was not alarmed. Instead, I and four others swam over to investigate.

Yup, that was a shark. He was gray and long and . . . not alone; he had a little friend. Well, not little. We swam closer. The sharks kept their distance but stayed on the reef with us for a few minutes. I was having, simultaneously, the scariest and finest moment of my young life.

Finally, the sharks meandered off the reef. As they did, we had the good sense not to go after them, not that we would have had a prayer of catching them. We made our way back to the boat, whereupon the seven folks with sturdier survival instincts than ours asked us what we were thinking.

Each of us, it turns out, was thinking the same thing: that we could swim faster than at least two of the other people in our group.

....

Every trip to the Keys is special. I've stayed at Bahia Honda, a state park with amazing beachfront campsites where I watched a glazed sun rise over the sand and sea. I've slept in "vintage" hotels that were tired yet clean, fronting a sea grove of red mangroves walking on awkward stilts across a shallow emerald sea. I've taken fast boats 70 miles off the coast to Fort Jefferson on the Dry Tortugas, where Dr. Samuel Mudd served a sentence for setting John Wilkes Booth's leg—until, that is, Dr. Mudd used his doctoring skills on the prison's yellow fever victims, including the guards. In the waters surrounding the fort I've snorkeled with a rainbow of fish, barracuda, and sleek, pointy tarpon. I've watched the tiniest of fish pick at minuscule food things in the underwater brick moat wall guarding the fort.

To be fair, I don't understand why everyone—including myself—doesn't live on this string of limestone pearls streaming off the edge of North America. If I am in love with the whole of Florida, I am obsessed and enchanted with the Keys. Things are different here, different even from the rest of Florida, where things are, admittedly, quite different already. Fishing and diving are the chief industries; they fill the void left by the lack of sandy beaches. The Keys have maybe three beaches, and aside from Bahia Honda, they aren't noteworthy. The real treasure here waits under the water. For divers, that's more than poetry, because along with artificial and natural reefs, shipwrecks make the area a beacon for scuba divers and snorkelers.

This is the end of the road, but it's the beginning of the Caribbean. The starfish and coral and eel and shark and barracuda and parrotfish and Sergeant Majors and . . . well, just about everything you can see under the sea . . . call me back.

....

As I said, Barry initially dreaded A1A. That's not an uncommon feeling; A1A is Florida's great misunderstood road. In a way, A1A is an extended metaphor for Florida: a smattering of everything, still more wild than you could possibly imagine, and entirely unlike anything else you've ever known. Everyone who has visited judges the road—and the state—by the part they have seen.

Florida, just like A1A, is more than the sum of its parts.

This is paradise. Welcome.

Acknowledgments

This book wouldn't have happened without a team of people constantly trying to save me from myself.

I've wanted to write since my fifth-grade librarian announced that I would. Good call, Penny Lawrence, good call. Along the way, great teachers like Ernest Johnson, Marie Grein, Frank Black, Joanne Roby, and Professor Thomas Hallock taught me how to beat words into submission. Dr. Jerry Smith introduced me to a Florida beyond beaches, which gave me something to do with all those words. Dr. Chris Meindl helped me think critically about Florida and its complex environmental issues. He's also a wonderful human being.

Fellow Florida Studies alum Theresa Collington was one of the original "Three Marjories" at USF St. Petersburg and an excellent traveling companion. She knows where to find the best oysters, even if she almost did get me killed, at least in my imagination (please see chapter 1). Daun Fletcher, fellow FSP alum and then-assistant for the Florida Studies Program, did no small amount of talking me off the ledge at questionable risk to her own tenuous sanity. In all honesty, though, the entire Florida Studies tribe at USF St. Petersburg to this day offers me unending support and love, and a home on our private "Island of Misfit Toys."

Maricris Loinaz, a hydrologist, provided endless hours of discussion about the Everglades Agricultural Area, the Kissimmee River, and nitrogen loads, much to the chagrin of our friends, who really wanted *just one* dinner party where I didn't launch into a rant about the Everglades.

Bob and Ann Loper, Barry's parents, generously loaned us their RV for this trip, not realizing it is indeed possible to drive 5,000 unique miles in the Sunshine State.

Every writer needs a brutal editor who doesn't just say "kill your darlings" but insists you burn their corpses so they don't ever come back to life. Shelly Wilson, who edited this manuscript long before it made it into the hands of my publisher, did this. I especially enjoyed her pithy comments, such as, "Fine, you don't want to capitalize the names of the rivers? Then don't. See if I care . . . [two pages later] OK, I care. I CARE. Also, yes, the panhandle has pine trees. WE GET IT. Feel free to mention something else."

This book is not a musty academic tome, in no small part thanks to Sian Hunter, my gifted editor whose first conversation with me involved me telling her that I didn't care if the Press put a stripper on the front cover if they thought it would sell more books. If you meet her, please buy her a drink. She's earned it.

My readers and Twitter followers sent me to the best places as I sunk ever-deeper into Florida's backroads. Craig Pittman, our state's preeminent environmental reporter, proved invaluable along my travels, ever-Tweeting and Facebooking suggestions for the panhandle.

My intrepid dachshund, Calypso, traveled most of these 5,000-plus miles in my lap. She has seen Florida from five inches off the ground and finds it no less fascinating than I. If you intend to travel the state, I highly recommend taking a hound. They rarely complain, will taste almost anything, and are great conversation starters.

Our Florida State Park rangers dug through musty archives for long-forgotten records, talked endlessly with me about my work and our mutual state, and are certainly the most underpaid and underappreciated workers in the state. They're also Florida's best PR people.

My mom and dad moved to Florida and never once uttered the words "that's not how we did it up north." Instead, they showed me how much better our lives were for Florida. They encourage me and love me no matter what dumb things I do (and trust me, there have been plenty.)

I could have explored Florida without Barry by my side, but I'm so glad I didn't have to. He inspires me, supports me, and makes me laugh. He also believes in me and somehow handles all my crazy and remains, through it all, my best friend.

Dr. Gary Mormino changed my life when he took me under his wing at the Florida Studies Program. He also didn't laugh me out of his office when I told him I intended to take this great Florida road trip. He is Florida's finest treasure, and I am blessed to have studied under him.

I owe, too, a debt of gratitude to Franklin Roosevelt, the entire WPA, and Federal One. These men and women left behind a treasure map, not knowing one day I would pick it up and try to follow the clues they left. I'm so glad they did.

Is it appropriate to thank a state? I must. Florida, you saucy minx, I have been in love with you for thirty-five years. At the risk of offending all the other states, you are my favorite.

Bibliographic Essay

The Florida canon of literature contains several essential reads that I used throughout this book. First and foremost, *Florida: A Guide to the Southernmost State* (New York: Oxford University Press, 1939), of course, offers a folk history look at Depression-era Florida; the final third of this book provided the framework for my great Florida road trip. *Land of Sunshine, State of Dreams: A Social History of Modern Florida* by Dr. Gary Mormino (Gainesville: University Press of Florida, 2005) is the essential Florida primer for our cultural history. During my travels, I relied heavily on the Florida Department of Environmental Protection's state parks website, www.FloridaStateParks.org. Here a reader can find all manner of information about each park, from history to geologic information.

Chapter 1. Salty Oysters, Sugar Sand, and Royal Reds (US 98)

St. Joe Paper Company, today called the St. Joe Company, forever altered the northwest Florida environment. Kathryn Ziewitz and June Wiaz tell the story in *Green Empire: The St. Joe Company and the Remaking of Florida's Panhandle* (Gainesville: University Press of Florida, 2006).

The Rise and Decline of the Redneck Riviera: An Insider's History of the Florida-Alabama Coast (Athens: University of Georgia Press, 2012), Harvey H. Jackson III's discussion of the cultural and social changes from Gulf Shores, Alabama, to Florida's Gulf Coast as far east as Panama City, brings this sandy stretch of Florida into clearer focus.

C. Vann Woodward's *The Burden of Southern History* (Baton Rouge: Louisiana State University Press, 2008) offers a clear picture of the challenges facing the Deep South—and Florida—when dealing with race and history. This book proves invaluable for anyone trying to reconcile some of what they may see and hear about race and the South.

Chapter 4. Gators, Skunk Apes, and Florida's Final Frontier (US 41, Naples to Miami)

Loren "Totch" Brown's life deserves much more than the passing nod given here. His autobiography, *Totch Brown: A Life in the Everglades* (Gainesville: University Press of Florida, 1993), can fill in the fascinating gaps.

Peter Matthiessen's *Killing Mr. Watson* (New York: Random House, 1991) combines bits of history with fiction to re-create the larger-than-life Mr. Watson mentioned in this chapter.

Marjory Stoneman Douglas's *Everglades: River of Grass* (Sarasota: Pineapple Press, 2007) told the Everglades' story first, and Michael Grunwald continues that story in *The Swamp: The Everglades, Florida, and the Politics of Paradise* (New York: Simon and Schuster, 2007). And, although I drafted much of this manuscript before its publication, Jack E. Davis also contributes to the essential Everglades reading list with *An Everglades Providence: Marjory Stoneman Douglas and the Environmental Century* (Athens: University of Georgia Press, 2009).

Chapter 11. Shells, Sugar, and 1928 (SR 80 and around Lake Okeechobee)

The stories I've recounted of the 1928 hurricane come from Eliot Kleinberg's *Black Cloud: The Deadly Hurricane of 1928* (New York: Caroll and Graf, 2003). No one can speak as eloquently as Kleinberg when it comes to the horrors borne by impoverished black men and women caught in this eerie foreshadowing to Hurricane Katrina.

Zora Neale Hurston wrote *Their Eyes Were Watching God* (New York: HarperCollins, 2006) while in Haiti, but the 1928 hurricane provides the backdrop for this Florida classic.

Chapter 19. Sour Orange Pie, the Green Swamp, and Strawberry Queens (US 301)

Marjorie Kinnan Rawlings's *Cross Creek* (New York: Simon and Schuster, 1996) breathes life into the Hawthorne area of this route. Likewise, her *Cross Creek Cookery* (New York: Simon and Schuster, 1996) offers vignettes of central Florida living interspersed with recipes that also speak to the time and place (black bear, anyone?).

Chapter 21. Paradise (A1A)

Herb Hiller's *Highway A1A: Florida at the Edge* (Gainesville: University Press of Florida, 2005) offers a town-by-town history coupled with anecdotes about the route.

Index

Yeehaw Junction, 83, 85, 87, 89–91,
206

Zellwood, 101–2
Zephyrhills, 194–95

CATHY SALUSTRI earned her master's degree in Florida Studies from the University of South Florida St. Petersburg, which, to those who know her, is no great surprise, given her intense passion for all things Florida. In 2011, Cathy traveled well over 5,000 miles along Florida's backroads in search of the Florida not often described in travel brochures. Not content to see Florida from a car, she also boats, sails, kayaks, paddleboards, hikes, and bikes the Sunshine State. Cathy writes and speaks for a living—usually about Florida. She is the "Arts & Entertainment" editor for *Creative Loafing*, the alt weekly paper in Tampa Bay. She lives with her hound dogs, cats, and partner, Barry, in Gulfport, a small town at the western edge of the Tampa Bay area and also, she likes to think, the quirkiest small town in Florida, which is no small honor. Most dinners at their home involve some sort of Florida food and at least one anecdote about Florida. You can contact her at CathySalustri@icloud.com; follow her on Twitter (@CathySalustri); or on Facebook (facebook.com/SalustriCathy). You can read more of her travels on her website, GreatFloridaRoadTrip.com.